The Political Web

W9-DGJ-842

Also by Peter Dahlgren

MEDIA AND POLITICAL ENGAGEMENT: Citizens, Communication and Democracy

TELEVISION AND THE PUBLIC SPHERE

YOUNG CITIZENS AND NEW MEDIA (*editor*)

YOUNG PEOPLE, ICTs AND DEMOCRACY (*co-editor with Tobias Olsson*)

The Political Web

Media, Participation and Alternative Democracy

Peter Dahlgren
Lund University, Sweden

First published 2013 by
PALGRAVE MACMILLAN

Palgrave Macmillan in the UK is an imprint of Macmillan Publishers Limited, registered in England, company number 785998, of Houndmills, Basingstoke, Hampshire RG21 6XS.

Palgrave Macmillan in the US is a division of St Martin's Press LLC, 175 Fifth Avenue, New York, NY 10010.

Palgrave Macmillan is the global academic imprint of the above companies and has companies and representatives throughout the world.

Palgrave® and Macmillan® are registered trademarks in the United States, the United Kingdom, Europe and other countries.

ISBN 978–1–137–32636–2 hardback
ISBN 978–1–137–32637–9 paperback

This book is printed on paper suitable for recycling and made from fully managed and sustained forest sources. Logging, pulping and manufacturing processes are expected to conform to the environmental regulations of the country of origin.

A catalogue record for this book is available from the British Library.

A catalog record for this book is available from the Library of Congress.

Contents

Acknowledgements

In writing the texts that became this book, I have been the beneficiary of much response and stimulation from many people in a variety of settings. Along with the large number of conferences and seminars that I have been privileged to attend and to contribute to, participation in the COST Action network 'Transforming Audiences, Transforming Societies', the European Science Foundation's programme 'Forward Look', and the EURICOM Colloquium network have provided inspiring contexts. Also, I am very grateful to have been a holder of the UNESCO Chair at GRESEC, Université de Grenoble 3, and a visiting scholar at Université de Paris 3; it was in these two settings in the spring of 2009 that I began the work that became this volume. For the various forms of help I have received along the way, I wish to offer many thanks – while taking full responsibility for the book's shortcomings – to the following: Claudia Alvares, Maria Bakardjieva, Patrick Baert, Bertrand Cabadoche, Nico Carpentier, Lilie Chouliaraki, Stephen Coleman, John Corner, Lincoln Dahlberg, Natalie Fenton, Christian Fuchs, Petros Iosifidis, Annette Hill, Igor Koršič, Bernard Miège, Fredrik Miegel, Yiannis Mylonas, Isabelle Pailliart, Michael Palmer, Tobias Olsson, Francesca Pasquali, Slavko Splichal, and several anonymous reviewers.

The most profound thanks go to Karin, to whom this is dedicated.

Some of the material in this book has appeared elsewhere, in a different form; I wish to express my thanks for permission to use selections from the following:

Dahlgren, Peter (2013) 'Online Journalism and Civic Cosmopolitanism: Professional vs. Participatory Ideals'. *Journalism Studies* 14(2).

Dahlgren, Peter (2013) 'Tracking the Civic Subject in the Media Landscape: Versions of the Democratic Ideal'. *Television and New Media* 14(1), pp. 71–88.

Dahlgren, Peter (2012) 'Contingencies of Online Political "Produsers": Discourse Theory and the "Occupy Wall Street" Movement'. In T. Olsson, ed. *Producing the Internet*. Gothenborg: Nordicom.

Dahlgren, Peter (2012) 'Public Intellectuals, Online Media, and Public Spheres: Current Realignments'. *International Journal of Politics, Culture, and Society* 25(4), pp. 95–110.

Introduction

Snapshots from a revolt

On a cold and cloudy morning in late January 2013, demonstrators were gathering in one of the main squares in Ljubljana as part of a one-day national strike of public sector workers. Similar gatherings were taking place elsewhere in the city – notably at university campuses – as well as in other urban areas of the small (population 2 million) country of Slovenia. The strike was part of a larger, growing protest movement against the government, specially the prime minister, and local authorities in some municipalities, that had been growing in size and intensity since the autumn of the previous year, though largely beyond the coverage of the international news media. Slovenia had been the most prosperous republic within former Yugoslavia; its transition to an independent state in June 1991 had proceeded with minimal bloodshed. Since independence, its economy had flourished; it joined both the European Union (EU) and the eurozone.

However, there has been a spiralling economic crisis since 2008, and the recent EU-driven austerity measures were not only further paralysing the country, but also making many private companies vulnerable to global finance speculators. These developments clearly served to mobilise many people, yet these citizens were protesting against more than the dire economic situation and the cuts in the public sector. They were also angered by patterns of corruption among political elites generally and the degradation of the judicial system. Not only the government but also the opposition parties in the parliament, for example, were largely perceived as part of the overall problem rather than offering any real alternatives.

1

One of the key figures in the coordination of the protest actions explained to me on that morning that the phrase 'the stolen state' had taken root among demonstrators. Many citizens had become enraged by what appeared to be a plundering of society's common assets, whereby politicians would sell off state-owned properties and holdings to others within the power elite networks. Such business transactions, often lacking in transparency, were done under the banner of neoliberal privatisation. Many demonstrators were thus calling for a whole new set of representatives; talk of establishing new parties was in the air.

Modern, post-communist Slovenia does not have a strong tradition of protest – which may correlate with its economic success story – but has had a viable democratic culture, including a wide array of civil society organisations, not least labour unions. Polling statistics (http://www.idea.int/vt/countryview.cfm?CountryCode=SI) show that voter turnout in parliamentary elections was impressively high at 85.9 percent in the first election held in 1992, and remained high at 65.6 percent in 2011 (while voting in the EU parliamentary elections in 2004 and 2009 was low, at 28.3 percent both times).

Interestingly, many new, spontaneous groups were now being formed to help facilitate the protest actions; these were collectives with rather flat and fluid organisational structures. Coordination throughout the country was effective; the protests were growing in size, and I was told that polls showed massive support for the demonstrators and that a sizeable number of them had already participated in at least one action.

Organisers at this demonstration spoke of the challenge of getting people onto the street, yet were happy with the results so far, noting especially the atmosphere of solidarity. In fact, some commented that the word had become very important within the movement, as the mobilisation was proceeding. The activists felt that the government had not only not engaged in any real serious dialogue since the protests began, but had been trying to discredit the protesters in crude ways. Top officials were in fact using Twitter a good deal to do this. Initial attempts to intimidate the protesters with police violence failed and only served to reinforce their resolve. The mobilisation was using Facebook a good deal for discussion and strategy coordination; e-mail was also much in use, particularly for discussion groups, as were cell phones.

Academic colleagues underscored for me that the dominant mass media and its journalistic activities were perceived to be doing a reasonably good professional job – indirectly confirmed, perhaps, by the government's frequent expressions of displeasure with the coverage. It was understood that the protection of journalism was important to the movement. A number of figures, some established public intellectuals, others representing newer voices, were being seen and heard in the mass media, while online there was a growing intensity of discussion and debate, with a few voices taking on some prominence in particular contexts or within certain groups. Along with the discussions there was also much effective expression of political views, including a good deal of satire and other forms of humour. Indeed the terrain of culture was being politicised, as the protesters and the defenders of the regime attempted to define themselves, the future, and even the past in terms intended to resonate with various segments of the population.

Five weeks later, in the last days of February, the prime minister stepped down under mounting pressure, and a new government was formed (with the country's first female prime minister). Yet many issues remain, and at the time of writing the protests continue, with a focus on corruption; how the political crisis in Slovenia will be resolved remains uncertain. While it is one particular case and we should avoid drawing major, generalised conclusions, these snapshots capture a number of important themes that I will be discussing in the chapters ahead. These have to do with the frustration and anger citizens feel towards the established political system and its representatives, and how they are finding alternative paths to democracy. Another theme has to do with the forms and character of political participation, as well as the conditions that facilitate it. Moreover, we can also see here the question of people's identities as political agents, how they emerge, and how they are reinforced; the social character of political activity thus becomes a significant motif as well. Also looming large in these snapshots is the specific role and use of various media in the political process, especially interactive digital media. The situation in Slovenia will continue to be shaped by the interplay of many different factors, and the future is definitely not pre-ordained. However, from the standpoint of democracy there was much that was both encouraging and analytically interesting on that chilly January morning.

The chapters ahead

In this book I will be pursuing these central topics from a variety of angles. I will be looking at political participation in various ways, exploring it conceptually as well as in concrete contexts, in an effort to elucidate its dynamics and evolution. My emphasis is on what can be called alternative democracy – efforts aimed at attaining social change by democratic means while circumventing electoral politics (I could have used the term 'democratic extra-parliamentarian politics' but it is a bit cumbersome). In choosing this focus I do not in any way seek to dismiss the significance of the party system. Rather, the growth of alternative politics can be seen in part as a response to the difficulties facing traditional democratic institutions and therefore merits attention on its own. Further, the link between politics and media becomes all the more important, given how these communication technologies provide the major spaces for political life today. And yet, as I will discuss, we risk major analytic error by ignoring other, non-mediated settings.

In regard to media, I will be highlighting what I, for the sake of convenience and with some technical imprecision, term 'the web'. I use this rubric to refer broadly to the converging digital technologies that are based on the computer, the internet, and telecommunications. When referring more specifically to social media or particular platforms I will of course identify them. Again, the chosen emphasis does not downplay the importance of that not chosen: the mass media (to the extent that they can be defined as distinct from online media given the processes of convergence) remain vital to political life. Yet, if we are concerned with alternative democracy, we simply find many more manifestations of it on the web.

The first section contains two chapters that set the scene by mapping the conceptual terrain of democracy, participation, and the web. Chapter 1 takes a brief look at the discontents of democracy, and then addresses the notion of participation, situating it as an analytic and normative horizon of democracy. In the final section of this chapter I introduce the first connections with media, noting in particular the debates that have been with us since the mid-1990s regarding the role of online media in democracy.

The second chapter explores the web as a daily (and increasingly mobile) environment that is also a site for politics. I address issues around mediated participation, which in turn link up with questions about subjectivity and power relations. I also take up basic contingencies of the web, that have to do with its political economy, technical architecture, and social patterns of use – and probe how these impact on the web's democratic potential.

The second section looks at emerging forms and newer contexts of web-based participation. In Chapter 3 the focus is on the first six weeks of the Occupy Wall Street movement, looking at the media strategies of the protesters and the dominant discursive environment in which they operated. I extract some lessons about media practices from this important historical experience.

The theme of public intellectuals is the topic of Chapter 4; it looks at the evolution of the idea of public intellectuals and this particular form of political participation, and offers a way of understanding how this archetypical political actor of modern democracy is evolving in the face of changing circumstances of the public sphere, the practices emerging on the web, and the evolution of the cultural and political climates.

Chapter 5 takes up the theme of cosmopolitanism and inserts it into the context of global activism – which often takes journalistic forms. Thus, I interrogate the discourses of cosmopolitanism as a foundation for transnational political agency, and analyse the new emerging journalistic practices among activists, highlighting the tensions between political participation and professional practices and norms in global web journalism.

The third and final section explores in some detail a variety of approaches to participation and media analysis, looking at key concepts and how they might be developed for continued critical investigation. The notion of subjectivity is often mobilised in a taken-for-granted manner within media and communication research; in Chapter 6 I compare a number of major traditions that have shaped our understanding of the subject and specified the nature of subjectivity. I argue that there are issues at stake in which traditions we use, including how we understand democratic agency. Yet no one version gives us all the solutions; each has something to contribute.

Finally, Chapter 7 takes a broad look at critical media and communication research and its revival in recent years. I begin by examining the multidimensional concept of critique; from there I highlight major currents in critical research, probe the notion of ideology, and look at critical discourse analysis as a methodology, bringing these to bear on the concept of participation.

Part I

Politics and Participation on the Web

1
Democracy, Participation, and Media Connections

Democracy: Discontent and resurgence

Troubling trends

That democracy is facing an array of very serious dilemmas has become an established and engaging theme within research and public discussions in the past two decades; foundations are earmarking ever greater sums to study the issues, non-governmental organisations (NGOs) are trying to tackle them in diverse ways, journalistic pundits analyse the difficulties, while political parties and governments are obviously troubled. Though the concept of 'democracy' is routinely invoked, at times almost as an incantation, we must keep in mind that the term itself is contested among theorists, who offer a range of ideal models (Held, 2006). Not least on the Left, there is a diversity of visions of its future (see, for example, Agamben et al., 2011).

Also, and significantly, actual manifestations of democracy in the world today vary considerably; there is no universal template, even if most would argue that there are a number of essential features to be included and criteria that must be fulfilled. Within Europe and the EU we find noteworthy differences and even tensions in regard to political traditions, notions of citizenship, assumptions about openness and access, conceptions of what constitutes civil society, and so on. At the same time, with the traditional nationalist frame for politics being problematised by globalised forces and regional structures, most notably that of the EU (with all its compounded dilemmas of distance between citizens and decision-making), this model is becoming increasingly problematic. This has been particularly evident in Greece, Spain, and Portugal, where governments carrying out EU austerity measures have evoked large-scale confrontations.

The problem was also glaringly illustrated by the elections in Italy in late February 2013, where a politically resurrected Silvio Berlusconi won approximately 30 percent of the seats in the bicameral parliament, and Beppe Grillo, the country's most famous political comic, who had turned to electoral politics, gained 25 percent. Among the planks on Grillo's very mixed protest platform was a call for a referendum on whether Italy should abandon the euro and default on its debts; the anti-corruption theme was also strong. Mario Monti, head of the so-called technocratic government that had recently been ruling Italy and attempting to establish an economic order along the lines set by the EU, received only 10 percent. Thus, a majority of Italian voters, of differing political persuasions, sent a strongly dissenting message to the EU (Grillo, whose electoral base is in the younger cohorts, may also signal the start of a generational change in Italian politics).

Growing strain around trust, belonging, individualism, legitimacy, and other issues makes it difficult for government to devise policies to simply promote citizenship as an all-purpose panacea for society's ills (Hurenkamp et al., 2012) Many citizens feel an estrangement from – and often a growing cynicism towards – governments and the political process; corruption scandals tend to confirm the view many citizens have of the power elites. The current civic discontent in Slovenia can be understood as a microcosm of widespread trends.

Democracy in recent decades has taken root in a number of countries that previously had authoritarian regimes, but it often remains precarious; in other parts of the world struggles are raging in an effort to establish something that might be called democracy. The older, Western democracies, for their part, are evolving as the social, economic, cultural, and political factors on which their political system is predicated are undergoing transformation in various ways (I summarise some of the extensive literature on this theme in Dahlgren, 2009). Globally, democracy has had a long and uneven history, as Keane (2009) demonstrates in his epic rendering; it remains an ongoing project faced with shifting circumstances and driven by actors with varying commitments. This form of governance is a complex, multidimensional enterprise for solving conflicts of interest and for making power accountable. It comprises many elements that must function together to make the whole system work, from the various formal institutions to tacit understandings, core values, and modes of practice. Any one aspect or 'problem' on which we may choose to focus quickly becomes prismatic and leads our attention to a number of other, related aspects and quandaries. So it is with the theme or 'problem' of citizens' participation and the factors that can promote or hinder it; this port of entry soon directs us to other related dimensions, including, as I shall shortly discuss, the character and use of media.

Political participation – or often, the lack of it – as a specific theme within the broader landscape of democracy, is also framed, not surprisingly, by a number of different theoretic traditions and conceptual schemes. There is full consensus that democracy needs people's participation, but views on what forms this should take and how much is desirable can vary significantly. As a normative ideal, for example, researchers using elite models of democracy will be less troubled by low participation than those with, say, a classic liberal or radical republican horizon. Likewise, the respective interpretations as to the origins of the problems and their possible solutions will vary – while still having to touch base with sociological realities (keeping in mind, of course, that these seldom have a permanent character). For example, devoting attention to politics requires time and energy, which are scarce resources in the context of the daily lives of many individuals. Moreover, we live in societies where many actors are competing intensely for our attention through the media. And Ben Berger (2011: 11) reminds us that just having an interest does not automatically mean we will take an interest, and more generally, that Western democracies are struggling with, among other things, what he calls attention deficit.

A further introductory point in regard to participation is that democracies today do not automatically guarantee extensive participation of citizens, either in electoral or in extra-parliamentarian contexts. Democratic systems in fact offer varying patterns of what are called structures of opportunity for participation. Within the same society there can be different obstacles for different groups; for instance, the workings of party machines, the lack of representation for some constituents, or the inaccessibility of power holders can all serve to deflect participation for certain categories of citizens. Participation of course also depends on the initiatives that citizens themselves take, but a basic point is that such agency is always contingent on circumstances. Thus, any perceived lack of participation should not be seen as simply a question of civic apathy, but must be understood in the context of the dynamics and dilemmas of late modern democracy more generally. And as we put these contours into focus, we see that there are strong patterns having to do with power, legitimacy, and meaning that impact on participation.

Neoliberal dynamics

A specific major structural problem for participation (and democracy generally) that has emerged in recent decades is the tendency for political power to drift away from the formal, accountable political system and into the private sector, in the logics of neoliberal versions of societal development (see, for example, Harvey, 2006, 2011; Fisher, 2009; Gray, 2009). This not only subverts democracy, but leaves social devastation in its wake (Bauman, 2011). Hay (2007) pinpoints a variety of neoliberal mechanisms in public life that tend to deflect participation from issues that require normative response; I quote him at length:

> I have suggested that privatization, the contracting-out of public services, the marketization of public goods, the displacement of policy-making autonomy from the formal political realm to independent authorities, the rationalization and insulation from critique of neoliberalism as an economic paradigm, and the denial of policy choice (for instance in discerning the imperatives of competitiveness in an era of globalization) are all forms of depoliticization. Each serves, effectively, to diminish and denude the realm of formal public political deliberation ... Moreover, the increasing adoption of a range of political marketing techniques has also resulted in a narrowing of the field of electoral competition.
>
> (Hay, 2007: 159)

When market dynamics come to be seen as the most suitable path towards a better future, democracy and the opportunities for meaningful political participation become eroded. Normative frameworks that concern justice are subverted, as economistic values seep into and put price tags on just about all areas of human life, derailing the foundations for democratic political discussion (Sandel, 2012). The upshot of such currents is often a process of depoliticisation, whereby issues that are normative and political in character become rendered in terms that are technical or administrative in character, undermining the meaningfulness of participation (see Straume, 2011, on this theme). This carries with it feelings of disempowerment and ultimately disengagement. Moreover, neoliberalism has become not just a polity horizon but also a cultural motif, shaping social relationships and visions of the good society (see, for example, Couldry, 2010; Lewis, 2011; Young, 2007).

Even in the wake of the global crisis of 2008–2009, there has been no serious rethinking of this paradigm or any effort to reform the international finance system among the power elites (Crouch, 2011).

At the same time, governments at all levels have decreasing margins of manoeuvrability in the context of increasingly complex globalisation. This in turn means that within nation states and local political units the practical requirements of governance become hampered, which can set further limits to what can be accomplished within democratic systems – and thus lead to more measures to restrain effective participation.

The decline in participation in the formal political arena can be traced to erosions of engagement at the subjective level – which in turn are fed by undercurrents of distrust, powerlessness, and ultimately meaninglessness. In commenting on these developments, Hay (2007: 39) specifies three basic perceptions that undermine public trust and legitimacy:

– Political elites subvert the collective public interest for party- or self-interest, while at the same time claiming to serve the public.
– Political elites are captured by corporate interests.
– Government is inefficient in using public funds.

Hay further argues that we should incorporate an historical perspective about civic disengagement, disaffection, and cynicism, with reference to earlier periods. Civic dissatisfaction is nothing new, nor is even the threat of delegitimation of democratic governments. In fact, one can argue that democracy historically has always been potentially vulnerable. Hay cites the British political philosopher John Dunn, who noted that politics has proved to be 'consistently disappointing'. What is surprising, according to Dunn, is not that democracy often disappoints its citizens, but rather that, given its track record of failures, thus far it has still managed to nourish reasonably high expectations. Indications are that these are in the process of being further reduced to troublingly low levels by an array of stresses and strains on democratic systems. Yet, if these trends contribute to a generalised sense of disempowerment and political disenchantment in a significant number of citizens, for others they become a signal to mobilise and to engage politically – to participate.

The explanations for political disaffection in formal electoral politics often turn to models of civic apathy, with their finger-pointing condemnation. While apathy is certainly an element (and can be found in most human endeavours to some degree), if we see politics in a broader sense, as extending far beyond the party domain, then such disengagement itself can at times be potentially understood as a political act, a considered and rational response under prevailing circumstances. Further, if we then look at the field of alternative political participation, the argument concerning apathy becomes more problematic, as we see many citizens engaging politically, but outside the electoral system. Often propelled by frustrations that the established parties are insufficiently responsive or even by a sense that the mainstream political system marginalises or excludes, many citizens are finding new routes to engagement and participation. Some forms of engagement are leading to new kinds of political practices, new ways of being citizens, effectively altering the character of politics in some contexts. Democracy needs both a functioning party system and a viable domain of extra-parliamentary politics; at present both are in transition.

Alternative democratic paths

Thus, parallel with the developments of declining involvement with electoral politics and an erosion of certain aspects of democracy, we also note a contrary narrative: a renewed engagement on both the Left and the Right – as well as within political shades that do not fit neatly into these classic categories – an array of groups, mostly operating outside the confines of party politics. They struggle hard to impact on legislation, entering the public sphere to pursue their own interests or their visions of a better world. On the political stage we can observe many established single issue organisations and loose collectivities, temporary issue publics, lobbying outfits, NGOs, social movements, protest activists, citizen networks, and other formations, active at local, regional, national, and global levels. The global crises are generating a good deal of critical analysis from a variety of perspectives, addressing the theme of existing, manifest political responses, as well as exploring, theoretically, the potential for further political confrontation with the neoliberal power arrangements behind the deteriorating situation (see, among such literature, for example, Badiou, 2012a, 2102b; Castells, 2012; Dean, 2012; Harvey, 2012; Mason, 2012; Žižek, 2012).

Engaged – and enraged – citizens in democracies from Slovenia to the UK, from Portugal to Australia, from Greece to the US are finding alternative paths to political involvement – though not always with great effect. One might look with dismay, for example, at how Occupy gained much attention when it was first launched, but failed to revive in a robust way the following year. On other, less crisis-ridden fronts, many citizens are also exploring 'life-', 'identity-', and 'cultural' politics, along with – or instead of – traditional politics. Indeed, the realm of politics is transmuting, as citizens broaden the notion of what constitutes political issues. In explicitly authoritarian contexts, the efforts to move society towards democracy have also met with varying success; in Burma there is a guarded optimism, while the protests in Iran after the 2009 election, Ukraine after the Orange Revolution, and Belarus after the regime aborted the elections of 2010 have not been able to claim significant and lasting gains. In Egypt after the Arab Spring, the situation remains ambivalent – and volatile at the time of writing.

Alternative politics operating outside party structures is hardly a new phenomenon within democracies, though its character evolves over time. A century ago, for example, much extra-parliamentarian politics in Western Europe and North America was embodied by unions and other mass movements striving for social transformations (for example, women's suffrage or temperance issues). Alternative politics of recent decades is shaped by many of the social and cultural currents of late modernity, not least the evolving character of democratic systems themselves. It is worthwhile to try to bring this into some historical relief, in order to understand the political context of alternative politics a bit more. These political manifestations can in fact be analytically linked to other developments in the evolution of contemporary democracy.

Such an effort can be found in the work of the French scholar Pierre Rosanvallon (2008, 2011). Looking at the US and France, he sketches a longer evolution of changes in the dynamics of democratic systems; indeed, he tends to underscore transformation rather than decline. While I sense he may end up with more optimism than is justified, his historical narrative is illuminating. Basically, he argues that the original design of electoral democracy saw political parties as important features for shaping collective identities and political will. They were promoting specific visions of societal development, with oppositional parties critically scrutinising those in government. Gradually the inadequacies of the model were becoming evident, in terms of insufficient response, catering to special interests, abuse of power, and so forth.

Insights of this kind paved the way for the rise of a whole constellation of state, public, and civic agencies, bodies, and actors that are geared to scrutinising government and to monitoring its actions, partly to prevent abuses of power, but also to pursue their own interests. If oppositional parties serve a certain monitorial function on government, and the courts become the first buffer to protect citizens against legislative and executive excesses and inadequacies, from there the playing field opens up to journalism, ombudsmen, commissioned inquiries, think tanks, lobby groups, NGOs, civil society associations, self-appointed civic watchdogs, and more.

The upshot of these developments leads to three key dynamics within contemporary democracy, which Rosanvallon identifies as

> *Oversight* or surveillance – I would term it monitoring: the capacity for representatives of citizens and citizen groups to monitor and publicise the activities of elected and appointed officials. It involves three dimensions, which he calls vigilance, denunciation, and political evaluation. He perceives growth in 'social attentiveness' as having fostered demands for transparency; he accentuates the role of the internet in this regard.
>
> *Prevention* or intervention – the capacity to mobilise civic resistance to specific policies.
>
> *Judgement* – comprises what he sees as the 'jurification' of politics, that is, the increasing use of the courts (especially in the US) as a vehicle for civic redress against officials.

Counter-democracy

These dynamics are the core of what Rosanvallon calls counter-democracy. He sees it as

> a form of democracy that reinforces the usual electoral democracy as a kind of buttress, a democracy of indirect powers disseminated throughout society – in other words, a durable democracy of distrust, which complements the episodic democracy of the usual electoral-representative system. Thus, counter-democracy is part of a larger system that also includes legal democratic institutions. It seeks to complement those institutions and extend their influence, to shore them up.
>
> (Rosanvallon, 2008: 8)

Within the established democracies where there is the frustration of feeling marginalised or excluded, and the sense that the established parties are insufficiently responsive, the strategic perception that pressure can be brought upon decision-makers becomes an empowering motif. Alternative politics can now be understood as the mechanisms of monitoring and in particular intervention, within the broader horizon of counter-democracy. The dynamics of counter-democracy involve bypassing electoral mechanisms to incorporate other actors who serve as watchdogs that speak and act on behalf of citizens, what he calls 'functional representation', thereby enhancing the responsiveness of democratic systems to citizens.

This can of course result in delays and gridlocks in the political process, as Rosanvallon acknowledges. Moreover, democracy requires what can be termed an optimal level of distrust, and he suggests that distrust can and does at times become excessive and dysfunctional. Yet, I take him to mean that this is part of the intrinsic character of the contemporary party system, which he sees as on its way out. He claims that elections really do not serve as a useful method of sanctions any more, since most citizens are no longer ideologically committed to particular parties and tend to mistrust most politicians. Also, punishing incumbents by voting them out takes place with increasing frequency, which, together with the lack of party loyalty, introduces a problematic dimension of instability. He surmises that the party system is historically on its way to being eclipsed by the emergence of what he calls monitorial democracy, which derives from the functional representation he describes.

Clearly there are a number of issues here. He is a bit quick to dismiss the party system; history may prove him right in the long run, but from present horizons this seems empirically remote and functionally problematic. There is a risk of elitism in the model of counter-democracy and its functional representation; already we have questions as to whom some of the various bodies actually represent and with what legitimacy. Moreover, citizens' access to these mechanisms is already quite uneven, which raises the issue of equality. Further, he does not say much about interest politics and the power of special interest groups. Politics for Rosanvallon is by definition a very public activity; thus he does not address the discreet exercise of power behind the scenes.

Yet, despite these and other questionable aspects of Rosanvallon's perspective – such as a view that treats politics as a rather rational communicative activity – his framework is helpful in contextualising alternative politics, highlighting the dilemmas facing democracy, as well as suggestive in proposing in which directions this political system may be evolving. Thus, alternative politics can be understood as a necessary extension of a long tradition of 'add-ons' to compensate for the inadequacies of the electoral model. The value and democratic character of any given alternative political intervention will have to be judged on its own merits, but the general enterprise of alternative politics, comprising new forms of political practice, is afforded a sound legitimacy in Rosanvallon's framework. Such political activity is seen as essential to trying to maintain democracy as a responsive and vibrant system.

The vision of post-party democracy is audacious and may or may not come to pass, but in contemporary contexts it does not seem to be on the immediate horizon. In any case, it would raise many new issues about how to do democracy. In the present circumstances, we understand that counter-democracy generally, and alternative politics specifically, cannot on their own provide long-term solutions to democracy's dilemmas. Given the perspective of democracy as an ongoing struggle shaped by protean historical forces, it would in fact be pointless to think about 'long-term solutions'; we do better by attempting to understand democracy in the present, informed by the past, and struggling to improve for the future – knowing that in the future we will have to continue to do so. However, Rosanvallon's contribution offers us some helpful tools to do just that, particularly in its focus on alternative political participation.

Participation as political agency

Delineating participation

The concept of participation is used in a number of different fields and discourses in the social sciences, and its meaning thus remains at times somewhat fluid, varying with the context of its use. Democratic theory embodies a diversity of views, given differing normative models of democracy. Rosanvallon (2008), for example, sees participation as a complex process embodying three conceptually distinct dimensions: expression (speech that gives voice), involvement (seen as assembly and banding together), and intervention (actual collective action). Such an approach can certainly be useful for some analytic purposes, but from our horizon it is less helpful as a starting point for illuminating the dynamics of communication, since in the context of the web it would often be difficult to empirically separate the three dimensions. Within the field of media and communication studies, the ubiquity of the term 'participation' can easily lead to it being taken for granted, with its meaning tilting towards the bland and uncontroversial. I will not attempt to offer a once-and-for-all definition, nor provide an inventory of possible usages. Rather, I will simply highlight what I take to be the key features of participation as it pertains to political agency and media (here I build on Carpentier's (2011) extensive treatment).

In this realm, participation becomes fundamentally an expression of political agency, and as such takes on relevance in the context of the political. 'The political' refers to collective antagonisms, conflicts of interest that can emerge in all social relations and settings (see, for example, Mouffe, 2005). This is a broader notion than that of politics, which most often refers to the formalised institutional contexts.

Thus, we can say that participation means involvement with the political, regardless of the character or scope of the context; it therefore always in some way involves struggle. Certainly some instances of the political will be a part of formalised politics and involve decision-making and/or elections, but it is imperative that we keep the broader vista of the political in view as the terrain of political agency and participation. Indeed, in the perspective I use here, democracy is conceived as something beyond a formal set of structures and procedures; democracy is understood as ultimately anchored in the cultural patterns of society, in its values, assumptions, ways of dealing with social differences, and so on. Without this cultural anchoring, without some degree of taken-for-granted democratic 'impulses' it is hard for the formal system to function as it should. Of course in the real world of Western democracy we are mostly dealing with situations of more or less and uneven fulfilment of such ideals rather than their total absence, and even under authoritarian regimes there can be found submerged traces of such thinking – which can nourish thoughts and actions of resistance.

At the most fundamental level, the political emerges through talk or other forms of communication – which may not necessarily be formalised deliberation at all. This can empirically vary enormously with the specific circumstances, local cultures, existing political traditions, historical experience, and organisational situations. I have elsewhere (Dahlgren, 2009) treated the process as akin to a continuum, where talk can be seen as moving from the pre-political, to the para-political (which manifests races and potential), and then to the full-blown political itself. From there it may enter the arena of formal politics. In more formalised methodological terms, one would say that the political emerges within discourses of different kinds, and to a large extent discourses in the modern world circulate through the media.

Political talk – that actually engages with the political – such as in a face-to-face discussion, or in an online forum or on Facebook, would be seen as participation; it is the enactment of the public sphere, where opinion can take shape. While this is an essential ingredient for democratic life, there is potentially much more that could politically be done. In fact, I would wager that much participation does not go beyond the phase of expressing and developing an opinion. This is quite understandable: most public spheres are 'weak' in the sense that their links to decision-making are remote, often because the formal decision-making structures are such, or because various mechanisms of exclusion deter the impact that opinion may or should actually have on decisions.

In both electoral and alternative political situations where activists want to pursue issues further and to achieve changes, the challenge is to develop strategies that will carry the mobilised opinion into a next phase of struggle where it can have political impact.

We can note that in today's society there may at times be some ambiguity as to where to draw the boundaries between participation in the political and the non-political. While we can largely dismiss as a misuse of the term those formulations that invite us to 'participate' in various commercial and promotional contexts, we need to be alert to possible subtle dimensions that may still have some significance for power issues (for example, Coleman's work (2007) on *Big Brother* comes to mind). We will simply have to tackle such ambivalence when it presents itself, but the central point here is that participation is conceptually linked to political agency and democracy, and the political is always potentially embedded in – and emerges from – anywhere in the broad terrain of the social. Carpentier (2011) emphasises that participation is often 'misrecognised' in the sense that what is often not understood – or is actually and actively rendered opaque – is that it pivots precisely on power relations, on what he calls 'co-deciding'. He states: 'Participation should remain an invitation – permanently on offer and embedded in balanced power relations – to those who want to have their voices heard' (Carpentier, 2011: 359).

I would add a point to this idea of making one's voice heard, namely that the subjective engagement behind it and the participation in which it results can have varying degrees of affective intensity, from the forcefully passionate and militant to the mildest and most lukewarm. The variance may have something to do with 'personality', but it is also the political circumstances that will shape the emotional character of the participation of individuals and groups.

Two axes

This raises a key question, namely, what degree of participation is normatively and functionally desirable. Carpentier (2011: 17) makes a basic distinction between what he calls minimalist and maximalist positions on this question; we can see them as forming the poles of a continuum within various strands of democratic theory. The minimalist position tends to emphasise the dynamics of representation, where power is delegated, and leans towards elite models of democracy; the role of citizens is largely limited to the selection of their representatives through voting. Politics here is seen in rather circumscribed terms, mostly tied to the electoral process; formal politics takes precedence over the wider notion of the political. Public opinion is treated as macro-aggregations of popular sentiment, rather than a dynamic process of interaction. I can add that minimalist positions tend to be congruent with liberal or elite models of democracy, while maximalist ones are more associated with republicanism or versions of radical democracy.

Maximalist versions of democratic participation, on the other hand (exemplified by, for example, Laclau and Mouffe, 2001; Mouffe, 2001, 2005), underscore the importance of achieving a balance between representation and promoting other, more extensive forms of participation. In attending to politics, it also keeps the broader view of the political in focus. Thus, participation is seen as multi-directional, and there is a conceptual emphasis on the heterogeneity of political voices and positions. Conflict and efforts to achieve compromise are more common, while the minimalist traditions are more likely to value the notion of consensus. These traditions are also prone to underscore the importance of rational deliberation. Maximalist versions of democracy can also value deliberation, especially in the context of actual decision-making, but point out that the demand for formal communicative rationality can at times be restrictive of expression, and even serve as a mechanism of exclusion towards groups with different patterns or registers of communication. Also, genuine deliberation assumes a degree of power equality that is often absent – and not likely to be attained merely by deliberation.

Carpentier (2011) has a second axis that intersects with the maximalist–minimalist one: that of conflict-oriented and consensus/solution-oriented participation. Again we can envision a continuum, where in some settings participation has a much stronger, confrontational character, and in others the circumstances promote mutual agreement and cooperative interaction. These two dimensions together can be useful in depicting specific contexts of participation. Also, I would add that they help keep open the door for normative and strategic reflection: since the ideal of maximalist participation strives for a 'balance' between representation and other, more extensive forms, it is not the case that in all settings the maximalist version is best and the minimalist is to be rejected; mechanisms of representation are unavoidable in large, complex democracies. Thus, particularly in consensus- and solution-oriented circumstances, maximalist versions may at times be deemed less suitable, and a minimalist approach (for example, when the use of representatives can be an optional choice, say within a large semi-organised social movement) may actually serve democracy better in the long run.

Media and political participation

In discussions about participation, media, and democracy, a traditional distinction is often made between participation *in* the media and participation *via* the media; these two strands have a long history of entwinement (see Carpentier et al., 2013). Participation in the media involves not only making use of the media, but also being active in some way in the creation of content. During the era of mass media such opportunities were few and quite constricted. Public service broadcasting, it could be argued, through its efforts to represent diverse voices and groups in society and with varying degrees of accountability built into the system, could be said to have been a major exception that facilitated (rather indirectly) participation in production. With the advent of the web and its affordances, participation in media has certainly been transformed. This is an important democratic step, and certainly the political can manifest itself in the media, within online networks focused on network issues. Still, we must bear in mind the distinctions in scale and impact between on the one side, small organisations, groups, and individuals, and on the other side, major corporate actors. The corporate colonisation of communicative space online and the growing domination of market logic on the web of course has implications for power relations online.

Participation via the media takes us into social domains beyond the media. Participation in these domains is facilitated by the media, but the focus of engagement lies with the contexts and issues that media connect us to. Increasingly our relation to the social takes this route, hence the contemporary attention accorded to the concept of mediatisation. A crucial point concerning this concept is that the media never serve as neutral carriers that simply mirror something else, but always, through their various logics and contingencies, impact on the relationship between media user and that which is mediated. Thus, democratic participation via media involves encountering power relations, yet the emergence of the political will always in some manner be shaped by mediatisation.

We should proceed with some caution in regard to this distinction, however: while the question of whether people are participating mainly *in* the media or in society more broadly *via* the media is conceptually useful, it may be difficult in some cases to resolve it empirically in absolute terms. This is due to the media's growing entwinement with social worlds beyond themselves and the ongoing developments of media convergences (a similar ambivalence emerges sometimes in distinguishing the *virtual* from the *real*). The actual extent to which people valorise the media experience itself in relation to that to which it connects them may thus always remain to some degree unsettled.

It might also be helpful here to clarify in passing that the media-based participation I have in mind should not be confused with what is called e-participation. This term can be defined as 'taking part in public affairs in a particular phase of the institutional policy process' (van Dijk, 2012: 112). It can involve online agenda-setting, consultation, petitions, campaigns and citizens' 'e-activism', and policy discussion and formation. These settings should definitely not be excluded from the horizons of alternative politics; they do hold potential, but van Dijk underscores that these are rather formalised settings, and tend to delimit the modes and extent of participation by the general citizenry.

Practices and civic cultures

As an expression of political agency, participation is predicated on an array of factors that can facilitate or hinder it, that is, participation has a number of contingencies. Carpentier (2011) maps the elements that can shape the material and discursive features of participation, showing how institutions, technologies, the attributes of communication, and identities, can all interplay. This framework provides a very helpful starting point for empirical analysis; one can begin to specify variables and examine how they interact in a specific context. A further way to explore participation, analytically and empirically, is to see it predicated on specific, concrete practices. That is to say, participation can take any number of possible forms; there is no one singular act that we can equate with participation, and no universal recipe for its realisation.

Practices can be mainly expressive and delimited, or more expansive and involve calculated tactics and long-term strategies. Yet, the practices that comprise participation always involve forms of communicative activities, which may mean not only live or mediated speech as well as writing via various media/platforms, but also other forms of expression, such as visual art (not least digital), theatre, comedy, music, and so forth. Even a sit-in using silence as a strategy involves communication; meaningful action therefore always has a discursive dimension (a methodological point I will return to below). Thus, the practices of participation are predicated on communicative skills and the mastery of relevant genres and technologies.

Further, the practices of participation, as embodiments of political agency, are dependent on what I call civic cultures (I develop this framework more extensively in Dahlgren, 2009). Civic cultures are a way of answering, analytically and empirically, the question of what facilitates or hinders people acting as political agents, from engaging in the practices of participation. This perspective addresses the contingencies of participation from the standpoint of people's everyday lives; it focuses on taken-for-granted resources that are available for different groups of citizens in historically various and shifting circumstances. Civic cultures serve as taken-for-granted resources that people can draw upon, while they in turn also contribute to the civic cultures development via their practices. The framework of civic cultures underscores that political agency needs culturally based supportive anchoring, that it is predicated on a set of dimensions that can serve as affordances for such agency.

Civic cultures are comprised of a number of distinct dimensions that interact with each other. If participatory practices themselves constitute one key dimension of civic cultures, others include suitable knowledge about the political world and one's place in it, democratic values to guide one's actions, and appropriate levels of trust. A minimal level of 'horizontal' trust, that is, trust between citizens, is necessary for the emergence of the social bonds of cooperation between those who collectively engage in politics; there is an irreducible social dimension to doing politics. Further, civic cultures require communicative spaces where such agency can take place: public, civil society sites for doing politics (clearly the web offers such sites, but these should in no way be the only ones, as I will discuss later). Finally, forms of identity as political agents are a major dimension of civic cultures; people must be able to take on a civic self, to see themselves as actors who can make meaningful interventions in relevant political issues.

While civic cultures can be strong in the sense that they can help empower citizens, they are not by any means free-floating and are also always vulnerable to structural factors such as political economy and organised power. They can be subverted or simply prevented from emerging by intentional, strategic measures. Moreover, sociocultural currents in society can impact on civic cultures; for example, consumerist individualism tends to compete with civic cultures. Media, of course, play a very significant role is shaping them; in today's world, media are no doubt the most significant spaces where civic cultures can flourish – as well as be obstructed. While I am largely dealing here with media practices, we must not lose sight of the offline contexts; indeed, as I discuss in Chapter 2, there are real dangers to limiting democratic participation exclusively to media activities.

Subjectivity and discourse

If identity as a political agent is a general prerequisite for participation, then engagement can be seen as the subjective disposition that motivates its realisation. Engagement is usually directed towards particular political questions or issues, although it may also be directed towards support for democracy more generally. For the moment we can simply say that subjectivity has to do with our inner reality and experience. This 'space of the self' as John Corner (2011) terms it, is on the one hand a source of individual agency; we develop our identities, make decisions, and take action based on the coordinates we have with us in our inner realities. On the other hand, this space is also a terrain in which society and culture is inscribed in us, making us not just human in general, but also providing us with specific influences. The net result at any moment is of course always some amalgam of agency and external impact. In addition, from the standpoint of psychoanalytic theory, our subjectivity is never fully unitary and centred, and we are never fully transparent to ourselves, since the unconscious always intervenes to some degree, operating, as it were, behind our back. Thus, agency may even be shaped by factors within us but which lie beyond our awareness.

A further important attribute is that subjectivity straddles the rational–affective distinction; thus political participation builds upon of the interplay of both of these aspects of our mental dynamics. Rationality can offer reasons, good or bad, for engagement and action, but affect provides the psychic energy. Politics is entwined with people's desires, anxieties, visions, and hopes, and all such subjective elements feed affective charges into their engagement, mingling with the rational, analytic elements. Indeed, even the seemingly rational act of voting is permeated by affective dimensions, as Coleman (2013) has cogently demonstrated. Thus in the broad media landscape, we find the political embodied not just in coherent political statements, but also in forms of expression from street humour to self-help therapies, from rap lyrics to detective fiction, from televised satire to theatre. So even while the coherent articulation of ideas still remains central to political life, political sentiments in the form of dominant and oppositional discourses are embodied by various modes of cultural expression, often comprising strong affective dimensions.

While some theorists of democracy and deliberation tend still to dichotomise rationality and affect (with the latter seen as a subversive threat), recent efforts are accentuating the fruitful and inexorable interconnections between reason and affect, aesthetics, and rhetoric. Rousiley Maia (2012: 16–24) discusses these developments in her recent work on mediated deliberation. It may be that one-sided models of 'rational man' [*sic*] – based on 19th century, pre-Freudian psychology – as blueprints for understanding political life are gradually losing ground.

Conceptually, subjectivity is informed by social constructionist premises, and is thus also characterised by tensions and fissures deriving from the social world. This means that subjectivity is never merely a 'private' reality, even if it will always comprise individual, personal elements; for example, two individuals may respond quite differently to the same set of cultural inscriptions. Moreover, in the context of politics, our emphasis is on the collective, social side of subjectivity.

From this rendering of subjectivity, we can understand that the subjective political engagement that prompts participation will always in part be conditional, shaped by shifting contingencies in the social world. A methodological approach to elucidating (collective) subjectivity is to examine discourses, that is, structured patterns of language use and the meanings they embody (I am basing myself loosely on Laclau and Mouffe's (2001) discourse theory). Discourses operate in and define specific social contexts, which we could say makes them the carriers of the meanings that are in circulation in society – keeping in mind that we are dealing here with what we perceive to be reasonable patterns: there will also be concrete sociological exceptions (individuals, groups) whose horizons of meaning may vary from dominant discourses. Still, this becomes a fruitful methodological step in elucidating how society and culture – via all their diverse modes of representation and expression – become inscribed in our subjectivity. While I will address the concept of the subject in more detail in Chapter 6, here I just want to establish the connection between subjectivity and discourse. We use discourses – but they also use us, and their entanglements with power relations are always potentially present.

The discursive foundation of engagement, which in turn is a precondition for participation, becomes evident in the work of a Swedish researcher, Erik Amnå, and his colleagues (Amnå, 2008 is in Swedish; an English summary is available in Amnå, 2012). Amnå emphasises that the development of political identities is always to some extent a process of larger self-definition and -production, carried on through encounters with the social environment and its evolving circumstances. He and his research team began with the basic question of 'why participate?' What are the motivations that propel or hinder young citizens from engaging in politics and the political? From a series of focus groups and individual interviews with young people who had been categorised as manifesting a range of degrees and modes of political engagement – including a large group classified as 'passive' – he was able to derive six categories of subjective disposition. Respondents could embody a mixture of several motivations, though for some of the respondents one motivation in particular was dominant. Amnå tags each motivation with an expressive phrase that helps specify the feeling behind it. From the theoretical horizon I am using, one can say that each tag points to a particular discourse that shapes the respective subjective disposition:

Obligation: 'One ought to.' This captures the imperative of basic civic virtue: the moral pressure to do one's duty. To not do it still seems to generate some sense of discomfiture, if not guilt, on the part of some of the respondents.

Importance: 'I have to.' This motivation can incorporate a number of different particular inducements, but is basically a more personalised expression of obligation. The sense of moral duty derives more from within the person, rather than from his or her feeling compelled by external obligation.

Ability: 'I can.' This is a clear expression of empowered citizens. The person feels that he or she is in possession of the skills and competences needed, and believes that they can influence political the situation.

Demand: 'I'm needed.' Amnå notes the importance of the personal invitation to participate; a perception that one is wanted by the political group or movement is an important psychological factor. A sense of belonging to a community is a key element here.

Effectiveness: 'It works.' Through a careful estimation of the circumstances, or often merely a kind of faith, the sense that participation would lead to a positive outcome is an important factor for many of respondents.

Meaningfulness: 'It gives me something.' The sense of participation being worthwhile generates a long list of values and benefits, of emotional and existential character, including personal joy and a sense of belonging.

It is relatively easy to see how each of these tags links up with larger, normative discourses circulating in society, and it is also apparent how engagement for various groups in various settings can readily mobilise mixtures of these discourses – or how they may for any one individual shift, prism-like, depending on the circumstances. Also, these discursive tags attest to the complexity of engagement, and signal that in our efforts to understand participation we should avoid reductionist logics and simple solutions. Any one group or individual can embody more than one of these discourses about participation, which may well serve to deepen and solidify the participation, but may also potentially generate dissonant subjectivity if there are tensions or other incompatibilities between them. Amnå and his associates were studying the fundamental question of participation or its absence; a second level of questions arise as we reflect on the particular issues that engage people, and how they position themselves in relation to the issues. Yet the basic attribute of participation as practices, anchored in political identities, manifested in subjective dispositions, and supported by civic cultures, is that it ultimately has to do with power relations. Let us probe this point in more detail.

The power connection

I discussed above that democratic political participation is inextricably connected with power relations. Carpentier (2011) posits that media-related participation should not be confused with a few associated terms. In particular, he distinguishes it from mere access to the media; this is a necessary element but not sufficient for genuine participation. Likewise, interaction, often lauded in the context of two-way communication structure, is also necessary, but does not fully capture the essence of participation. What is it that these two terms lack? Basically they avoid the issue of power relations. Today, we find all too many settings in which participation is rhetorically evoked, but remains at the level of access or interaction ('Go online and express your views to the city council – participate in local government!'). Democratic participation must at some point and in some way actualise and embody power relations, however weak or remote they may seem. Formalised representation and voting – assuming validity and transparency – embody participation, as do innumerably more micro-contexts of citizen input.

Participation is ultimately about power sharing, and if this is structurally absent or systematically undermined, then whatever is being called participation must be seen with the utmost scepticism, or indeed labelled fraudulent. This may seem like a severe criterion, but fundamentally this is what democracy is about. In what has by now become a classic article, Sherry Arnstein (1969) offers a 'ladder' of citizens' participation, with eight rungs, ranging from manipulation and therapy, up through consultation (which she sees as 'tokenism'), and arriving at delegated power and citizen control. This model reminds us that participation should not be understood in either–or terms, as present or absent, but rather as a question of degree, a continuum. One could develop other possible versions of this suggestive conceptual framework and apply them analytically in concrete situations. However, all actual and potential – or ideal – participation must be gauged against a specific set of circumstances: the character of existing organisational frameworks and decision-making procedures, and more general expectations of participation as defined by normative cogency of the democratic culture of the given situation.

'Power' is one of those major terms within social science that loom large in importance while remaining multivalent in their meaning; once again the plurality of intellectual traditions, while enriching, also leaves us with conceptual problems. While we would no doubt wait in vain for a once-and-for-all ultimate definition, I will briefly sketch an angle on power that is congruent with the perspective on participation that I am developing here. While there are many disparate approaches to power, a few authors have strived to structure and to some degree integrate the various strands to form helpful ports of entry into this convoluted semantic space.

One approach offers a three-way prism for thematically talking about power: Morriss (2002) from a philosophical point of departure makes a basic distinction between three contexts in which the term is used: practical, moral, and evaluative. Practical contexts involve analysing the realistic possibilities and limits of actors in concrete situations where power relations are salient; there are practical, realistic aspects of what participants can do and accomplish – as well as what power holders can achieve. Moral contexts have to do with allocating responsibility and blame to actors – ethical judgement of all parties entwined in power relations – in relation to their actions and the power they have at their disposal. Evaluative contexts refer to passing overarching normative judgements on power relations within social systems or their sub-parts – political arrangements, government, and so on – using democratic norms of assessment. Here the question is not about the actions of individual or group actors, but about power arrangements more broadly; the extent to which, for example, citizens can in fact impact on the decisions that affect their lives. This tripartite division can be quite useful in organising discussion and research, clarifying which aspect of power we have in focus.

In his landmark study on the major traditions of power, Lukes (2005) distinguishes, among other things, between three empirical layers of power: first, the explicit layer, which involves the threat of force – I would term this *coercion*; secondly, what he calls agenda-setting, which defines and delimits the terms of discussion and debate – I would term this *constraint*; and thirdly, what he calls core values, which operate at more subjective and subtle levels – I would call this *influence*. This scheme situates the problematic neatly in several traditions of media research (see Corner's discussion of this in Corner, 2011: 85–95) and takes take us into the realm of hegemony, ideology, and discourses. It resonates also with Foucault's idea that knowledge is inexorably linked to power, as well as with Bourdieu's notion that power operates through symbolic means, for example, via language. In deploying the terms 'coercion', 'constraint', and 'influence' I am merely reinstating into Lukes' scheme a traditional set of concepts found in the literature on power and which retain some analytic utility.

The problem with Lukes' otherwise admirable contribution is that it – like many others – tends to view power largely in terms of domination, as the one-way 'power over' others. This misses the reconceptualisation of power most associated with Foucault, which emphasises, in simplified terms, power as dispersed, embedded in the micro-contexts of social life, and not deriving from particular centres. It can best be grasped by looking at how it operates upward, from below; seen thus, power is enabling, not disabling. This is an important corrective to the tradition of power as domination, but I would underscore that it complements but does not supplant it. Centres of power are still very much with us, as is domination. But this intervention into the theory of power helps us to better accentuate the relational aspect of it, and takes on clear relevance in regard to participation.

Hearn (2012) offers a genealogy of theories about power where he takes into account Morriss, Lukes, and a large number of other theorists. In his distillation of these many currents, he insists that power is not uniformly dispersive in society, but in fact concentrated in various centres. He claims that power tends to be enduring, 'dispositional', which is to say not merely the upshot of an event or the effect of circumstance. It tends to have, in other words, structure. Yet Hearn argues for a dialectical perspective of agency and structure: 'Power is not a matter of agency *versus* structure, but of agencies *in* structure, which is part of the account of its variable distribution' (Hearn, 2011: 211–212). Structures, of various kinds, can thus be understood as constituting key contingencies for agency, but by no means eliminating agency.

From this follows the distinction between 'power to' and 'power over', which is not only conceptually serviceable for analysis, but also invites questions of legitimacy: who should have what power over whom, and why? What sorts of 'power to' should citizens have, and why? Also, Corner (2011) reminds us that the idea of 'power to' invokes the indispensable notion of empowerment. Finally, Hearn makes the distinction between asymmetrical versus balanced power. Behind this couplet hovers the general democratic ideal of checks and balances of power, and accountability, as well as the more fundamental idea that the power of domination can and should be met by counter-power. Systematic relations of subordination and domination, of suppression and exploitation, thus do not sit well with the democratic ideal. This compels us to examine the balance, to register relative symmetry and asymmetry.

Thus, when we define participation as at bottom concerned with power relations, we have a set of concepts that can address this theme with a good degree of conceptual precision. The distinction between practical, moral, and evaluative contexts can provide a first step of specification of conceptual clarification. The empirical distinction between coercion, constraint, and influence also serves as a helpful analytic signpost in elucidating specific contexts of participation and/or its obstruction. The idea that power derives from specific centres, is to a great extent structural, and can readily take on the character of domination, is axiomatic. Yet that is also contingent, operates differently in different contexts, and can have a dispersed character which offers a complementary view. That power can beget counter-power, even in the small corners of social life, that citizens can become empowered, gives us a dynamic, relational view. Moreover, the idea of asymmetrical power, and the ever-present potential for the critique of domination, underscores the normative forcefulness that still resides – despite all the difficulties I have been discussing – in democratic theory itself and its invitation to participation.

The web and democratic hopes

More media, more democracy?

In the modern world power in the form of constraint and influence is exercised and negotiated to a great extent via the media, although power as coercion is also present – and no doubt growing as authoritarian regimes make use of digital media to target and threaten those who dissent. In liberal democracies established power structures strive for control of agendas and to exercise influence – over competing structures of power (such as other political parties or organised interests) as well as over the prevailing climate of political discussion and over citizens generally. Power is wielded in a variety of ways; the legitimate power to represent citizens and enact legislation is of course part of the democratic arrangements of power, while, for example, the influence of corporate interests via personal lobbying to impact on legislation raises issues of transparency and accountability.

In media contexts power as constraint and influence is manifested discursively and directed to the realm of people's subjectivity. Thus, while the experience of powerlessness that many people have derives from existing, 'objective' circumstances of their situation, the sense of being disempowered always has a 'subjective', experiential side as well. This generally derives from and is maintained by the discursively mediated ecologies that dominate everyday life. These dominant and routine representations in the media convey, in complex ways, impressions about the social system and one's place in it. The messages of these hegemonic 'lessons' often serve to promote a constricted sense of a political self; we are discursively positioned as agents of delimited efficacy in relation to the major structures of power.

Particularly in the era of analogue mass media, the mechanisms of such discursive exercise of power operated in many effective (and familiar) ways to reinforce prevailing views and deflect critical initiatives. The power to define the issues, set the terms of discussion, present the options, and generally specify what constitutes the realm of 'realistic' and 'legitimate' political alternatives is a classic attribute of all established power structures; even the promotion of particular values and attitudes is part of the repertoire. The discourses emanating from centres of power tend to prevail over their competitors, that is, they have hegemonic status. Critical observers will discern in many specific situations asymmetries of power, normative deviations from democratic ideals, often involving domination and exploitation.

History of course does not stand still; circumstances change, and hegemonic powers can be confronted with counter-hegemonic ones. These may arise within party structures, but as noted above, in recent decades we find the challenges increasingly located in alternative politics, in the manifestations of counter-democracy. An important part of the historical changes that can impact on power relations and participation is the character of the media technologies available. Media affordances are of enormous significance for political practices and strategies – both of the more powerful and of those contesting the arrangements of power. Thus, with the increased mediatisation of power, and of citizenship itself, the media take on all the more significance, a development that has only been accelerated in the digital age.

This is certainly the case with the web, especially in its incarnation as Web 2.0. It has generated considerable optimism in regard to participation and the general enhancement of democracy; on an obvious level the web permits many forms of political practice that are unquestionably empowering. While this enthusiasm is not unfounded, there is a tendency to overstate the case, not least by downplaying the significance of mediatisation processes. Further, while media alter the conditions for political life, they do not automatically transform power relations. As mentioned above, democratic participation involves more than media access and interactivity.

Discursive hegemonies can be and are continuously challenged; it is built into the concept of hegemony that it can never be fully secured but must be continuously re-accomplished. This is notable in the realm of alternative politics, which relies heavily on the net for its horizontal communication, and where many citizens feel that there are more openings for political communication and engagement, for political contestation – and thus for agency. Various movements, organisations, activist collectives, or just networks of people on Facebook find new ways to act as citizens, addressing many kinds of issues. Sometimes they meet with success, many times not; the vicissitudes of power relations are complex and not always predictable.

Contested perspectives

The newer digital media are of course a part of the larger social and cultural world, intertwined with the offline lives of individuals as well as with the functioning of groups, organisations, and institutions (see Couldry, 2012, for an integrated sociological perspective). This dramatic transformation of the media landscape and the social world has of course also had implications for democracy. Since the mid-1990s, research and debate have explored a number of themes in this regard. In this extensive and diverse literature we find currents of strong optimism in, for example, the work of Benkler (2006), Castells (2010), and Shirky (2008). More sceptical and critical voices, who argue that the democratic possibilities of the web have been seriously oversold, are found in Fuchs (2011b), Hindman (2009), Goldberg (2010), Song (2009), and Morozov (2011).

Despite the contrasting views from these and many other authors, one perspective that stands out is that the web does not operate in a social vacuum, and it should not be seen as some simple solution to democracy's problems. The sceptics remind us to avoid reductionist thinking and see that the realities of the web and its social and political consequences are shaped by a variety of factors (Loader and Mercea, 2012). The web as we know it is partly a result of policies pursued by various stakeholders – and could thus in principle be politically altered (Colemand and Blumler, 2009; Feenberg, 2010; Feenberg and Freisen, 2012). Popular rhetoric can lead us astray with techno-utopian formulations, for example, when the uprisings during the Arab Spring become simplistically framed in as 'Twitter revolutions' (for more analytic views on such developments, see for instance, *The Communication Review* (2011) and *The Journal of Communication* (2012)).

Research also indicates that using the web for political purposes (at least defined in traditional terms) comes quite far down on the list of activities, far behind consumption, entertainment, social connections, pornography, and so on. Today the opportunities for such involvement are overwhelmingly more numerous, more accessible, and more enticing for most people, compared to civic or political activities. Even in public sphere contexts, we should bear in mind that the density of the web environment results in an enormous competition for attention; getting and holding an audience is no easy matter. Also, while the net is an impressive tool of historic dimensions, it does not, by itself, politically mobilise citizens who may otherwise lack engagement (see Gustafsson, 2012).

On an even more fundamental level, while many proponents enthuse about how this new world of information is having an immensely positive impact on everything from personal development to the character of our civilisation, other voices, such as Carr (2010) argue that it is undermining our capacity to think, read, and remember. If many observers laud how the participatory 'wisdom of the many' (as manifested, for example, in Wikipedia and the blogosphere) is producing new and better forms of knowledge, others, such as Keen (2008), warn of the dangers of participatory Web 2.0, arguing that it erodes our values, standards, and creativity, as well as undermining cultural institutions.

And yet, while many authors distance themselves from simplistic hi-tech help for democracy, they also continue to underscore the vision of the internet's potential for extending and deepening democratic involvement. The web clearly contributes to the massive transformations of contemporary society at all levels, and it would be odd if it did not also alter the premises and infrastructure of political life. In making available vast amounts of information, fostering decentralisation and diversity, facilitating interactivity and individual communication, while providing seemingly limitless communicative space for whoever wants it, at speeds that are instantaneous, it has redefined the premises and character of political engagement. As power and political issues take on an ever stronger global character, the web facilitates protest and solidarity in the global arena, as Hands (2011) argues. Also, while politics remains a minor net usage, the vast universe of the web makes it easier for the political to emerge in online communication, especially within the new kinds of alternative politics that are on the rise.

Clearly it is not a question of coming to some simple resolution, a neat, all-purpose truth about the web and political participation. We are faced with the age-old question of 'What kind of difference makes a difference?' That is to say, what is the significance, for political participation, of the changes that the web has helped bring about? The answer is predicated on the premises we use as a point of departure; I have sketched a number of them in this chapter. We have seen how, against a backdrop of increasing crises, alternative politics is on the upswing, and how democratic participation involves connecting with power relations. Participation must be seen in the broad terms of the political and not just limited to institutionalised politics; it embodies a maximalist impulse, though this not suitable in absolutely every context. Political agency is manifested in practices and is in turn predicated on modes of subjectivity, which evolve through experience, practices, and discursive frames. This first look at the web and participation gives us a somewhat uneven picture, yet with a few useful signposts. Let us now probe further into the dynamics of democratic participation via the web.

2
Force-Fields of the Web Environment

The web can be thought of as a communicative space – or rather, an infinite universe of spaces, where new spaces are constantly being generated by users. This environment is characterised by a number of features that shape the experience of the web as an everyday phenomenon; there are also aspects of it that have impact but may not be directly experienced as such by those who use the web. From the standpoint of participation, more generally, there are tensions that serve to both augment and diminish the web's democratic character. I explore some of these force-fields in this chapter, beginning first with some features regarding the web as a daily environment and resource, then addressing more specifically some of the main tension-ridden attributes regarding participation. In the third section I look at three sets of contingencies that shape participation on the web, illustrating them with glimpses from Google, Facebook, and the highly individualised mode of participation that tends to prevail.

The everyday web

A daily environment

The web as somewhat of a catch-all term includes not least what we call social media, which is often the aspect of the web that is most relevant for participation. The term of course encompasses a variety of forms. Without claiming to be exhaustive, the most common ones are as follows: *blogs* are online journals, whose purposes, content, duration, and impact can vary enormously; *microblogs* involve blogging with small-scale content('updates'), distributed online and via mobile phone networks, with Twitter as the obvious leader here; *social networks* like Facebook are built on sites that allow people to generate personal web pages and to connect and share with others; *content networks* organise and share particular kinds of content (legal as well as illegal) – the largest is of course YouTube; *wikis* are websites where people add and modify content collectively, generating a communal database, with the most significant one being Wikipedia, the online encyclopedia; *forums* are areas for online discussion, usually focused on specific topics and interests; *podcasts* make audio and video files available by subscription, through services like Spotify and Apple iTunes. I offer this little list with more of a rhetorical than an informational intent, to emphasise that when we analyse social media, we must be quite specific – and careful about drawing conclusions about one form based on evidence from another. For an overview of the developments of social media, with an in-depth analysis of several of the major platforms, see van Dijk (2013).

This mediated terrain of social life can be understood as predicated on several parallel processes of convergence (Meikle and Young, 2012). Firstly, there is the basic ongoing technological convergence of computers and digital media, where older media are constantly being reinvented and reformatted to mesh with the new possibilities. Upgrades are incessant. Seen from this angle, the web is technologically constantly in motion. Secondly, there are organisational convergences, perhaps most significantly between the older institutions of the mass media and the newer online actors, with new trade-offs and syntheses steadily emerging. The actors here are many, and the competition, fusions, buyouts and bankruptcies continue apace, with a very few giants emerging to dominate the web landscape. Thirdly, we have the convergence of one-to-one communication with the one-to-many; this blend of mass and interactive communication is at the heart of social media and signals a historically new communicative capacity accessible to large segments of the world's population. Finally, we have a number of convergence models regarding content: multimedia (where words, images, and sounds can be combined integrated on the same device by virtue of the shared digital language); transmedia (where the same content is dispersed across a variety of platforms); and mash-ups (which involve sampling, remixing, and reconstituting texts). Even to call the web an intensively dynamic milieu may well seem like an understatement.

The web has come to constitute an ever more ubiquitous social environment, where more and more people spend much of their time for an array of purposes. From social interaction with friends to gossip blogging, from music perusals to news, from shopping to finding a partner, the web environment is becoming the taken-for-granted site where much daily life is increasingly embedded; it has become interwoven with our social worlds. Online media offer possibilities that are harnessed and mobilised in varying ways across the societal landscape, and impact on the strategies and tactics of everyday life and the frames of reference that provide them with meaning. We can and should still distinguish between on- and offline contexts, but our daily lives have become dependent on their entwinement.

Moreover, people can develop their practices and skills in online settings as they find new and often creative ways to use them. The tools become more and more effective, less expensive, and easier to use; access and collaboration are increasing, and we are evolving from being mostly media consumers to include many media producers – or 'produsers', as they are sometimes called. The possibilities for participation *in* media are quite staggering, and no doubt must be often experienced as socially or civically empowering, even if the participation is not of the political kind.

Mobility is a key theme in the theoretical landscape of late modernity (Adey, 2010; Urry, 2007; Elliott and Urry, 2010), and communication devices are a central feature in this development (Ling and Donner, 2009; Moores, 2012); we have moved from mobile phones to handheld computers that connect to the web, and we can store and retrieve huge amounts of data in 'clouds'. The mobile character of the new communication technologies has important consequences for daily life; while the significance of place does not simply disappear, its relevance in many circumstances can be muted by mediated connectivity. We can become more reachable than before, and our lives generally more portable and flexible as we take our networked connections with us wherever we go; much social coordination and organisation can be done from a distance. Surveillance can also be enhanced by mobile technologies, by authorities for a variety of purposes (crime-fighting, political suppression), by peers, by parents (who often want their children to carry a cell phone). Old relationships can be transformed, new ones, both 'real' and 'virtual' established, with mobile devices.

Most fundamentally mobile devices function to dissolve – or rather, to redefine – the boundaries between public and private space (Meikle and Young, 2012). The private can now be inserted into just about any space which would otherwise be perceived as public, for example, a personal conversation overheard in a public setting; public space can thus be 'customised' or 'reformatted' in a variety of ways and for different purposes. The accumulation of such measures means that the basic coordinates of our social geography are evolving. In daily life mobile devices are largely used for mundane purposes, but in other contexts they can take on political significance. They can be used to augment or challenge the news services of established media organisations, even becoming an essential element of the regime of mainstream journalism, while it is undergoing major historical transition (Russell, 2011; Vobič, 2012). Such devices can also facilitate various forms of alternative or citizen journalism. Political mobilisation and coordination make ample use of mediated mobility; protest movements today are dependent on them. From daily life to revolution, mobile communication technology has become part of the overall media landscape.

Today's web-based media culture is becoming all the more difficult to grasp as an analytic totality. As Lievrouw aptly describes the situation:

> Media culture in the digital age has become more personal, skeptical, ironic, perishable, idiosyncratic, collaborative, and almost inconceivably diversified, even as established industries and institutions seek to maintain their grip on stable messages and audiences and to extend their business models online.
>
> (Lievrouw, 2011: 214)

What she captures here in fact are some of the definitive textures of the late modern situation, with their cross-currents of power relations and their particular sensibilities and affect. It is against this historical backdrop, as I indicated earlier, that we have to understand contemporary political participation. Lievrouw's analysis underscores the interplay between the affordances of communication technologies and the practices by which people utilise them for their own purposes. In this interface,

> people adapt, reinvent, reorganize, or rebuild media technologies as needed to suit their various purposes or interests. As they innovate, users combine new and old techniques, or adapt combinations of familiar technologies in new ways... New media are recombinant, the product of the hybridization of existing technologies and innovative techniques.
>
> (Lievrouw, 2011: 216)

This perspective on creative development helps us to understand how web-based practices can result – in the best of circumstances – in the progressive evolution of civic cultures themselves; new practices become established as resources that future participation can draw upon. At the same time it would be foolish to deny that people can also find the web environment a rather confusing and perplexing place, as daily practices, identities, and relationships are transmuted (Lovink, 2011). Thus, until one has attained a certain degree of mastery, the tools that the web makes available can also appear to be a rather daunting set of instruments. Yet, with the skills also comes a dramatic expansion in what is perceived as personally pertinent: one's zones of relevance expand, as may well the stress of keeping up with it all – also known as FOMO (Fear of Missing Out, cited in Rainie and Wellman, 2012: 104).

The differing possibilities of various web platforms are also significant in relation to practices. In regard to an activist group's differing activities and strategies, we might conceptually distinguish between, for example, (a) discussing ideas and debating; (b) developing collective identities; (c) mobilising members; (d) striving to reach out to new members; (e) trying to get mass media coverage; (f) coordinating on-site during a demonstration. Facebook could well serve (a) and (b), Twitter may be very serviceable for (c) and (e), YouTube might be useful for (d), and mobile phone calls and SMS be especially useful for (f). There is nothing hard and fast here, yet one should be aware of how different platforms offer divergent affordances, and how this may shape the patterns of use. Moreover, the various platforms can be and are used in convergent ways, with relays, feeds, and sharing across the platforms (see, for example, Thorson et al., 2013; Neumayer, 2013, demonstrates how different platforms are used for different purposes in the media strategies of two confrontational groups in Germany).

Networks and democracy: Yes, but ...

In regard to democracy generally, an important attribute of the web is a capacity to facilitate horizontal communication: people and organisations can directly link up with each other for purposes of sharing information as well as affect, for providing mutual support, organising, mobilising, or solidifying collective identities. These features reflect the web's network character. Mediated social networks take the form of polycentric nodes, thus offering a communication structure that is seemingly well suited to fostering non-hierarchical democratic social relations. The notion of the network has become a central theme in social theory more broadly, and has obviously been intensified recently in the light of the growth of the web.

Jan van Dijk (2012: 37–43) identifies a number of 'laws', or properties, regarding the web, which neatly illuminate and summarise the substance to the rubric 'network society'. These attributes are: that social *relations* tend to gain influence over the social *units* that they link; the more people participate in a network, the more likely others are to join (a 'snowball' effect, in other words); networks tend to grow too big and soon require intermediaries to link the various units within them (think portals, search engines, and sub-networks like Facebook groups); in large networks, units are aligned in clusters with fairly strong bonds, but can still in principle reach any other unit in the larger network, with weaker bonds (the web is de facto structured by nodes and clusters, not by an even randomness); with every unit in principle capable of communicating with every other unit, the competition for attention becomes acute; power in the form of the accumulation of links tends to accumulate: those who already have many gain more, while most remain with only a few; and finally, networks tend to amplify and reinforce social and structural trends by virtue of their connectivity (things can readily 'go viral').

What we have here are the contours of a sociology of the web, and of social networks more generally. The properties that van Dijk puts forth underline that networks are dynamic. They are constantly evolving in response to internal and external impact, adapting as circumstances change; they are contingent, not fully determinant on their own. Also, while social relations in networks are taking on greater significance than individual social units that they connect, this does not eclipse the sociological import of actors – it rather signals that power, broadly understood, resides in the cooperation of many. A number of the properties van Dijk presents are also picked up and framed in more popular, 'user-friendly' versions by Rainie and Wellman (2012), who choose to put the individual, not social units, in the centre. They point to the 'triple revolution' of social networking, the empowering capacity of the internet, and the capacities of mobile devices for promoting a historically new version of dispersed self-hood: networked individualism. This 'osmotic self' absorbs elements from a multiplicity of social networking contexts in which it can find things in common to share.

They see a trend whereby people are moving beyond their original core social groups and investing in loose, or bridging, relationships on many fronts, developing new ties in new social circles. In the process, new skills or 'literacies' are emerging: to deal with the visual graphics of screens, to navigate the geography of the web, to handle the shifting contexts and connections of networked social life, to multitask and to focus on the essentials at the same time. These patterns are real; they derive from empirical evidence and are in many ways encouraging; however, Rainie and Wellman (2012) are only emphasising part of the reality. They do take up some issues such as privacy and copyright, yet their rendering of networking leans towards the upbeat versions of the techno-future and avoids discussion of power relations.

If we juxtapose van Dijk and Rainie and Wellman with the better known version of networks found in Castells (see, for example, Castells, 2010), some interesting observations emerge. Castells shares the basic optimism of Rainie and Wellman, but his notion of networks' emphasis is precisely the theme of power. In fact Castells' core argument is that networks make possible a historically new form of social power. While it is always tempting to hang on to optimistic horizons, we should be careful that they do not lead us astray. Critical scrutiny of Castells' arguments about networks reveal some problems that cannot be readily dismissed. Van Dijk (2012: 110), from his angle of what we might call sceptical sociology, points out that Castells tends to downplay the negative implications of networks, such as the fact that they can also be used by oppressive regimes to quash dissent – something that Morozov (2011), on the other hand, firmly underscores; much, again, depends on context.

At bottom, the difference in perspective derives from a social theoretic stance. Castells posits that networks have become the basic unit of social life – supplanting actors such as individuals, groups, and organisations. Van Dijk counters with the argument that while network logic is increasingly shaping the modes of organisation and structure in modern society, networks are not the fundamental reality of society. Such a line of reasoning gives priority to forms instead of substances. The social networks analysis following this approach emphasises the morphology of ties and nodes to such an extent that that it downplays the attributes of the social units and what happens inside or between them' (van Dijk, 2012: 33). From Castells' horizon, it would seem that the conceptual importance of social agency, and the subjectivity that shapes it, becomes eroded, replaced by the formalistic idea of network structures, with its inklings of techno-deterministic thinking. This becomes particularly problematic when we turn to political participation and activism, which are thereby seen as existing largely through and thanks to the web (Fuchs, 2012, who argues that there is a strain of essentialism in Castells' social theorising about networks).

Thus, we have to see social networks – and the media that facilitate them – as important enabling features that are becoming all the more prominent in modern society, but which do not in themselves guarantee any particular direction of social development: democracy is never automatic. Moreover, we should not lose sight of the actors that networks link together, the practices in which they engage, and their societal circumstances – which networks are of course important in shaping. Indeed, there is another line of argument in regard to social networks that specifically underlines their benefits for the participants, a more theoretically ambitious one than we find in Rainie and Wellamn (2012); one that flies the flag of social capital.

Social capital as a conceptual Trojan Horse

The version of social capital that has the widest circulation today derives from the work of Putnam (2000). At its most basic, the argument suggests that social groups, with their cooperation and the preferences accorded their members, have value; this is what generates social capital. Members invest in the groups and in return can draw upon a number of benefits, including enhanced efficacy in dealing with the social world. Putnam highlights the virtues of civil society, such as trust, cooperation, sociality, and community action and participation; he sees an unfortunate decline in these virtues, and the negative social consequences that follow. The decline in social capital, the argument runs, is serving to weaken civil society – understood as the social terrain open for citizens to freely gather and associate, to speak publicly, and pursue mutual interests; in other words, the prerequisite for democratic life. Civil society has a number of theoretical models (see Edwards, 2009, for an introductory overview), but its main value from the perspective of the present discussion is the extent to which it recognises, permits, and facilitates the political.

One could say that social capital is just a metaphor; however, analogous to its economic counterpart, it turns out that unequal social capital often tends to beget still more inequality: the rich get richer, the poor get poorer, when seen through this lens. This stands in contrast to the hopes and expectations that have surrounded the social capital concept and its extensive deployment, expressly in a vast array of policy measures. Even the introduction of the internet does not seem to alter this pattern; in fact it often exacerbates it (Kadushin, 2012: 183). While compelling in some ways, it appears that the idea of social capital does not seem to help pave the way help for enhanced democracy as was intended. As we further probe the concept, we find there are aspects that may account for this, aspects that we may also want to avoid being entangled in – and being an accomplice to. Somers (2008), in her ambitious effort aimed at defending the idea of a robust and socially inclusive citizenship in the face of neoliberal political advancements and their discursive manifestation as market fundamentalism, confronts the notion of social capital in a cogent manner.

She begins her reflections by recalling that the social at bottom is irreducibly about relations: society is more than an aggregate of individuals. This is the foundation of all sociologies. She then contrasts this with the idea of methodological individualism, which has become the foundation for an alternative theory of society that emerges in mainstream economics and rational choice theory; both see the basic unit of social analysis to be the individual, who pursues a utilitarian path of happiness maximisation. Trust, solidarity, and other virtues have little bearing on the 'bottom line' of economic rationality, as Sandel (2012) demonstrates in his analysis of how such instrumental logic bulldozes over just about all other values. The individual converts her social relationships into capital by 'investing' in them for future use; the social world of networks becomes transformed into a form of private property geared to maximise individual happiness (which, within this logic, can only be measured in quantitative terms). The proof is in the pudding: Somers discusses how the idea of social capital has become orthodoxy in neoliberal policy circles, and the World Bank makes considerable use of it in its analyses and strategies for development.

Somers cites the prominent neoclassical economist Gary Becker, who in the early 1990s spoke proudly of a new 'economic imperialism', whereby all the social phenomena important to sociology and anthropology would become accountable within a framework of new economic theory. In this conceptual colonisation, sociological variables, not least power and politics, would be reduced to and incorporated into economic theory. (We can note that this echoes another conceptual notion of colonisation, namely Habermas' view of how the instrumental logic of the 'system' encroaches on the normative terrain of the 'lifeworld'.) She also contends that too many sociologists believe that the use of the social capital concept in economics now means that economists have begun to incorporate real social perspectives into their theorising. However, she argues, the truth is quite the opposite: the economists have captured the social and chained it to economic rationality, isolating it from the realm of social relations. Thus, the concept of social capital has become a 'Trojan Horse' by bringing the market into the core of the social, evacuating and marketising it.

That neoliberal discourses would appropriate the social capital concept in this way is certainly not what Putnam had in mind for its future. Despite her conviction that Putnam is completely committed to democracy and justice, Somers argues that he bears some responsibility because of the loopholes inherent in the concept and the way that he uses it. She writes:

> He excludes the entire spectrum of the very institutions of governance, rights, and power without which civil society could not be sustained against the corrosive effects of unregulated market forces. These absences, moreover, are ... the very essence of the theoretical work that he wants social capital to perform. Putnam never comes to grips with the fact that the theory of social capital extends market principles to those noncontractual arenas of social life where utilitarian ethics will do nothing less than corrode the very social ties and civic practices he so celebrates.
>
> (Somers, 2008: 235)

She further asserts that Putnam's perspective never really touches on the exercise of power, nor does it connect civil society with the public sphere; moreover, he completely ignores the neoliberal restructuring of the economy, with all its downsizing, outsourcing, undermining of trade unions, and dismantling of the welfare state. 'Instead, we are implored to go bowling' (Somers, 2008: 234). Finally, she also criticises Putnam and others for ignoring the 'dark side of social capital' – extreme right-wing movements, with racist and/or xenophobic views, or religious groups justifying regressive political views on theological grounds, also accumulate social capital.

Clearly social networks offer benefits, and certainly among these is enhanced social efficacy and support. There is something almost commonsensical about the notion of social capital – it conceptualises the advantages of networks in a manner that is easily graspable. We do not need to be puritanical in our relationship to the term, but simply cautious about what theoretical weight we give it. We do not want to be ensnared by its utilitarian associations. 'Mere' metaphors can readily have a rhetorical impact on our thinking, and we should avoid gravitating towards a concept that by logical extension turns trust and solidarity into commodities. It is more fruitful to underline the *social* side of social relationships, rather than their individualistic 'economic' gain. To reinsert this discussion into the framework of political participation, we do better to keep in our sights how the political is always embedded in the social. In other words, the approach should be to elucidate in the social the presence of power relations – seeing power as 'power to' (enabling) as well as 'power over', in the form of coercion, constraint, or influence. These valences are always active in social networks, and shape the character of political participation via the media.

Dynamics of mediated participation

Sociality – and its antithesis

I have stressed that the political emerges in and through talk, broadly understood. Sometimes this may be in the context of a highly politicised atmosphere which draws much talk to itself. At other times it may be in the casual, meandering messiness of everyday conversation, or more focused topical discussions on shared involvement, that the subjectivity of political agency will become unexpectedly mobilised. Pre-political talk can move into the para-political, and perhaps then on to the political in explicit terms; such talk can help keep the door open for the political, and is thus indispensable for the vitality of democratic life. Freedom of speech and association in the private sphere, in civil society, as well of course in the public sphere, is thus essential.

Mediated social networking involves considerable sociality. Baym (2010) offers a detailed analysis of how the web's reach and capacities for interaction, the modes of social cues, temporal structures, mobility, and other features serve to facilitate social networking. The specific affordances and practices vary with different platforms of social media, so, for example, visual Skype contact offers considerably richer possibilities for deepening sociality than, say, Twitter. These communicative aspects are significant for the dynamics of networked interaction, but I would further insist that this digital lubrication of the social is also essential for the emergence of the political. Political participation is fundamentally a social act, based in human communication, and contingent upon sociality; doing politics in an effective way requires a degree of social skills or competence – the criteria of which of course vary considerably with the context. All too often analyses ignore the importance of sociality in stimulating and maintaining participation, of how interaction with others actually serves to support (or not) participatory activities. In short, social interaction is a prerequisite for the maintenance of participation.

The forms that online social interaction can take vary greatly, from supportive sociality to uncivil and unsavoury forms of communication. Freedom of speech does not guarantee adherence to communicative ethics; anonymity (which remains an important and complicated regulatory issue) can afford a certain power for unhampered 'netbullying' –

online harassment – of those one dislikes. This dreadful use of the web is obviously not a form of democratic political participation, and many people are cruelly victimised. There are many unfortunate examples of how not just baleful individuals but even entire symbolic 'lynch mobs' can emerge in social media. However, netbullying becomes too mild a term when the harassment turns nasty and involves threats of physical harm, even of death, to the person or his/her family. At the time of writing there is an intense debate in Sweden on how to handle this phenomenon in regard to women who are active in public, as journalists, editors, programme hosts, and debate bloggers. They often receive vile messages from anonymous male senders who increasingly go beyond vulgar verbal abuse: the women are many times explicitly threatened with sexual violence and even death – including targeting their children.

This obviously results in severe psychological stress and at times requires the mobilisation of police protection and other security measures. Further, several of these women have stated that there are particular topics that trigger such responses – immigration and issues of multiculturalism, as well as gender questions, especially with a feminist slant. However, with these public women, it is rare that the harassment actually addresses the ideas that have been put forth; for the most part the abuse is simply directed at them as persons, mostly focusing on their gender and their bodies. Several of the women have said that they find themselves applying self-censorship to avoid the harassment. This is understandable, but such a pattern can quickly become a serious threat to democracy.

The police are required by law to pursue all serious threats, but this is rarely done. Tracing the senders is a large and often challenging task, and the legal framework still has loopholes: it is often difficult to ascertain genuine intent. Interestingly, some journalists managed to trace some of the abusive men and interview them (though none who actually sent any threat of physical violence). While some expressed remorse about getting carried away 'in the heat of the moment', many simply shrugged and said to the effect, well, if I were face to face with her, I guess I would not say such things, but this was just a Facebook comment, or an SMS, or an e-mail – it was just some text. It's no big deal – she shouldn't take it so hard. One might interpret this as an example of the brutalisation of public speech; it certainly is a manifestation of a mode of sexist behaviour that some observers fear is becoming normalised. In any case, sociality cannot be legislated, but there remains the regulatory challenge of dealing with anonymous harassment that can stifle public discussion – in ways that will still safeguard freedom of legitimate speech.

Public sphere topographies

I mentioned above that mediated social networks are structured in clusters; online traffic tends to gather around key topics and people, and even align itself with other networks perceived to be of significance (facilitated, for example, by hyperlinks). Political participation via media often goes through this route, not least through social media. At this point in the discussion it can be worthwhile to pause for a moment and reflect on how this picture of the web as a platform for participation in alternative politics can fit with the traditional idea of the public sphere – understood as a complex multidimensional entity. The original Habermasian model was augmented with notions of alternative, counter, and subaltern public spheres (Negt and Kluge, 1993; Fraser, 1992; Wimmer, 2012). But how would we today, given the character of the media landscape, situate this role of the web on a topographic view of the public sphere?

There are of course many models of the public sphere in circulation, and they can quickly become quite convoluted – with diminishing returns in terms of their edifying capacity. I find that the approach of Bernard Miège (2010) in this regard is optimal. Adapting it slightly to harmonise with my conceptual framework, we have a three-tiered pyramid-like representation. At the top is the elite sphere, with the organs of the state together with legislatures and the upper echelons of the corporate sector. Political discussion here is linked to decision-making powers; it is a 'strong' public sphere. The middle tier is the mainstream sphere, mostly played out in the dominant media; vested interests, parties, and other actors with varying power dominate here. The lowest tier is the societal sphere, seen as a sprawling, amorphous arena which people can readily link up to, where communication can take a vast range of different forms, and where the political can take shape in the proximity of people's everyday lives. It is, however, largely remote from the major centres of decision-making, and is thus a 'weak' public sphere. The web has a prominent position here, even if it is also growing in the mainstream and even elite spheres. The three tiers are connected by various lines of communication and (mostly asymmetrical) influence.

Despite its somewhat bare bones, the virtue of this model is that it incorporates contemporary perspectives on social and cultural factors that shape political communication and agency – giving deserved attention to processes of micro- and meso-political activities and processes and the operation of power at these levels. Yet it also retains a focus on the traditional – and still so decisive – structured forms of power and decision-making that shape society, as represented by the top and middle tiers. This model conceptually affords great leeway to the processes by which the political can emerge in the societal public sphere. It facilitates focus on if, how, and to what extent political expression from the lower tier makes its way to the middle and top tiers; one can chart the mechanisms by which the political views from below become discursively framed then impact (or not) on the two tiers above. Miège on the one hand underscores the messiness of the empirical world, with its often porous boundaries and contradictory trends, and on the other hand offers an analytic map to help bring some degree of order. The model is a starting point for empirical analysis – and may even end up becoming more complex as empirical insight is added.

It is in the broad societal public sphere that Miège sees the possibility for alternative politics arising, facilitated to a great extent – but not only – by the web. We can situate the phenomena of alternative politics and understand their relation to other elements of the public sphere and established power. With the vast multiplicity of ever-changing sociopolitical circumstances and media convergences, this domain of the societal public sphere can need a good deal of ongoing topographical mapping. The point of such work, as far as it might go, is not just to develop some abstract picture of a totality (a goals whose chances of success are quite limited), but rather to alert us to the specifics of each situation, and see how they compare – are similar and different – to others. This can help us to shed light on contrasting sets of contingencies, the different modes of practices involved, varying subjective grounds for agency and for political efficacy. I will just briefly provide two examples from recent empirical investigations that illustrate some of the heterogeneity of this societal public sphere.

Mattoni (2012) offers a study of workers in Italy, who, finding themselves in very 'precarious' positions of short-term contracts, job insecurity, and a diminishing social safety net to fall back on, engage in political opposition on media fronts. Over a period of years, social movements have been mobilising more and more to politically confront, from the bottom up, the decision-makers who have shaped the prevailing socio-economic circumstances and working conditions. Gradually the practices veered towards media strategies, to make visible the notion of 'precarious workers' and to challenge the mainstream media's negative picture of these workers, and to provide an alternative interpretation of the crisis. In short, the precarious workers became engaged in a class-based struggle to contest the hegemonic discourses of the power elites and their media.

In the analysis, Mattoni gives special attention to what she calls relational media practices. This is a multidimensional approach, whereby activists did not simply go online and stay there, but rather used the complexity of the whole media landscape – with its technologies, institutions, and key actors – to develop their strategies. What comes into view is a typology of four media sectors: mainstream and alternative media, each with a specified non-digital and digital sector. The mainstream media's non-digital sector is basically the traditional mass media, while the digital mainstream is comprised of online newspapers social network sites, commercial blog sites, and so on. In the alternative media, the non-digital sector includes alternative radio, street TV, theatrical performance, leaflets, posters, and magazines, and so on. The digital alternative media sector is the terrain of activist websites, alternative information websites, alternative blog platforms, and so on (see also Marden, 2011). While ongoing convergence will no doubt require conceptual redrawing of these boundaries, the important point here is the multimedia character of these counter-hegemonic struggles; online social networking is just one political communication component among many others. Relating this to Miège's model, the media practices of the precarious workers make it part of their strategy to move up beyond the societal public sphere and 'infiltrate' the middle tier, that of the mainstream public sphere.

Askanius (2012) examines the media practices of various activist elements within the broad alterglobalisation movement who use YouTube as a site for their practices. It is a platform that increasingly contains content developed by big media corporations, and is used as a promotional site by powerful interest groups (for example, the EU and the Vatican). Moreover, it is relentlessly exploited for marketing purposes. Yet at the same time it retains a decidedly popular profile, providing space for – and encouraging – cultural participation. Anyone is permitted to upload and share videos. Also, there is a space for commenting the videos, which often can engender discussion and intense debate, of varying quality and civility. The fact that YouTube has become the largest repository of videos in the world means that many people watch it, but any one video is thus situated in an environment where viewers are confronted with a seemingly endless universe of material.

While this kind of political practice remains mainly within the larger societal public sphere, from the standpoint of alternative politics there are still tensions involved in operating within the framework of this platform, both normative and strategic ones. For instance, while participation in YouTube is compelling and engages many, the extent to which participation in the political via this platform is effective remains ambivalent. Moreover, the question arises: what happens to mediated radical politics when it leaves its own smaller media and inserts itself into the frame of a large, pleasure-oriented commercial platform? Also, the alterglobalisation movement is socially and politically disparate; how does one develop and maintain collective identities and social bonds in these media circumstances?

We have here, manifested in the public sphere, two (out of innumerable) contrasting societal contexts, political goals, social profiles, media strategies, obstacles to confront, and criteria for success. Yet they are united in a shared critical view of the prevailing order and its neoliberal mechanisms, and in their insistence on the importance of media for their respective struggles.

Individualisation and activism

As I mentioned earlier, in the media landscape there is a profound rivalry for people's attention. If public spheres can be conceptually rendered as I indicated above, we must bear in mind that within the media landscape this accounts for only a small portion of the terrain of possible attention; there are massive amounts of non-political participation on offer. We may understand this larger terrain in terms of media forms, genres, and content, but also as forms of social relations other than the political, that mobilise different modes of subjectivity. Discursive structures tend to privilege certain specific patterns of attention and understanding, and therefore the boundaries between public spheres and other media terrain remain fairly stable – yet always precarious, always contingent. And in recent decades, late modern sociocultural patterns have evolved that alter the contingencies and increasingly challenge the stability of the boundaries.

One such pattern is the familiar 'hybridisation' of media formats that can genre-wise blur the distinctions between the public sphere and its 'others', such as entertainment and even advertising. On a deeper level, there are also the processes of individualisation in society, whereby life courses become individual 'reflexive projects', less guided by traditional norms and collective identities than in the past, as manifested by, for example, social class, civil society organisations such as unions, and political parties (see Beck and Beck-Gernsheim, 2002). These processes of individualisation are coupled with a media environment (and societal logics) characterised by intensive commercialisation and values that increasingly affirm private fulfilment over social solidarity.

Together they promote the trend towards the personal character of politics and the political, that is, political engagement is subjectively experienced more as a personal rather than a collective question (see the work of Lance Bennett and his colleagues on these themes of new political modes in regard to web-based activism: Bennett, 2012; Bennet and Segerberg, 2011, 2012; Segerberg and Bennett, 2011; Bennett et al., 2011; Bennett and Toft, 2009). Thus freed of the weight of traditional political 'isms', this development opens the door for new areas of political contestation (culture, identity, lifestyle, and so on) and deeper personal significance – while at the same time engendering such problems as weakened political efficacy and avoidance of confrontation with more traditional centres of power.

It can be worthwhile to schematically fill in the terrains that 'compete' with the public sphere generally, and with political participation more specifically – not with the aim of analysing them per se, but rather in order to encourage conceptual and empirical sensitivity to the borderlands. There are basically three; let us look briefly at them: consumption, popular culture, and civil society. As might be surmised, the borders between these three are also permeable to a degree. And while the political can in principle appear anywhere and the public sphere may therefore 'seep' into terrain where it is not normally present, the flow can of course also go in the opposite direction, especially with consumption flooding into the public sphere.

Terrains of engagement: The borderlands

With 'consumption' I refer to societal participation via commercial logics. Engagement here proceeds through market relations that offer us that which we need to survive and that which we might desire: the promise of satisfaction and pleasure. Consumption accounts for a vast amount of online participation. It should be understood that consumption is always embedded in an array of macro- and micro-power relations, and that democratic issues are always to be articulated. Thus, poverty, for example, can be seen as a reduced capacity for consumption that points to exclusionary mechanisms that raise questions of justice. Moreover, politically motivated consumption is certainly on the rise (see among others, Micheletti, 2003; Barnett et al., 2010) even if it remains a minority phenomenon. Consumption is a powerful gravitational force, and it is not surprising that our identities as consumers are generally much more easily mobilised than as citizens.

The massive and heterogeneous terrain of popular culture also has a compelling allure; there is something here for everybody. It is often entangled with consumption (and advertising), yet also increasingly overlaps with public spheres (see, for example, Street, 1997; van Zoonen, 2005; Riegert, 2007). It usually has an accessible, welcoming character that can express significant democratic values; it invites participation, offering easy access to symbolic communities, to a world of belonging beyond oneself. This can at times be preparatory for civic participation by offering what Hermes (2005) calls 'cultural citizenship'. It can invite us to engage – with both our hearts and minds – in many questions having to do with how we should live and what kind of society we want. It allows us to process, to work through positions having to do with contested values, norms, and identities in a turbulent late modern sociocultural milieu, even at times actualising conflicts where a 'we' and a 'they' can be identified. Indeed, popular culture, in contrast to consumption, allows for discursive patterns that can problematise and at times even challenge prevailing hegemonies.

With 'civil society' I signal a terrain that in some way or other involves free association for a common purpose outside both the market and the private sphere of the home. There are no doubt lingering issues with the concept, but the idea of civil society emphasises that in a democracy people can exercise the freedom to communicate, assemble, and interact in pursuit of their shared interests. This is the foundation for democratic public communication. For instance, dealing with colleagues, communities, associations, and social networks for non-commercial purposes are all a part of civil society. There is an almost infinite realm of participation in meaningful and pleasurable activities around sports, music (e.g. amateur contributions on YouTube), fandom, wikis, and so forth – though it is often not possible to completely keep market logics of consumption out. While the political conflicts may emerge within any such constellation, the idea of civil society suggests that the purposes and goals of such groups need not by definition be directed at politics, and most often are not.

However, the freedoms associated with civil society are absolutely essential for democratic public spheres; rather than collapsing the two concepts, I see it as more useful to treat civil society as a prerequisite for public spheres and for democratic political life, a perspective underscored by Cohen and Arato (1992). Civil society is always a potentially vulnerable terrain, one that must be defended against anti-democratic trends. Like popular culture, but perhaps even more so, the potential for

the political to appear is ever-present – and to be expected, given civil society's conceptual proximity to the public sphere.

Bakardjieva (2010) uses the term 'subactivism' to describe a form of civic preparation among people at moments in everyday life, where norms are questioned, challenged and negotiated, where moral horizons are applied to the social world, where issues of justice are raised – before the political has surfaced or any connections with politics have been made. Empirically ascertaining when subactivism turns into the political or veers into fully fledged politics may not always be easy, but pursuing the challenge will undoubtedly enhance our sensitivity to the subtleties that participation encompasses. A fascinating analysis in this regard, which crosses both popular culture and civil society with the horizons of the political clearly in sight, is found in Kraidy, (2010). In the Arab world, the introduction of popular television programming, especially of the reality genre, has engendered extensive debates, not least on the web. With some conservative religious leaders denouncing some of the programming, discussions ensue around norms and values, pertaining to gender, liberty, and propriety, putting such issues up for public discussion in totally unprecedented ways. Kraidy shows the varying specific preconditions for such debate in the Arab countries, ranging from the highly repressive circumstances of Saudi Arabia to the more liberal climate of Lebanon.

Going public: Voice and visibility

A particular aspect of political participation is voice. Couldry (2010) suggests that while we often use the concept of voice as a metaphor to refer to expression of opinion in political contexts, it is at least as important to see it as a value in itself. Fundamentally, voice is a process of giving accounts of oneself and of the circumstances in which one acts. Such narrative is a basic element of our humanity, and thus to deny it to others is, at least implicitly, to deny their humanity. Particularly in the context of contemporary neoliberal social arrangements where voice, along with so many other social values and visions, becomes marginalised by political design and/or economic rationality, voice becomes something to be protected, to be promoted, to give witness to the human reality behind, for example, financial statistics about austerity measures – as illustrated by the precarious workers in Mattoni (2012). Voice is a social process, intertwining the lives of collectivities, not a collection of atomised personal stories. It requires resources and access to take material form and provide distribution. There are many factors that impact on generation, viability, and distribution of voice;

mechanisms thus have consequences for the character of the character of the public sphere.

Visibility is yet another conceptual port of entry into the public sphere and a central aspect of participation. The notion of visibility points to complex, social technical and political arrangements; it is not simply a question of being visible or invisible. Brighenti (2010) suggests that there are what are termed 'regimes' of visibility, and suggests two basic models that are pertinent for the present discussion. First, the public sphere is a mode of visibility where one can *be* in public; this is where the 'synchronicity of attention' can be said to (in its better moments) give rise to a certain regime of democratic visibility.

The second model is the public realm of social visibility, of interaction, where the gaze and recognition of general or significant others becomes central to the constitution of self, of identity. I would call this 'intervisibility'; it relates to general perspectives such as Meade's idea of how our sense of self emerges through interaction or the 'presentation of self' à la Goffman. It also has a more specific dimension that concerns the encounter with strangers, a public mode of interaction that involves optimal distance, recognition, but not intrusion. This is the terrain of civic interaction, and we can readily relate this to the sociality of loose bonds – where on the web in particular, strangers become visible to each others to various degrees in order to cooperate.

Being visible in public can involve varying cultural sets of postures, behaviours, roles, and expectations, but what is of primary interest here is the basic logic of each model and a potential tension between the two in regard to participation. To function, the public sphere mode of visibility – in the sense of political participation – is in fact predicated on the intervisibility mode. Its weakness or absence will undermine the public sphere mode. This line of reasoning can lead us back to the idea of civic cultures and the practices and trust that sustain or erode them, thus reiterating the importance of sociality – the interactive social experience and confirmation that political agents give each other.

There are other, negative regimes of visibility associated with discipline, and surveillance can make the lives of citizens accessible by centres of power for purposes of control. We also have the hegemonic visibility of state- or corporate-based power, as well as the reverse: the hegemonic invisibility of centres and agents of power (Green, 2010, builds a democratic theory around the concept of forced visibility of power holders). From the perspective of democratic participation, however, public sphere visibility and social intervisibility remain both conditions for and payoffs of participation. Beyond that, however, these regimes of visibility take on particular pertinence with the emergence of the network as the new dominant social topology and contemporary phase of global capitalism. We find here a mix of flexibilisation, decentralisation and de-hierarchisation on one hand, and heightened inequalities, cleavages, and overall worsened social conditions on the other. Our two regimes of visibility become one of the key force-fields of the web environment. Brighenti (2010: 93) captures this tension well:

New media make users more vulnerable to surveillance and other forms of control. Perhaps never before has the distinction between empowerment and vulnerability, between recognition and control, been thinner.

Web logics

A three-part scheme

The prevailing structures of established power in society tend to align themselves on the web as well. These structures are mediated, negotiated and challenged via online media, resulting, for example, in the kind of tension in regard to autonomy and agency that Brighenti (2010) identities around the theme of visibility. The contingencies of agency on the web – the factors that both facilitate and hinder participation – are many and complex, as I suggest in the previous section. Here I want to call attention to what are no doubt the most fundamental ones, but perhaps also the least apparent from the standpoint of the experience of agency. Further, it would be helpful to organise these various kinds of factors into a basic scheme; Oblak-Črnič and Prodnik (2012) offer such a device.

They present a three-part scheme of the biases, or what I what call the contingencies of the web. Relabelling them to fit the discussion here, we have, first, the *technical* ones deriving from the basic architecture and infrastructure of the web. These are manifested in its general network structure, with its links, as well as in the specific technological affordances of given tools and platforms. Secondly, *social* contingencies are basically sociocultural in character, embedded in user practices: digital competencies, patterns of use, and the dynamics of network social relations. These contingencies can evolve as practices change, but at any given moment serve as significant parameters that guide web use. These connect to wider social relations and discursive hegemonies, for instance, in regard to norms, values, and hierarchies. The third category of contingencies is the *political economic* ones. These contingencies direct our attention to concentration and privatisation of ownership and the commodification of value of and on the web.

Keeping in mind that contingencies are sets of conditions that make possible and delimit phenomena in particular ways, Oblak-Črnič and Prodnik (2012) demonstrate that these contingencies operate in complex relations of reciprocity; they can reinforce or contradict each other, though the political economic dynamics tend to dominate. They impact on both the technical and the social contingencies, shaping, for example, the character of specific applications and social hierarchies with their relations of power. A new technical web tool may enhance autonomy by providing the possibilities for new and empowering practices in user-generated content, but its full potential may be constrained by political economic features that translate such content into commodified forms via ownership regulation. The lines of structural contradictions and societal antagonisms visible in the offline world are very present on the web as well, where they are solidified, negotiated and challenged.

As often is the case, the neat conceptual distinction may at times be difficult to specify in detail, but the interplay between political economic, technical, and social contingencies (to take them in reverse order) offers a general approach for examining the key dynamics of the web. I will illustrate this with a brief look at Google, Facebook, and the strong individualised use pattern of the web, which in regard to political participation engenders what I call the solo sphere. The interplay of the three sets of contingencies is present in each case.

Google's grand design

The role of Google in shaping how the web functions can hardly be exaggerated, as Vaidhyanatha (2011) and Cleland and Brodky (2011), among others, delineate. Moreover this behemoth has become the largest holder of information, both public and private, in world history, shaping not only how we search for information, but also what information is available and how we organise, store, and use it. In many ways it is an utterly astounding development and has become a completely decisive feature of the net's architecture. For the year 2010, over 85 percent of all searches worldwide were carried out by Google; by comparison, its nearest competitor, Yahoo, accounted for just over 6 percent, as Fuchs (2011a) indicates. That Google has also become a verb is indicative of its status.

With the search logic built on personal profiling – the filtering of results to 'fit your known locality, interests, obsessions, fetishes, and points of view' (Vaidhyanatha, 2011: 183) – the answers that two people will receive based on the same search words may well differ significantly. This can wreak havoc with the whole concept of public knowledge. Members of insular groups can well get their biases reinforced instead of challenged by this filtering process (Pariser, 2011), in the long run potentially jeopardising the democratic culture of debate between differing points of view.

Though often locked into tough competition with its competitors, especially Microsoft, on a number of fronts, Google has taken major steps in establishing its premier position on the web – while also consolidating its position in other areas, such as academic books. The company has grown into an enormous concentration of power that is largely unaccountable, hidden behind the cheery corporate motto 'Don't be Evil' and built on the considerable trust that it has managed to generate. But increasingly very serious questions are being raised, about copyrights and privacy, about how Google is using its information, about Google's own agenda in striving to organise knowledge on a global scale, about its role in democracy. All this is not to detract from its truly impressive accomplishments; rather, the issue is that the position it has attained, and the activities it pursues (which are quite logical given its position), raise questions about information, democracy, accountability, and power in regard to the web.

Fuchs (2011a) examines the political economy of Google and highlights, among other things, its monopolisation of the search engine market. Google's global dominance in this area poses a threat to the democratic nature of knowledge. Google is also involved in what he calls reality distortion and stratified attention: the company tends to prioritise certain sites at the expense of others, particularly favouring those that are backed by wealthy and powerful interests, thereby jeopardising the public and democratic character of the web. Further, Google engages in surveillance and privacy intrusion of citizens in the gathering of consumer-related data, while at the same time denying transparency in regard to, for example, its PageRank algorithm and Google Scholar search process (see also Beer 2009).

While Google presents an image of itself as a flat, decentralised organisation, it acts as an extreme force for centralisation, aided by a techno-determinist discourse. This mode of reasoning asserts that the solution to society's problems lies in information technology – and not in, for example, in dealing with unaccountable power in the private sector. Its cooperation with the Chinese government between 2005 and 2010 in censoring politically sensitive search words also calls into question its commitment to democracy.

The surveillance business in which Google is involved is of particular importance: with its complex system for ranking search results, it matches ads to the search parameters, gathers private, sellable databases, and auctions them to the highest bidder. We are all strewing personal electronic traces around us daily; these are gathered up, stored, sold, and used for commercial purposes by a variety of actors, not just Google. This selling of personal information is done with our formal consent, but often via discrete, seemingly friendly strategies. And if we refuse, we effectively cut ourselves off from the major utilities of the web. As Goldberg (2010) suggests, all participation on the net, even the most radical political kind, feeds data into the commercial system that is its infrastructure.

The more time people spend online, the more Google's economic power is enhanced. Turow (2011) explains how the surveillance data routinely gathered on us is used by the new kinds of high-tech marketing and advertising firms. They integrate and analyse personal data from many sources in order to develop individual and household profiling and media customisation – much of it channelled through social media. This not only undermines much of the rhetoric about consumer power and initiative – we are decidedly not in the driver's seat here – but rather at the receiving end of carefully planned strategies to offer us products and services the marketers think we should have, based on our profiles.

One can of course respond that this is merely a minor irritation; we can put up with silly commercial pop-ups and even the gathering of our commercial data if that is the price we have to pay to use the web and social media. However, the dilemma is more profound than that, since it erodes large segments of our personal privacy and could, with only a slight change in circumstances, have consequences for our political freedom as well. While the personal information is mostly for commercial use, its relevance can easily change under altered circumstances (as already happens in cases of deliberate misuse, technical errors, hacking, and so forth), and in the hands of other actors, significant for social and political purposes beyond consumption patterns. Much information about a person deserves to be forgotten – details about the past that only make sense in their context. Yet such digital information is not forgotten; it is archived, and can be retrieved and inserted into new contexts of a person's life; many cases have shown that it can at times be very damaging.

Society benefits immensely from what Google has accomplished, but these problematic aspects are becoming a high cost for democracy to pay. The prevailing neoliberal climate has made it harder to confront this private enterprise with demands about the public good, and the global character of its operations renders all the more difficult any attempts at national regulation. Google is unquestionably the most powerful actor on the web, but the critical questions of political economy arise across the whole web landscape. For instance, user-generated content (UGC), which is such a mainstay of the web, is riddled with issues having to do with the social good, commercial interests, copyrights, control and exploitation (see the paired articles McKenzie et al., 2013 and McNally et al., 2013). Who should be able to lay claim to the value that UGC generates? How should producer, labour, and consumer be defined in these contexts?

More broadly, the monopoly tendencies of the web landscape, which is dominated by a few giant firms, results in a massive concentration of power, as McChesney (2013) lucidly discusses. He notes: 'It is supremely ironic that the Internet, the much-ballyhooed champion of increased consumer power and cutthroat competition, has become one of the greatest generators of monopoly in economic history' (McChesney, 2013: 123). In the US the interface of corporate, military, and government interests in the web makes for a situation that poses a profound danger to democracy. What is ultimately required, as MacKinnon (2012) argues, is a global policy that can push regulation of the web such that it will be treated like a democratic, digital commons; we have a long way to go.

Is Facebook your friend?

While we cooperate indirectly, or de facto, with Google in providing personal information, with Facebook we are very active in feeding personal data into the system, and we should be all the more concerned about what kind of information about ourselves we are making available to whom. Social media sites such as YouTube, Facebook, and Twitter have become important channels for political communication as well as outlets and sources for journalism; they are a major part of the public sphere of political discussion. They are used for both parliamentarian and alternative politics, blending the political and the social with the personal, civil society with consumption and pleasure. Notably they have become the sites for massive marketing efforts, as Dwyer (2010) underscores. The click of the 'like' button sends signals out on to networks where the like-mindedness pre-structures considerable trust, and where this credibility becomes translated into a promotional asset for marketing.

In Facebook's role as a site for political discussion, the 'like' button takes on another significance. While it is only human to be drawn to people who are like oneself and think in the same way, this is not necessarily a healthy pattern for democracy or for the enhancement of political participation. One clicks to befriend people and ideas who are 'like' oneself, generating and cementing networks of like-mindedness (there is no 'dislike' button). As time passes, and people increasingly habituate themselves to encountering mostly people who think like they do, we can postulate a danger to democracy where citizens lose the capacity to discursively encounter different views, where the art of argument erodes, and where deep differences to one's own views ultimately become seen as expressions of the irrational. Time will tell; meanwhile we have the very immediate issues of surveillance and privacy on Facebook.

Facebook, now with about 1 billion users, compiles massive amounts of data on individuals, largely freely given. José van Dijk (2013) shows how, since the middle of the last decade, the logic of Facebook (and other social media platforms) has moved towards what she calls 'connectivity' – which she sees as automated connections via platforms driven by technology and economic models. This replaces the original mode of user-driven and controlled social connectedness; it also appropriates sociality in a predatory manner. The notion of 'friend' becomes corrupted and inserted into market logics, merging with the role of customer (generating the category she terms 'frustomer'). The economistic rationality of the concept of 'social capital' takes on particular congruence here.

Over the years some Facebook users have reacted over privacy issues, with a number of organised protests and class action suits, but the platform has not been greatly affected and has not altered its strategy; indeed, commodification has only increased. A full Facebook profile contains several dozen pieces of personal information, with a variety of tools available for users to search out and add potential contacts (in this discussion I draw upon Grimmelmann, 2008). The so-called Wall posts can convey personal information about the poster. The payment mechanism for Gifts generates strong links between a profile and offline identities. To upload and tag a Photo of yourself documents your appearance; it also documents that the photographer knows the person photographed. And there is more: for example, each game of Scrabulous you plays gives some sense of your active vocabulary; one's list of Causes tells others what principles are meaningful to you; answering a Quiz reveals your knowledge, beliefs, and preferences. And so on.

The interesting question sociologically is why so many people trust Facebook with so much personal information. Basically it has to do with the fact that people have *social* reasons for joining *social* media sites. They gain social connections, and the sites become forums for developing identities and networks. These are strong motivations and can explain, at least in part, why so many users tend to ignore the rather well known risks to their privacy. The sense of collective identity suggests that we are basically alike and thus we are in this together. It may be that an element of groupthink prods people into thinking that if everyone else is involved, it must be safe; if people collectively, on an implicit level, define this as private, well then, it *must* be private. This can be seen as a case of misplaced trust, to which the recurring breaches in privacy attest.

As with Google, the data gathered is for commercial purposes, but again, changing social contexts can generate new uses and meanings of personal information. With Facebook, the spillover from private to public is much easier (many examples are now part of urban folklore), resulting in embarrassment, entanglements, loss of employment, and/or defamation. Data theft is also easier, and has apparently been accomplished a number of times; hackers today are very clever, whether they are motivated by amusement, a political cause, or simple nastiness. Large digital storage systems are simply not fail-safe, as witnessed when hackers today have even entered high-security military databases. Thus, to participate in Facebook and similar social media is to expose oneself to surveillance and to have one's privacy put at risk. The issues around so-called big data become serious concerns for democracy (see Boyd and Crawford, 2012; Oboler et al., 2012). We can in fact see a transition as social media platforms emphasise in their advertising that providing big data is their basic business model. It may well be that the daily habituation to *not* reflect on these issues can prove to be most problematic in the long term. Power-driven socialisation that facilitates acquiescence to hegemony – what we could term 'discipline' – proceeds precisely by establishing patterns of thought and behaviour.

The seductions of the solo sphere

A further pattern that seems to be emerging, and which is worrisome in regard to participation and the culture of democracy, is a form of what we might, in expanding on Brighenti's (2010) categories, call personalised visibility, which includes self-promotion and self-revelation. When (especially) younger people do turn to politics, it seems that the patterns of digital social interaction increasingly carry over into the political. Papacharissi (2010) argues that while digitally enabled citizens may be skilled and reflective in many ways, they are also generally removed from civic habits of the past. For example, it is not so obvious among the young citizens of some democracies that demonstrations in the street or other forms of live assembly are necessarily an appealing or effective form of political practice. Obviously what is tactically optimal in each phase of any given political context must be evaluated separately, but the tendency to just stay with the screen can only in the long term undercut the political impact of participation. Morozov (2011) writes with unabashed disdain about the illusions of 'slacktivism' – the comfortable media-centred mode of political engagement where feeling good takes priority over political commitment; see also Dean (2010) for an extended treatment of this argument.

According to Papacharissi (2010), much political behaviour today has its origins in private environments; she suggests this is giving rise to a new kind of 'civic vernacular'. This analysis is definitely on the right track, but while she labels this setting for political engagement as the private sphere, it seems to me that this term may be misleading. It readily evokes the traditional, cosy family or home milieu. This is no doubt a part of the setting, but I would call it instead the solo sphere, to indicate its historically new character. The Bourdieuian term 'habitus' seems quite applicable here. The term points to the ensemble of practices, dispositions, taste, and horizons of expectation of particular group; this is established in the context of their everyday lives and serves to mediate prevailing patterns of societal hierarchy into the domain of subjectivity. The solo sphere can be seen as a new habitus for online political participation, a new platform for civic agency (see also Papacharissi and Eston, 2013, for a fuller discussion of habitus in regard to web use). Papacharissi (2010) suggests that this habitus fosters a retreat into an environment that many people understandably feel that they have more control over; a networked yet privatised mode of sociality emerges.

From this networked and often mobile personalised space, the individual engages with a vast variety of contexts in the outside world.

On the web s/he is confronted by the terrains that compete for attention with the public sphere and the political, in particular consumption and popular culture. We need not launch into any essentialist distinctions between on- and offline realities; it suffices to simply indicate that they to some extent build on different sets of conditions, cue some different kinds of social skills, and most importantly offer differing spaces for social interaction, with often differing implications. These contrasts can be significant for political participation. It may be that the online setting, with its powerful technical affordances, discourages engagement beyond itself: social, technical, and political economic contingencies may thus interplay to prioritise participation *in* the media and constrain the significance of over participation *via* the media. However, we should be wary of falling into techno-determinist reasoning; I would suggest rather that it is more the political contingencies that shape the mode and extent of participation.

The solo sphere, as a historically new and problematic mode of participation, arises therefore, not so much as a direct consequence of the web's technology, but rather in the interplay with its technical, political economic, and social contingencies, in specific societal circumstances. I mentioned earlier that participation can have varying degrees of affective intensity; the solo sphere would probably often correlate with low intensity participation, the routine political involvement in which many people may engage now and then. Where engagement is lukewarm, the distractions and enticements of the other terrains of participation become more compelling, the retreat into one's own experiential reality easier. High intensity participation, such as militant protest or even revolutionary activity, set in motion other dynamics. Aday et al. (2010), for example, based on data from the use of social media in the Iranian protest actions after the presidential elections of 2009 specify five interlocking levels that capture these dynamics: individual transformation, intergroup relations, collective action, regime policies, and external attention. These five levels address much of what has traditionally been described as the aims of much protest activity: to impact on how people think and act, dampen or intensify group conflict, mobilise collective actions, provoke responses and change from regimes, and attract attention from the broader public and internationally. In such a setting, the solo sphere has little relevance.

Part II
Evolving Forms and Practices

3
Occupy Wall Street: Discursive Strategies and Fields

The year 2011 witnessed intense political protest in many countries. This includes the Arab Spring, which began in Tunisia and Egypt, where the revolts led to the removal of these countries' dictators; in Libya a civil war emerged, leading to a democratically committed leadership taking power, though the situation remains unstable. In Syria the peaceful protest movement that began in 2011 was met with brutal violence, and at the time of writing a vicious civil war rages with reports of huge casualties daily. In Europe, most noteworthily in Greece and Spain, revolts against the economic crisis and austerity measures began – and continue today, in these and other countries in the southern part of the EU. In the US, the Occupy Wall Street (OWS) movement spread from its New York City origins to other cities in the US and abroad – but largely dissipated the following year. It is this latter protest movement that is the topic of this chapter; despite its short-lived character, it is a very instructive case in regard to alternative politics and participation via the media.

In it we can find evidence to provide more nuance to some of the debates about the web and politics that I mentioned earlier, including the specific role of such media in participation and the question of participation beyond the media. More fundamentally, I want to look at this case from the standpoint of the conceptual notion of context, trying to illuminate how the elucidation of specific contingencies can help us to understand the dynamics of media practices within alternative political movements. While the Occupy movement is often thought of as a phenomenon of the streets, it had a very strong media component. On the one hand its media practices were integrally tied to the physical assemblage of activists and also served to extend OWS's reach to other locations; on the other hand, its life in social media quickly became a central component that not only countered the mainstream media's portrayals of it, but also facilitated an extensive web-based engagement, with much discussion, debate, and global linkage (DeLuca et al., 2012; see also Caren and Gaby, 2011). Indeed, the use of multiple platforms – for example, sharing YouTube content via Twitter and sharing current cell phone footage as well as historical archive materials – were central to the media practices the movement developed (Thorson et al., 2013). Moreover, since the movement and its media practices were contextualised by the broader discursive environments of the mainstream US media, these efforts constituted important counter-hegemonic efforts.

These phenomena differ greatly in circumstances and character, but in all cases they make use of up-to-date media technologies, especially portable variants. Many among the activists are what are called political 'produsers', that is, while they are users in the traditional sense, they also specifically make use of these communication technologies to produce their own materials. These materials in turn express and in part constitute their political activism. When researchers and journalists write about these practices, they tend to speak about the activists as people with an established political agenda, using the communication technologies as tools in their efforts to reach their goals. And on a common-sense level, such of course is generally the case. However, particularly when we are dealing with the more fluid end of the political spectrum characterised by social movements, impromptu activist networks, and other less established, more alternative modes of political participation, we would do well to keep in mind the basic truism that people act from the circumstances in which they find themselves, that is, their actions – and their identities – are shaped by context.

At the same time, to invoke context, or the more conceptually ambitious term, contingency, is also to insist on the open-endedness, the non-deterministic character of phenomena and agency; there always remains a fortuitous, unpredictable dimension, characterised neither by logical necessity nor impossibility. That agency is contingent, that people adapt their practices as circumstances change, is hardly news, yet it is easy to lose sight of. To underscore the shifting circumstances behind agency helps us to better understand its character.

If we apply this line of reasoning to political produsers, this means that we avoid thinking of them as already-formed actors with a firmly set political compass, and open up the perspective of seeing their actions (including their communication) as well as their political agendas and identities, as to some extent responsive to circumstances that are evolving and may also contain contradictory elements. Further, this contingency derives to a great extent from the political milieu itself, the discursive fields in which they are operating. Thus, to analyse a political movement with a strong web presence means to follow and chart the adjustments, shifts, and adaptations in its political actions and identity, as politics unfolds in the media – its own media as well as the broader media milieu of which the movement media are a part. While the research results of such efforts may be less neat and tidy than a result based on an idealised expression of the political vision of the protagonists, this 'messiness' may be more in keeping with what is actually going on.

In this chapter I will be exploring this perspective of contingency with reference to the first six weeks of the OWS movement that began in New York City in September 2011. My aim here is to use their media representations as well as some online news coverage and commentary to illustrate the dynamics of contingency in the context of alternative political movements. The actions and identities of political produsers – especially within new movements, but the argument holds for politics more generally – are involved in a continual process of adaptation, even while we often – out of habit or at times seemingly even out of analytic necessity – 'fast freeze' our definitions of them. I will also look at the dominant political environment, as manifested in the mainstream media, to highlight the discursive field that OWS was operating in. My hope is that this approach will provide us with a more nuanced understanding of the conditions of online political produsers and the kinds of practices and skills required of them. Not least, the larger media environment in which the media practices of alternative politics must operate in is in constant evolution, presenting constant new challenges (see Askanius and Gustafsson, 2010).

In pursuing the analysis, I will begin by connecting again with the discourse theory of Laclau and Mouffe (2001), extracting a simplified analytic frame. Thereafter I situate and summarise the first six weeks of OWS based on an analysis of their media materials, looking specifically at their communicative strategies and identifying a few key discursive phases. From there I explore the OWS material and look at online media news coverage and commentary, in order to elucidate discursive shifts in practices and identities, as well as in the overall media milieu. Thereafter I probe the responses that emerged from various media corners, and typify some of the major features of the dominant discursive media field in an effort to shed some light on the larger contingencies that OWS had to deal with; I also look at some basic sociological attributes of US society – which did not always fit well with the OWS narrative. In the final section, I return to the OWS media practices and situate them in some of the broader analytic horizons about media and participation that I addressed in the previous chapter.

OWS from the start prompted much analysis and led to a large literature emerging, as it spread across the US and into many other countries. Many genres of books appeared, including social histories, eyewitness accounts from within and beyond the movement, ethnographies, and political analyses. Popular articles, research studies, pamphlets, debate texts, and political analyses, debates, journalistic reportage, and basic news coverage were also a part of this huge textual production – which says something about the perceived significance of the successes and failures of the movement.

An analytic framework

There is today a variety of approaches for analysing the discursive dynamics of politics, to focus on the formation and contestation of meaning and identities in the force-fields of power. One such approach, deriving from Laclau and Mouffe (2001), is called discourse theory (DT) – not to be confused with discourse analysis, although there are points of intersection (I take up DT again in Chapters 6 and 7). It is clearly post-structural in its approach to society, knowledge, language, and the subject. This is markedly evident in its emphasis on contingency: Laclau and Mouffe argue all our knowledge, and the discursive modalities that it takes, are predicated on particular circumstances; no human practice or subjectivity exists outside the specific conditions that both make them possible and delimit them. At bottom, DT is a rather dense philosophical enterprise with detailed ontological premises and has given rise to considerable debate.

The details of DT and the debates around it are beyond the scope of this book (for a useful introduction see Smith, 1999; Jørgensen and Phillips, 2002). Rather I want to extract from DT a basic methodological platform for discourse analysis. In contrast to much of the rest of their text, Laclau and Mouffe's analytic categories are relatively straightforward and quite applicable. In recent years media studies has begun to make use of DT in a variety of ways (see, for example, Carpentier and De Cleen, 2007; Uldam, 2010; Askanius and Uldam, 2011; Dahlberg and Phelan, 2011). For applications to wider cultural analysis, see Carpentier and Spinoy, (2008). We find in DT a few key concepts that together provide a useful analytical framework that can be used in empirical studies.

DT posits that meaning arises via *articulation* – the positioning of signs, words, and actions in relation to others; this is what gives them their sense. The key, definitive signs within a discourse are called *nodal points*; these are important for fixing the meanings within the discourse; we can think of them as the core concepts or vocabulary of a discourse. *Discourses* as such are structures of fixed meanings that arise as linguistic and material practices within a particular context. Some discourses, in relation to others, have *hegemonic* positions, that is, they offer preferred or dominant meanings. Here we have the pivotal point of politics, where prevailing discourses are challenged by alternative ones – of course always in the context of concrete societal circumstances. Since meaning is always to some extent shifting and contested, even hegemonic discourses can never be fully secure – even if discourses and society in general are characterised by large degrees of inertia.

In this regard, DT has another important concept to offer, called *chains of equivalences*. These become significant for developing counter-hegemonies; activists can use such discursive chains to try linking together the social and political demands (and visions) of various political groups (even while risking a dilution of platforms of the individual groups). They can coordinate their efforts so that they come to discursively define the problems – and especially the 'antagonists' – in ways that facilitate the building of coalitions and alliances. Further, if politics has to do with antagonisms between groups, between an 'us' and a 'them', discourses can serve as mechanisms of inclusion and exclusion. Discourses 'interpellate' subjects, addressing them and providing them with *subject positions*. In the context of public spheres and politics, subject positions can be understood as political identities made available by pertinent discourses. However, given the often contradictory, contested and generally disorderly state of discourses circulating in society, it is often the case that subjects are to varying degrees *over-determined*, which means that they are not fully at home in any one discourse, but are pulled in different directions and put into different positions by competing discourses. Their political identities thus fragment; the us–them divisions become less self-evident, and chains of equivalence can be confronted with *chains of difference*.

DT is engaged in exploring the conditions that make specific identities, meanings, and practices possible, and how the dynamics of power support or alter them. Public spheres become not just sites of political communication, but rather the spaces that discursively construct specific political subjectivities, with all their complexities and contradictions. In the spirit of classic critical theory DT offers a form of analytic practice that encourages us to look beyond the surfaces and to probe the factors that maintain particular existing arrangements – with the aim of 'thinking and doing otherwise'. It invites us to imaginatively envision alternatives, and explore what conditions might be necessary for their realisation. Yet, politics is never finished; democracy never reaches a point of equilibrium: new contestations and antagonisms always arise. Let us now, armed with the DT toolbox, turn to the OWS movement.

The strategies of situated produsers

The first six weeks

The original idea for the protest actions is usually credited to *Adbusters*, a Canadian-based activist magazine critical of consumerism and its consequences. During the summer of 2011, on their website (http://www.adbusters.org/blogs/adbusters-blog/occupywallstreet.html) they launched the idea of a demonstration on Wall Street as a way of protesting corporate influence in politics. The idea quickly snowballed through the alternative media, and the slogan 'We are the 99 percent' began to take hold. This slogan points to the gaps in wealth between the richest and most powerful sector of the population, and the vast majority, a gap that has been growing rapidly since the late 1970s. Very soon after this initiative, with various groups getting involved, the demands for change began to cluster around corporate greed and the corrupting effect it has on government, and the impact of lobbyists, along with economic inequality more generally.

The demonstrations began on 17 September 2011, with the protesters occupying Zuccotti Park, near Wall Street (they were not permitted on Wall Street itself). Tents and other facilities were set up; a few hundred protesters were there, in shifts, more or less permanently, while their ranks swelled to many thousands as particular demonstrations were organised. The occupation continued until 15 November, when the police raided the park, evicted the whole occupation, destroying even the tent with the OWS People's Library with over 5000 books (Goodman and Moynihan, 2012). Yet with the media coverage, the Occupy movement rapidly gained visibility and had already spread to over 1000 other US cities and towns, and internationally as well, with General Assemblies (GAs) and Working Groups (WGs) developing and coordinating an array of protest activities as well as an oppositional political culture. Occupy very quickly went global; this spilling across national borders is of course nothing new – the revolutions of 1848, the anti-colonial movements of the 1940s and 1950s in Africa and Asia, the upheavals of May 1968, the anti-communist movements of Eastern Europe in the 1980's, the Arab Spring in 2010 and 2011 – all established transnational connections.

After first trying to ignore the movement for almost a week, the mainstream media began to pick it up, and news coverage, blogs, alternative media and social media were spreading the messages of the movement, analysing, supporting, and criticising them. Media coverage took an upward turn early on, not least with mass arrests and the circulation of amateur footage showing unwarranted police violence using pepper spray against peaceful women demonstrators on the Brooklyn Bridge, which generated a political scandal and sympathy for the demonstrators. Goodman and Moynihan (2012) document the military-like suppression of journalistic activity by the police at many demonstrations and occupations around the US. However, cell phone cameras and social media were able to document and quickly publicise police abuses. On the whole though, the use of live video streams increased interest in the OWS story within mainstream media. Getting reasonably fair coverage there always remains a goal of protest movements; television is still the main medium through which most Americans get their news.

Support for the protests grew, some unions aligned themselves with the demonstrators, a large number of liberal celebrities expressed their support, and by 9 October the movement was spreading fast with the help of media coverage in the US as well as abroad; a global 'Occupy' movement was taking form. There emerged, not surprisingly, a massive flow of communication within the movement and between it and the outside world. It soon became a very dense and complex discursive milieu. For example, on YouTube, after six weeks (the end of October) a search yielded approximately 70,000 results, including contributions from the OWS movement itself, as well as groups and individuals across a vast global political spectrum: from the Defeat Obama Campaign to RT America, a Russian English-language 24/7 television news service that promoted the movement and saw it as symptom of America's decline. Al-Jazeera had given it considerable and favourable coverage, both in news reporting and by its regular bloggers.

The profile of the participants in the first week was largely young, white, and middle class, but as time went on it became somewhat more mixed – though OWS's demographic profile remained a problem. A survey conducted with about 1600 visitors to the OWS website (Captain, 2011) found that a third of them were 35 or older and one-fifth were 45 or older. Half were employed full time, while 20 percent worked part-time and just over 13 percent were unemployed. About 15 percent could be considered affluent (earning between $50,000 and $80,000 per year), and another 15 percent quite wealthy (earning over $80,000 per year). A big majority – 70 percent – saw themselves as politically independent, with just over 27 percent identifying themselves as Democrats and about 2.5 percent as Republicans. Two-thirds of the respondents were men – it was not clear if this is representative of the movement – and the number of non-whites was small, and largely remained so.

Some more detailed information on the views of the protesters emerged in a smaller survey (see Paybarah, 2011), done on site with about 200 respondents on 10 and 11 October. It found that a big majority had supported Obama during the election, but now about half no longer did so. Also, 65 percent asserted that government has a responsibility to provide affordable health care, a college education, and a secure retirement. They want to see higher taxes for the rich. On the question of what frustrates them the most, 30 percent answered 'The influence of corporate/moneyed/special interests.' Only 6 percent said 'Income inequality' and 3 percent said, 'Our democratic/capitalist system.' To the question 'What would you like to see the Occupy Wall Street movement achieve?' 35 percent answered 'Influence the Democratic Party the way the Tea Party has influenced the GOP' and 11 percent said, 'Break the two-party duopoly.' Only 4 percent responded with 'Radical redistribution of wealth.' Between the two surveys it is not clear how many actually support the Democratic Party, but overall there is a strong impression of a movement that is broad, even if far from representative of the 99 percent.

Also, the results suggest that it is largely left-reformist and populist rather than radical or revolutionary. But in keeping with the contingency perspective, we should remember that a survey at best captures something of people's political subjectivity at a particular moment under specific circumstances, and that it is not set in stone. These data can provide us with an interesting starting point, but they should not be reified. Also, they say nothing about the depth of commitment.

Much criticism has been levelled at Occupy for not specifying their demands. While the movement had been decidedly reticent in this regard, Sachs (2012) posits that it was not difficult to piece together the basic political vision that drives the movement, despite variances and differences in emphasis between different wings of the movement. He offers these main points (Sachs, 2012: 473):

– Politics in the hands of the 99 percent, not the 1 percent that control the large corporations.

- Rebuilding a mixed economy with a proper balance of markets and government.
- Ending reckless wars and downsizing the military.
- Shifting public funds into training and education so that young people can develop the skills needed for gainful employment.
- Taxing the rich and the financial sector, including a financial transaction tax.
- Building or rebuilding a social safety net and active labour-market policies more along the lines of northern Europe.
- Reinventing key services, such as health and education, to bring them within the reach of everyone, rich and poor.
- Global cooperation to put this agenda into effect.

This is really not an anti-capitalist agenda, intending to do away with capitalism in a revolutionary surge (although, again, there are/were such voices within Occupy). Rather, it is quite reminiscent of a classic social democratic vision familiar, indeed, from northern Europe – one that was never quite fully implemented (but, more alarmingly, has undergone severe erosion in the past three decades of neoliberal development).

The produsers' self-representations: Subject positions

A mix of prevalent discourses, with their varying positions, fissures, and contestation circulate in the media, constituting the relatively stable hegemonic discursive milieu in the mainstream media. From the perspective of DT, the occupation of the park near Wall Street, the demonstrations, and other on-site activities of the movement enter into and confront this milieu; this in turn is picked up and given varying forms of representation in the media. In looking at the OWS phenomenon I have made use of a variety of online transnational mainstream media resources: BBC, CNN, and as a sort of counterpoint to these two sites, Al-Jazeera, which offers a 24/7 global news service with a journalistic profile that at times varies from the two Western sites (Barkho, 2010). Also, the *Huffington Post* site was used, especially for its commentary, as well as a few other sites of varying political colours. For the movement itself, I have restricted myself to the main New York OWS website http://occupywallst.org/. (There is also a more specific New York City General Assembly of OWS, http://www.nycga.net/, which is a detailed record of the discussions and decision-making processes of the movement.) The website was actually established well ahead of the occupation, on 14 June, and is used here as the main evidence of the produser side of the movement, even if most of the production takes the form of text messages, that is, the website does not have much in the way of multi-media interventions, which can be found on other sites, such as YouTube.

In the horizons of DT, the major contingencies for the movement are the definitive characteristics of American society, its (historically anchored) overall sociopolitical attributes, as well as the key elements that define the contemporary crisis; these contingencies as are embodied in the discursive milieu. The movement inserts itself into this discursive context. On the main OWS website we find an interesting presentation and evolution of political identity. It was clear from the beginning that the movement was very heterogeneous, with a broad array of viewpoints gathered under its umbrella; after all, given the rhetoric of 99 percent of the population, it must encompass quite a spectrum of political identities. A virtue was made of this heterogeneity, while at the same time there emerged some effort to give it some definite shape.

On 26 July we can read a statement that sets the tone for the months to come:

> As the two U.S. political parties unite to dismantle Medicaid, Medicare and Social Security, it's clear: The bankers are looting decades-old peoples' programs and the Democrats can't help us. Obama can't help us. Elected officials can't help us. It's time for the people to meet and take the bull by the horns! [...] The current depression-level crisis is not due to lack of revenue. It's due to theft. The trillions that the banks are sitting on right now? That's our money. Whether through taxes; the looting of pension and social security contributions; or the wealth we created from our labor – all of that belongs to us. Come to Wall Street August 2 and strategize – on how to get that back!

The theme of accountability is underscored on 7 September: '#OCCUPYWALLSTREET is all about breaking up that cozy relationship between money and politics and bringing the perpetrators of the financial crash of 2008 to justice'. And the reiteration of the 'We are the 99 percent' serves to cement it as a slogan.

Thus, among the key nodal points in the discourse of OWS are: the people, 99 percent and 1 percent, democracy, and corporate greed. From the outset, OWS presents itself as an all-inclusive movement with no barriers: it is a large and sprawling 'us' mobilised against the 1 percent 'them', consisting of the economic and political elites. The movement offers a view of itself as horizontal, open, transparent collectivity, united in its victimisation by the 1 percent. An ethos of sharing and empowerment is established on the very first day, where it defines itself as an open-source project, making available all its internal deliberation for others to use and build upon. A supplementary element was soon articulated to this set of nodal points: given the ban on loudspeakers in the park, the demonstrators make a democratic virtue of necessity by developing the 'People's Mic' method of verbal relay. What a speaker says to the crowd, without any amplification, becomes repeated, in successive waves. This is a cumbersome process, but a practice that is inclusive and participatory.

The movement itself presents a leaderless collectivity (though there are a few key spokespeople, notably Keith Olbermann), based on a number of WGs and a general assembly, with no hierarchy. This was modified in early November 2012 with the introduction of a 'spoke council' at Liberty Square (3 November), which aims to make more effective internal coordination of the movement. Yet the aura of direct, participatory democracy remains a core element of the movement's identity.

Concern and consideration for people living near the park is expressed; meetings are held to discuss the noise (especially in regard to drumming), with the neighbourhood (13 October). On 9 August the website offers a link to a practical 'quick guide on group dynamics in people's assemblies' – a sort of instruction kit for how-to-do direct democracy. The frequent reference to 'the people', however, is somewhat of a 'floating signifier' one, as DT would call it: it is not fully anchored (and is traditionally one mobilised by political actors to point to their support base).

The signifier 'the people' articulates strong American traditions (e.g. Carl Sandberg's poem *Yes, the People*), yet can also galvanise socialist traditions – something seen as very un-American in mainstream US society. Thus, when the People's General Assembly is introduced on 4 August, the signification becomes cloven. A reference (20 August) to President Franklin D. Roosevelt's speech on an economic bill of rights is framed with reference to early socialist thought and the French Socialist party, indicating not only a perspective far to the left of almost all Americans, but also an intellectual identity presumably not shared by the majority within the 99 percent.

The dominant political tone on the website is what might be called 'strongly reformist'. But many voices are contributing, and we also see phrases such as 'We call for workers to not only strike, but seize their workplaces collectively' (17 September, the day the occupation begins), and 'we are foremost here to oppose the growing power of the ruling class' (30 September). Such terminology evokes images of socialist rev-olution, suggesting problematic internal fissures. While the daily flow of messages underscores the inclusiveness of almost all Americans – and soon this is expanded to global contexts – we also see the celebra-tory presence of left intellectual stars such as Slavoj Žižek and Cornell West, and the textual support of others, like Noam Chomsky. These are figures who are either unknown to or seen with suspicion by many mainstream Americans. There is also a strong theoretical profile in the critiques of consumer culture, materialist values, and so on (most promi-nently on 12 September) – evoking the issue of the role of intellectuals in OWS movement. Also, this generates a parallel discourse to the one concerned mainly with economic justice and democracy: themes clus-tering around values and culture are now also discursive elements of the movement.

DT puts much emphasis on building alliances. There are OWS allies – potential and actual – that are named, as well as ignored; we could say there is some problematic juggling between the chains of equiva-lence and the chains of difference. Some Democrats in Congress express their support, but little is made of this on the website; OWS defines both of the political parties as part of the problem. Much of what OWS has to say is perfectly in harmony with the discourses of the World Social Forum (WSF) and its alterglobalisation stance; yet the WSF is not mentioned, probably because it has not had much public visibil-ity in recent years and is not associated with any concrete successes. However, exchanges of solidarity with the demonstrators in Greece and activists in Cairo are made public on the website, as well as of course Occupy efforts going on in other American cities. At the end of the six weeks, the website refers to the large Israeli demonstrations, cit-ing them as evidence of anti-neoliberal politics; no mention is made of the plight of the Palestinians, which could be divisive in the US context.

Potential articulations of all kinds, hovering in the background, are part of the overall contingencies of a political movement. Those deriv-ing from popular culture have a particular kinetic energy because they are so ubiquitous and circulate quite freely. Thus, popular culture often offers easily applied articulation of meaning that can at times be enabling (e.g. the undermining of hegemonic discourses via televi-sion comics), but also problematic. Many commentators linked OWS with the film *Network* (popular among journalists), from 1974, which featured the frustrated TV anchor opening the window of apartment and shouting 'I'm mad as hell and I'm not going to take it anymore'. In the film this sets off a mass wave of people following his example. The problem with this articulation, aside from the possible frivolity of popular culture association, is that the depicted movement had no political impact. It was easily absorbed by 'the system'. While this particular articulation was visible for a while, it never really became definitive.

Thus, the subject position of the OWS has certain problems of ambiguity. It is multi-vocal, with a variety of valences, but is not heavily over-determined, that is, not profoundly torn by competing internal positions; it largely works. Given the genuine heterogeneity of the movement, OWS manages nonetheless to offer a reasonably coherent political identity of the morally enraged, economically victimised, and politically disenfranchised majority. While a few voices give evidence of replacing capitalism (with what is not clear) the dominant vector is, as mentioned, reformist. It is a populist Left movement; comparisons with the Tea Party movement become inevitable, but even if there is some analytic foundation for some overlap (based on shared distrust for the power elites, for example), there is little confusion about their political trajectories. The specific demands that OWS put forward, however, are not so clear; it is difficult to make a powerful political slogan of 'less corporate greed'. This lack of clear political proposals has been one of the main themes in the media coverage of the movement.

The fields of mediated hegemonics

Political response: A shifting discursive milieu

OWS at first functioned somewhat like a floating signifier that quickly became contested: on the Left, commentators could invest it with the visions of a fuller, more vibrant democracy where the people challenge the power and corruption of the corporate elite and their impact on government, while on the Right the discursive strategy was to paint it as either a mob of spoiled brats or a dangerous gang of revolutionary troublemakers trying to foment class warfare.

As mentioned, the mainstream media coverage was at first slow to take off, and as it began to focus on OWS, it was initially wary. Yet, public opinion surveys showed quite strong support, especially among New Yorkers: one university poll found that 67 percent of the voters of the city approved of the movement, while only 23 percent disapproved

(Quinnipiac University, 2011). A poll by CBS News/*NY Times* (2011) showed that 43 percent of Americans agreed with OWS, while 27 percent disagreed. The brutality of the police in a few incidents in the first days of the coverage no doubt helped the movement win sympathy, and many of the positive commentators – in particular found on Al-Jazeera blogs – underscored that the basic message of the movement was clear and had no difficulty resonating with large numbers of Americans.

In fact, a number of mainstream commentators could accept the lack of organisation and structure, as well as the absence of coherent political demands. They understood that OWS is not a traditional protest movement that struggles for specific political goals against a targeted enemy. Rather, as some commentators suggest, the protest is less about victory than about inclusion, participation, and consensus. Benjamin Barber (2011), a theorist of democracy, writes:

> To understand what's going on, look at what OWS is, not what it does. Start by taking seriously the ubiquitous signs asking 'What does democracy look like?' and answering 'WE are what democracy looks like!' Look at the process, which is a bold attempt to embody a 'horizontal' paradigm of participatory engagement as an alternative to 'vertical' big league moneyball democracy... The protesters' principles are in their processes, which stand in radical contrast to how we normally conduct business.

Support has come in from many intellectual figures, and a good number of unions, as well as a few major business leaders, most notably George Soros (The Huffington Post, 2011). This in turn triggered a response from the Right, with some commentators (for example, Newman, 2011), claiming that Soros was funding this 'anti-capitalist' movement. Soros denied this claim, but it is interesting to note the semiotic dissonance that emerges when 'Soros' becomes articulated with 'anti-capitalist'. As noted above, a few Democrats in Congress expressed support (not least House Democratic leader Representative Nancy Pelosi), and President Obama said he could sympathise with 'the frustrations that many Americans feel'. From the Republican side, among the presidential candidates, came, not surprisingly, negative responses, such as those from Herman Cain and Newt Gingrich. Interestingly, the presidential front-runner, Mitt Romney, showed a subject position that was over-determined, that is, self-contradictory: on a YouTube clip (http://www.youtube.com/watch?v= iJ_orudj6hA) he characterised the OWS protesters as 'dangerous' and claimed that they were 'inciting class warfare', yet soon after he is quoted as saying 'I look at what's happening on Wall Street and my view is, boy, I understand how those people feel' (Geiger and Reston, 2011). Further out on the right wing, commentators such as Glenn Beck and Rush Limbaugh confirmed their reputations for rabid rantings, with the latter referring to OWS as 'this parade of human debris' (Limbaugh, 2011).

Such responses are not startling – however, the extent of public support may have come as a positive surprise to many within the movement. The expressions of reaction in a way embody the basic political contingencies of political realities in the US: there is clearly a well-entrenched discursive hegemony that supports and justifies the prevailing arrangements and thus condemn OWS, yet it is a hegemony that has cracks in it. Romney's remarks give clear evidence of the cleavages: a defensive reflex for the system, together with a capacity to empathise with those who are so dissatisfied with it. For OWS, seen as a collective of online producers, to navigate its way through such a complex and contradictory landscape as they in fact managed to do in the first weeks of their movement must be seen as a significant political accomplishment.

Despite inconsistent rhetoric, they kept a fairly consistent political identity on the website (which may in fact gloss over backstage differences, but that is a different issue). Moreover, via their discursive nodal points, they were able to create chains of equivalence with allies within the Occupy movement across the US as well as abroad. They soon elicited considerable public support, drawing a number of important elite politicians and other public figures, as well as some unions, to their side. Perhaps most significantly, they managed well to make visible and accentuate the cracks in the dominant discourses and open up public debate in the US in an unprecedented manner, at a time of crisis when such a transformation is sorely needed.

The trouble with class

Class is one of the key signifiers in the OWS, but one often submerged precisely by the narrative of the 99 versus 1 percent. Ehrenreich and Ehrenreich (2012) point out that the 99 percent comprises a very wide range of class elements; while all within this category can distinguish themselves from the super-rich top 1 percent, the large category includes everyone else within the entire class structure of the US: from the unemployed, the working poor, the stable working class, middle management, small business people, middle class professionals, and so on. The political economic and social realities of the world, and especially a huge country like the US, are messy and confusing; there are tensions and conflicts present that problematise the basic Occupy narrative: many people look at the groups around them and compare themselves with these others. People tend to see the class divisions that are more visible in their own everyday lives, and situate themselves in frameworks that are coloured by their own habitus, rather than a macro-sociological perspective.

Thus, in a firm, employees may be more cognisant of differences between, say, lower and upper-middle management personnel; such distinctions can take on great salience in the experiences of daily life. The US is crisscrossed with many divisions beyond the basic distinctions of the 99 and the 1 percent also can evoke resentment. For example, older age cohorts generally are doing much better than younger ones: comparing the relative wealth of households headed by 65-year-olds with those aged 35, we see that the wealth gap has increased from 10:1 in 1984 to 47:1 in 2009 (Cowen and de Rugy, 2012: 415). Sachs (2012) adds that more than 70 percent of Americans between 25 and 29 do not have a bachelor's degree – not least because many are forced to drop out due to financing difficulties. Looking at ethnically based divides, we can see that among Hispanic men of the same age only 11 percent are enrolled in higher education. More African-American males have prison experience than a college degree. The 99 percent is riddled with diversity, and it is understandably difficult to forge a unitary narrative that is convincing. One could say that the discursive accomplishment of establishing chains of equivalence is countered by troublesome sociological factors – and thus in the long run will not succeed as a powerful counter-hegemony.

Meanwhile, on the Right, the strategic discourse about the 'liberal elite' had been circulating for several decades This populist, mythic construction identifies the liberal/left-leaning 'East Coast' intelligentsia, media people, academics, managers, and so on as a powerful political group – espousing 'political correctness' – who look down on the middle- and working-class Americans and their lifestyles. Moreover, this elite champions reckless government spending and often highly unconventional lifestyles that threaten traditional family values (for example, gay marriage). While always a profound sociological distortion, this particular narrative became increasingly difficult to maintain as the recession took hold (Ehrenreich and Ehrenreich, 2012). Not just the poor and the working class were feeling the adverse effects, but large numbers within the middle and upper-middle classes were also going into an economic and social tailspin, losing jobs and homes, as manufacturing, the service sectors, health care, education, and the cultural sector all began contracting. Thus, the partially hegemonic idea of the liberal elite had taken a beating during the growing crisis – but the OWS counter-hegemony was not strong enough to fill up the gaps that emerged and fully replace it.

Yet, one may well ask, why were OWS's demands for redistribution of wealth not more forcefully presented? Research by Kuziemko and Norton (2012) indicates that most Americans believe that the inequality of wealth in the US is too high, but there does not seem to be any group who actually call for its elimination. For varying political reasons, US citizens feel that some degree of economic distinction is justified and are very reluctant to support measures that facilitate redistribution of wealth. In fact, support for such policies has actually fallen since the start of the recession in 2008. This mechanism, whereby people seemingly act against their own interests, has long been a puzzle on the Left. To invoke the classic refrain of 'false consciousness' does not shed much light on the paradox.

The authors propose that the notion of 'last-place aversion' might offer some clarification. This concept basically proposes that, first of all, people carry a strong loathing for ending up in or near the bottom, and secondly, people near the bottom of socio-economic hierarchies tend to 'oppose redistribution because it might allow people below them to catch up with them, or even worse, to leapfrog past them' (Kuziemko and Norton, 2012: 282). The research results of the authors 'suggest that people in last place are willing to risk losing money for the chance to jump over the players just above them, and second-to-last players feel they need to defend against this possibility'(Kuziemko and Norton, 2012: 283).

The relevance of this in regard to the Occupy movement is that it wisely seems to anticipate these mechanisms by providing, in its narratives of contemporary society, an engaging alternative that switches the attention of all groups away from those just below them, and encourages them to look critically at those far above them, that is, the top 1 percent. This became a new and challenging discourse in the American public debate, though a short-lived one. Despite its internal heterogeneity, OWS in fact made available on a broad scale an alternative conception of politics as such – one that offers not just a vision of a more equitable society but also one that provides through its own practices and discourses a vision of what democracy should be. Yet, despite the fissures it accentuated and OWS was not able to dislodge the key hegemonic parameters around social hierarchy in the US.

Weschler (2012) sees the movement's most significant contribution as being that with its narrative meme of the 99 percent, Occupy had reinvigorated a moribund discursive field that challenged very basic assumptions about politics and economics in the US; it was now 'becoming imperative that the movement find a way of ratcheting the narrative up another several notches' (Weschler, 2012: 401). This, however, did not take place. Similarly, Castells (2012) argues that the most important impact of the Occupy movement is to have generally raised awareness of the inequalities of income and wealth and have injected social class into mainstream political discourse. This awareness will no doubt linger very long in public consciousness, as the crisis continues.

However, the mainstream media began to decrease their use of phrases such as 'inequality' and 'corporate greed' as soon as the movement began to subside from the headlines (Knebel, 2012), even if the phrases 'the 99 percent' and 'the 1 percent' continued longer. Hegemony was discursively contested in these media for a few months, as alternative narratives began circulating. However, in the absence of the impulse provided by continuing media coverage, a discursive 'normalisation' took place, restoring the prevailing outlook on these matters. As Knebel notes, 'changing the conversation' has no automatic permanence.

Media practices – and live assemblage

I turn now to a few aspects of media practices, organisation, and the question of participation in the offline mode. Based on extensive research, Costanza-Chock (2012) describes what in a short time developed into an intense multi-media approach to spreading the protest, which included social media sites (SNS) and mainstream media:

> Occupiers produced and circulated media texts and self-documentation across every platform they had access to...SNS were crucial for the spread of media created by everyday Occupiers, while media, press, and tech WGs worked to build SNS presence (especially on Twitter and Facebook), create more highly produced narratives, edit videos, operate 24-hour live streams such as Globalrevolution.tv, organize print publications such as *The Occupy Wall Street Journal*, design and code websites such as OccupyTogether.org and wikis such as NYCGA.cc and build autonomous movement media platforms and technology infrastructure (see Occupy.net). Members of

these GAs also worked with members of the press, from independent reporters and local media outlets to journalists from national and transnational print, television and radio networks.

(Costanza-Chock (2012: 4)

He characterises the media practices as based in an awareness that, given the ambition to represent a broad and heterogeneous segment of society (the 99 percent), many activists and potential participants would not necessarily have high-tech media skills. Thus, there was a concerted effort to also develop offline, analogue counterparts, chiefly print forms, used for posters; the overall approach became a *transmedia mobilisation*. His data show that in the 24-hour period prior to his interviews, media use by individual activists to gather information to keep up with the movement was spread across all the major technologies and platforms. Nearly half said that face-to-face discussion had also been a part of their communicative experience. In terms of media-making to spread the movement, about three-quarters used Facebook and an almost equal number used face-to-face conversation, while about one in five replied that they had written blogs and one in ten made some kind of video.

Though self-described as 'leaderful' rather than 'leaderless' in ways similar to many contemporary social movements, OWS had structures and persons who filled leader roles, especially in relation to media practices. Differing normative views regarding leadership emerged, which pitted openness and equal participation for all against privileging those who worked harder and more consistently with Occupy and/or had more social movement experience elsewhere. Further, the dominance of white, educated straight males from middle- and upper-middle class backgrounds soon emerged as a dilemma; the movement struggled with this and attempted to rectify it in various ways, but with only partial success.

There was a considerable body of media expertise with social movement experience within Occupy; this was a small yet important minority. Many media productions, such as the live television stream and other genres of visual documentation, were highly significant in spreading the movement, both in the US and internationally. As an interesting contrast, notably at GAs, what became known as the People's Mic, to which I referred above. This inclusionary social device for relaying non-amplified speech through a crowd not only served an immediate practical purpose, but also underscores the value of face-to face side of political work and participatory culture.

Gerbaudo (2012) offers a very insightful analysis into the uses of social media in the dynamics of protest movements, building upon research he has conducted on the Arab Spring, the Spanish Indignados, and OWS. He begins by inserting himself into the debates on the role of the web and social media for political protest by first rejecting the easy optimism of observers like Shirky (2008) and Castells (2010), but also by positioning himself against the very pessimistic views of Morozov (2011). Gerbaudo's point here is that on both sides one tends towards an abstract, essentialist view of the communication technologies, seeing automatic (though opposite) consequences of their use. His own perspective on these media underscores 'their interaction with and mediation of emerging forms of public gatherings and in particular the mass sit-ins which have become the hallmark of contemporary popular movements' (Gerbaudo, 2012: 5). Further, he underlines that each setting requires a situational analysis, one that deals with how social media practices interplay with other forms of communication as well as with the physical geography of the mobilisation.

He launches the term 'choreography of assembly' to signify a process whereby specific public places (for example, Tahrir Square, Zuccotti Park) take on symbolic meaning for a movement and also guide, in practical ways, the physical assemblage of a heterogeneous constituency. His strong contention is that the use of the web, social media, and other communication technologies does not on its own lead to spontaneous engagement and genuine participation. Rather, he sees influential leadership emanating from key figures via social media, what he calls 'choreographers'. The adjectives he uses to describe such leadership – soft, emotional, invisible, dialogic, and so forth – clearly signal its character and resonate with the notion of choreography. Thus, there is not absence of leadership in these kinds of movements, but one that promotes 'liquid organisation' and tends to take a different form compared to traditional political organisations. Moreover, the idea of pure spontaneity as a way of understanding this kind of participation crumbles as he demonstrates how media-based interaction has pre-figured subjective engagement, prior to the physical gathering.

In regard to the Occupy movement, Gerbaudo (2012) concludes that despite the launching of the idea by *Adbusters*, and its spread across social media sites, not much really happened until people began the process of choreographing assembly and the movement took to the streets, did it begin to gather broader attention. Moreover, he found that while there was massive web-based discussion within and outside the movement, these conversations were led and moderated by a handful of core organisers managing influential movement Facebook and Twitter accounts. Such activists came to acquire a role as invisible choreographers who by using social media to publicise the movement's plans and events had much influence in shaping its manifestation. If the activist spaces created by Occupy and other groups are indeed characterized internally by a strongly participatory character, their initiation and maintenance nevertheless requires the work of a few committed activists.

(Gerbaudo, 2012: 132)

On this point, Juris (2012), though somewhat tied to a Castellsian view of networking, still accentuates the importance of aggregation. He claims that the loose bonds established through mediated networks can have a certain stability, but that physical aggregation is important for activists: 'These individuals may ... forge a collective subjectivity through the process of struggle, but it is a subjectivity constantly under the threat of disaggregation ... hence the importance of interaction and community building within physical spaces' (Juris, 2012: 266). We are reminded here how the screen-based solo sphere, as a mode for political participation, becomes a subject position doomed in the long run to relative inefficacy.

4
Online Public Intellectuals

The status and significance of public intellectuals (PIs) continue to be debated. Even if PIs themselves tend to dominate these discussions, we would be foolish to dismiss the issues as merely an expression of vanity among a small coterie, because, as I will argue, PIs still play an important role in democracies. They represent a particular form of political participation, often within the realm of alternative politics, and while there may be in some corners a misguided tendency to dismiss PIs as 'elitist', their significance persists, despite changes in their circumstances, activities, and practices. Most of the familiar questions remain and will no doubt continue to be discussed: are PIs in decline or not, in quantitative terms? How should we view the quality of their contributions today? Who is/is not a PI? What are the consequences of their increased academic profile? Who are the audiences for contemporary PIs? In fact, these questions, as we shall see, take on new pertinence with the advent of the web.

Whatever answers one might propose, it is important to take into account the societal changes that impact on PIs, their situation and activities. In this chapter I explore some of these transformations; my aim is to elucidate the factors that make possible as well as delimit and alter the phenomenon of PIs in contemporary democratic societies. Thus, after a review of some of the main debates about PIs, I look at three sets of evolving contingencies in which PIs are inexorably embedded: the *structural* setting of mediated public spheres, with a particular emphasis on the web, the dynamic realm of *practices* associated with online political participation more broadly, and, lastly, the cultural and political *climates* of democratic societies confronted by serious dilemmas.

Traditional PIs, contemporary distinctions

In the history of modern democracies, the public intellectual is a figure who has played a significant if fluctuating role. While the somewhat romantic or heroic image of the rugged individualist can at times occlude sociological insight into the phenomena of PIs, their capacity to independently address matters of contemporary concern has contributed to the dynamics of public opinion. While they are politically engaged, their commitments have largely been to the truth (as they see it from their various political perspectives); most have not sought power or political careers for themselves. At times they have expressed a minority opinion that may then take hold and sway popular sentiment and/or decision-making by elites; at other times they have had harsh responses from both power holders and the general public. The success rate of their causes has been less significant than the fact that they participate in vitalising democracy and animating the public sphere, even if success, of course, inevitably adds to the heroic status (Émile Zola's intervention in the Dreyfus affair in France in late 1890s remains the paradigmatic model). They have largely been driven by ideas – and they have had a communicative capacity to reach and engage large audiences.

PIs and their contexts

There is certainly a dose of caricature in this image, but it does capture something of the significance that democracies have attributed to PIs. A basic shortcoming of this depiction is that it is sociologically uninformed; it is fixed on individuals, and can easily veer towards a Great Men of History stance. While the dimension of individual agency is of course essential here, we must also keep in sight the circumstances that shape PIs as a societal phenomenon in any given setting. Much of the research literature (see below) has been filling in the sociological horizon, and we increasingly understand that analytically, the phenomenon of PIs, like all social phenomena, resides in a conceptual force-field comprised of agency and very particular historical contexts.

One important aspect of the context for PIs is of course the national setting, and we see even today a wide range of different national cultures in regard to PIs. While I will not be addressing national differences or individual PIs in this discussion, it can be worth noting that France retains a degree of 'exceptionalism' here; French culture still accords more weight to PIs than just about any other democracy. They have considerable visibility in the mainstream media; along with profiling individual PIs, the French media also continue to address the general state of PIs (recent contributions include, e.g. Rimbert, 2011; *Le Nouvel Observateur*, 2010).

A quick look at Pierre Bourdieu, the French sociologist who passed away in 2002, can illustrate the importance of specific contingencies. Swartz (2003) shows how Bourdieu by the 1990s had made the transition from professional university researcher (with a massive international standing) to a (mostly national) PI. He had become publically engaged in issues of poverty in France, in the role and character of television and journalism, and in the anti-globalisation movement. Swartz demonstrates that there were both continuities and changes in Bourdieu's activities, and along with his own obvious forceful public initiatives there were a whole set of factors that shaped his persona as a PI. These have to do with his movement to a central position in the French academic field, how this field itself was evolving (expressly in becoming more 'mediatized', as was much of French cultural and political life), the political failure of the French socialists, and the galvanising national issue of globalisation. What Swartz underscores is that Bourdieu did not simply launch himself, unilaterally, on a PI trajectory, but rather was continuously responding in strategic ways to the shifting situation in which he found himself – an agency operating within the vectors of circumstances.

PIs have evolved, unevenly and ambiguously, in Western democracies over the past century or so. It recent decades it has become understood that the classic or traditional PI has become a problematic category; indeed, many of the contemporary discussions about PIs evoke a nostalgic sense of a lost golden age (see for example, Jacoby, 1987, a landmark book on the theme). Later contributions include Michael, 2000; Small, 2002; Etzioni and Bowditch, 2006; Posner, 2003; Melzer et al., 2003). At the same time, in the more sociologically oriented parts of this literature we find various sets of distinctions that can help us both grasp the heterogeneity of PIs and understand some of the issues at stake in the debates today.

Institutional affiliations

A key theme is the institutional affiliation of PIs. A quarter of a century ago in the US, Russell Jacoby (1987) underscored that the insular logics of university life increasingly deflect academics from becoming PIs, or render them irrelevant in the role, a perspective that he has reiterated more recently (Jacoby, 2008). Within academic circles, being a genuine 'populariser' has long been suspect; this tends to detract from one's professional status, even while university professors are admonished to engage themselves in – or 'provide service to' – society outside the academic world to advance their careers. To fulfil this criterion for academic advancement, corporate or governmental consultation is usually a safer route. In recent decades, the growth of the 'new public management' ethos within academic bureaucracies, with its built-in market logic, has affected the criteria used in evaluation for appointments and promotions (for example, the importance of the quantitative bibliometrics of citations). There is also across the board an increasing managerial rationality in the organisation of academic work, more difficulties in getting research financing, a growing emphasis on team efforts, and so forth. These trends all serve to impede the robustly independent PI – assuming that s/he is also trying to pursue an academic career.

However, one can ask: what are the viable institutional alternatives for PIs? Beyond academia, PIs have traditionally also been associated with 'bohemia', which generally signals an economically vulnerable situation. Here we have the classic figures of the 'writer' and the 'philosopher'. In today's world they are increasingly rare, given the difficulty in subsisting largely on freelance publications. While there are many writers and not least journalists who do survive as freelancers, the demands of the market often get in the way of being a PI: such forms of writing are usually not the most lucrative.

The somewhat romantic figure of the PI is on some fronts being replaced by PIs affiliated with think tanks. These tend to reflect technical expertise rather than the humanistic traditions. Some are independent, but most think tanks have some connection with interest groups, powerful organisations, or government. Also, NGOs have become modern homes for some PIs; here too one sees connections with particular interests or advocacy causes; the status of 'independent' can at times become compromised, though NGOs tend to provide more room for explicitly politically engaged expression than think tanks do. Beyond NGOs the terrain can blur into various extra-parliamentarian activist groups, networks, and social movements. Some are very established, such as Greenpeace, who can provide research and engage in public debate, while others – and their PIs – are more transitory and ephemeral. We might find new versions of 'organic intellectuals', as Gramsci called them, working in education projects or loose social movements contexts (see Borg and Mayo, 2007), but these are very much the exception. Thus, what we might call the traditional model of the PI is in some ways being edged out by institutional changes both within and beyond the university that erode the viability of economic and ideological independence.

Further distinctions

From another perspective, PIs can be identified either as generalists, or as specialists in a discipline. The generalist PI will commonly address a range of issues, where pre-existing knowledge is seen as less important than the ability to reason, analyse, and argue. Discipline specialists as PIs base their authority on their expertise in a particular field, which means that in the long run, generalists often have more options and flexibility to operate. A further distinction has to do with the actual disciplines from which a PI derives: some PIs have their origins in the humanities, while others derive from the technical or natural sciences. PIs with a social science profile split the difference, with some leaning more towards the humanities – emphasising norms and values, for example – while others present their expertise more as a form of 'hard' science.

The late Christopher Hitchens, an undisputed PI with a profile that would warrant the adjective 'traditional', defined a PI as someone 'who makes his or her living through the battle of ideas' (Hitchens, 2008). Another commentator robustly expressed the differences between a perceived traditional model of the PI and the more specialised versions that we see today:

> In the past, public intellectuals would answer big questions, and primarily philosophical ones...They would ask, earnestly and unashamedly, about humanity's place in the cosmos. They would diagnose the moral sicknesses of their age. They would ask whether civilization was in decline, and why or why not. Public intellectuals today, by contrast, are most interesting on matters of detail – the future of Chinese monetary policy, the prospects for the next climate change summit, some newfangled trend in ethical theory. Their banality increases exponentially in proportion to the generality of their topic.
>
> (Anonymous, 2011)

The distinction evoked here is obviously not just between generalist and specialist; it also has to do with intellectual horizons and moral engagement. The specialist tends to be less normative, less oriented to 'grand ideas'. Several commentators (e.g. Hitchens, 2008; Dezner, 2008a), note another difference between PIs now and those of the immediate post-World War II decades: the political leanings of PIs today are much less leftist and not always secular. There is an increasingly conservative and even theological presence. To the extent that one is looking at mainstream PIs this is probably true, and can no doubt be explained at least in part by the ascendency of neoliberal politics over the past three decades. However, as I discuss below, in the online context we see more diversity.

Another distinction has to do with a PI's proximity to power, be it political, economic, or cultural. There are PIs that have a decided elite profile; they interact with, or at least have access to power holders, while others are seen as more 'popular' (and are usually generalists), in the sense that they are situated outside the centres of power, and thus their public persona differs less from that of their audiences. Does a PI speak to or with power? This is decisive; the classic PI wants to impact on society, usually via public opinion, but generally does not seek to hold power. However, we see governments making use of 'house intellectuals' (Tony Blair's recruitment of the sociologist Anthony Giddens comes to mind). This of course enhances the power of the PI, but may also risk eroding his/her perceived independence as an intellectual. Of course, on a personal level, given the celebrity culture that permeates the mass media, PIs can engage in self-promotion at the expense of engaging in ideas – for purposes of enhancing their own position, as Habermas (2008) recently pointed out, echoing one point of his classic critique of the modern mediated public sphere (Habermas, 1989).

From another angle it becomes significant to consider the contrast between what I would call national and cosmopolitan PIs. National PIs are active in the public spheres of their own countries (even if this may involve only local or regional settings), while cosmopolitan PIs function in more 'global' contexts. This can mean travelling for live presentations as well as just publishing abroad. Thus, some cosmopolitan PI's from small language countries may publish extensively in English, and thereby have very small publics in their home countries. Finally, in today's media world, we can also distinguish between traditional PIs and those of a less traditional character, who are emerging in the new online media. I will return to this development later.

Close proximities: Pundits and journalists

Drawing the line between those who are (genuine) PIs and those who are not (genuine) is an issue that seemingly will never fade. In some areas the distinction remains fairly clear, despite occasional efforts to deceptively cloud it: the demarcation between PIs and public relations specialists, spin doctors, image managers, and advertisers is for the most part quite apparent. There are more problematic grey zones, however, for example, between pundits, in the sense of journalistic commentators, and 'genuine' PIs (see Joffe, 2003). While many intellectuals view pundits as often shallow and superficial, it is also true that many PIs make use of journalistic formats to express their views in popular and accessible ways. Pundits, as media-based practitioners, have become increasingly important in recent decades in the dissemination of what count as 'ideas' in modern society, even if the intellectual dimension often can and should be challenged. The categories of pundits and PIs have come in closer proximity to each other.

Jacobs and Townsley (2011), in the US context, examine the mainstream 'spaces of media opinion', mostly filled by elite editorialists and commentators, as a major component of the public sphere. With an admirable sociological stoicism they concede that such spaces 'are limited, fragmentary, exclusionary, contradictory, and filled with artifice' and that they 'typically fail to satisfy minimum standards of reason or rational deliberation. Opinion columns and television talk show programs provide distortion as often as they provide clarity, and self-serving performances are at least as common as careful deliberation' (Jacobs and Townsley, 2011: 5). They capture, in a pithy manner, the dynamics of this sector of the public sphere:

> While it would be nice if public debate emerged from the ground up, emanating from the bowling leagues to the halls of power, this turns out to be a rare occurrence. More typically, public debate is organised through media, and public opinion is articulated in conversations among journalists, politicians, experts, and insiders, all of whom are jockeying to represent the public interest
>
> (Jacobs and Townsley, 2011: 6)

This depiction, aside from reminding us of the difficulties that stand in the way of the realisation of a Habermasian vision of the public sphere, also signals structural aspects of the mass media, as well as their media logics. The public sphere representations of the mainstream media are populated and dominated by journalists, pundits, establishment political figures, and so forth; they facilitate or give direct voice to political issues that usually reside comfortably in the prevailing discourses. These are not settings that are normally conducive for traditional PIs; as spokespeople for views that often put them in the category of minority or alternative voices, and as actors whose interventions are guided by a strong identification with the realm of ideas, the fit here is not the best. When they do engage in these settings, they often find the discursive terrain for their expression quite circumscribed – both in terms of the substance of ideas and the by the logic of sound bites and audience ratings. They can of course adapt, and some do, though the extent to which their participation can be deemed that of a traditional PI becomes less certain.

There are of course different ways of being intellectual, and differing ways of being public – and with the web, the options are increasing, as I will discuss shortly. PIs have no inner essence; a PI is not a job, nor a career, but rather a role that certain people assume, and may even at some point leave behind them, thereby becoming less, or post-traditional. There is no official register – even if lists based on vote-ins such as those offered by *Prospect Magazine/Foreign Policy* (Chatfield, 2009) or by elite selection, as in *The Guardian* (Naughton, 2011), continue to grapple with the issue of who should count. Such lists are of course always controversial; *Prospect* admitted that there was evidence of campaigns to get some names on the list (from non-Western cultures, indicating at least a cosmopolitan engagement in the issue). Debates around inclusion/exclusion to PI status often centre on specific criteria on which agreement is absent; such interchanges can easily feel inconclusive. Thus, in a recent exchange, Dezner (2008a, 2008b) argued for a broader, more inclusive and popular view of PIs against Gewen's (2008) perspective, which accentuated a more traditional, elite version. Normally this encounter would have been deemed a tie, but there was a particular element in Dezner's argument that indicated a new turn in these debates, namely his insistence on how the web has altered the premises for PIs. Let us now turn to this evolving media domain.

Structures: New media landscapes

The media, broadly understood, constitute the array of communicative spaces in society where citizens can engage most readily with the political, and where public opinion can develop; it is here PIs connect with their audiences. A decisive attribute of the current media landscape is its turbulence. For one thing the number of media outlets and the content available continue to grow at an astounding pace. We are awash with media, an abundance that easily becomes disorienting, and most of it is obviously not overtly politically oriented. Even if journalism and current affairs in the media have increased in recent years, the growth in the realm of advertising, entertainment, and popular culture is much larger. Thus a definitive aspect of the contemporary media landscape is its density and the intensifying competition for attention, a situation of considerable relevance for PIs.

The new world of books

The media industries are following the general patterns found in the global economy, with large conglomerates acting under loosened regulatory controls, and driven by an ever more brutal commercial logic. This of course has impact on content, especially in the mass media sector, and poses serious dangers for pluralistic public spheres, as many authors have written. At the same time, the emblem of Web 2.0 points to the newer electronic media and their affordances, signalling also the creative practices that emerge in tandem with them, as I discussed in Chapter 2. Yet, as the traditional media industries restructure, economically, institutionally, and technically, new spaces for PIs can be taking form. Let us look at two specific media spheres in the context of these transitions that are of particular relevance for PIs: books and journalism. The book format has also been a key genre for PIs, and that industry is certainly going through a turbulent period (see Thompson, 2010; Striphas, 2009, for recent analyses); this too impacts on PIs' opportunities to reach the public. The intensified economic pressures for short-term profits lead to strategies aimed at launching bestsellers; this tends to reduce the likelihood of intellectual books aimed at smaller audiences being published, a discouraging development for PIs. However, technological changes also provide new options.

Pasquali (2011) shows how digitalisation is altering not only the infrastructure of publishing, but also the social practices of reading, as well as the very 'status' of the book. Moreover, and perhaps most relevant for our perspective here, digitalisation is also transforming the relationship between authors and readers. The enhanced opportunities for dialogue between authors and readers, and collaborative environments, are fostering new, participatory forms of online writing. The act of reading, as it evolves more and more into an electronic activity, becomes integrated into a broader array of cultural consumption spread over a variety of media platforms. The reader takes on simultaneously the role of a technology 'user', a 'consumer' and member of a 'media audience'. In this makeover of the culture of books, and print generally, the playing field for PIs becomes modified in ways that can be promising for those who are willing and able to adapt to the new environment. For the more strongly traditionally minded among PI's there is a risk that their arenas will contract. There are no doubt nostalgic voices who may point to what is lost in this transition, but these circumstances suggest that what we see are important modulations of PIs, certainly not their exit from the historical stage.

Evolving journalism

Turning to another key element of the public sphere, namely journalism, we can note that much of the development in the last two decades or so has served to further erode traditional news values, while audiences for journalism are fragmenting into more specialised niches (and the elite press is in serious economic trouble). Among the Western democracies, this 'crisis of journalism' has probably gone furthest in the US (see the annual reports *State of the News Media* (2013), now in their tenth year, from the Pew Research Center's Project for Excellence in Journalism). For our purposes here we can note that journalism was quick to move onto the internet in the 1990s, and today we see many forms. Mainstream journalism institutions have been adjusting to life online, with among other things its 24/7 schedules and uncertain financial models; they are also eliciting assistance from citizens ('Are you at the scene of the riot? Send us your material!') as well as making use of social media.

There is also a variety of sites that blend news, commentary, group advocacy, and discussion forums, making journalism more de-centred, dialogical and participatory. What is called 'opinion journalism' has blossomed, spurred on in particular by the increased deployment of journalistic modes for advocacy purposes. Notably we also see many versions of citizen, amateur, or alternative journalism taking, including full-blown alternative news networks (e.g. Indymedia). The growth in journalism as a facet of user-generated content on the web is of course also dramatically altering its parameters and even its professional centre of gravity (see Forde, 2011). Patterns of news consumption are also evolving, especially among the young, with a gradual shift from mainstream journalism to social media networks now under way (Bennett et al., 2010) This heady brew of course gives rise to issues: the boundary between journalism and non-journalism becomes all the more blurred, and we also see a decline in the controls for veracity, accuracy, balance, transparency, and accountability, even if critics may rightly claim that these attributes have always been somewhat deficient. PR and news releases from special interest organisations are at times disguised as news, while the broadened ideological terrain has also come to include hate groups and other anti-democratic actors.

This digital transformation of the public sphere has significance for PIs. There are today many more, albeit smaller, public spheres that can be accessed, and there are more media outlets online that are eager for more opinion content. The more porous boundaries between journalism and other, often hybrid media genres mean that PIs have more options in their form of expression. There are pitfalls and problems with these digital public spheres, yet overall these developments are encouraging and have been embraced by a variety of scholars with a more sanguine view of the web's potential (Castells, 2010; Benkler, 2006), allowing for at least some guarded optimism. And for PIs in particular, while the evolving online book industry clearly holds out potential for new initiatives, it is the growing terrain between traditional journalism and newer modes of advocacy that offers the most potential for their activities. However, in this media terrain PIs certainly have no monopoly.

Practices: Evolving online expression

The web: A new scene for PIs

The newer digital media are of course a part of the larger social and cultural world, intertwined with the offline lives of individuals as well as with the functioning of groups, organisations, and institutions. That more people do not automatically become active citizens on gaining access to the web should not be a sociological surprise; while the web offers vast new horizons, it does not necessarily alter the way people think – and act – in regard to power or politics. Yet, if the web does not offer any neat solution to democracy's difficulties, it has continued to nourish the vision of its potential for extending democratic involvement. Minimally, based on what we saw in Chapter 2, one can say that the web is redefining the premises and character of political engagement for those who choose to engage. While politics remains a minor usage of the web, its vast communicative universe offers many forms and formats for political participation, from the websites of political activist groups, to public discussion and debate forums, to the materials from political demonstrations and confrontations uploaded on YouTube. Research underscores the interplay between the affordances of communication technologies and the practices by which people utilise them for their own purpose (Lievrouw, 2011).

For PIs, the upshot of these features has several aspects. First of all, the web obviously provides PIs with new ports of entry into the public sphere – as it does for all citizens who want to engage. Further, there are now many more citizens who might be pursuing activities similar to PIs – that is, expressing opinions, formulating ideas, engaging in debate – regardless of how we might want to evaluate or rank such efforts; political talk has become more commonplace for more people in a public culture – mainstream and alternative – where opinion as personal expression has become more prevalent (and perhaps increasingly at the expensive of factual grounding, we might add). Thus, PIs are in some ways less unique in this newer milieu than they were in the context of the traditional mass media; there are more people today doing things at least somewhat similar to what PIs do. Further, what constitutes politics, what is deemed to be political, has not only become more heterogeneous, with growing numbers of causes, issues, trajectories, and styles, but also people online can more easily move in and out of the political. For better or worse, one can easily pass through the boundaries separating politics, consumption, entertainment, civil society, personal relations, and so on with just a click. PIs can easily jump into this fray, yet their status and impact will be challenged by the torrential cacophony of the web. How they navigate it is thus very significant.

The digital amplification of traditional PIs

For many PIs of a more traditional bent, however, much actually remains the same when they enter digital public spheres. The visibility of traditional PIs is in fact being enhanced by the web. Danowski and Park (2009), in analysing the social network links of 662 of the traditional PIs from Posner's (2003) list, found that in fact they have higher visibility via Google and Google Groups than in the mainstream mass media. Moreover, the authors ascertained that the internet also supports – counter-intuitively, we could say – discussion of deceased PIs better than the mass media. Turning to online newspapers and major news organisations like CNN, the BBC, and Al-Jazeera, we can note that these outlets all have bloggers, who function much like the commentators of the printed press, and in their ranks we find PIs. Some such bloggers appear regularly, others are very occasional. And the issue of deciding who is and is not a PI even in this setting remains ever with us; many are journalists and established 'pundits', but some are academics or experts in a special area. Newer versions of journalistic practices like the Huffington Post aggregate many other blog sites, offering high visibility to the connected bloggers, including many PIs.

Sites such as these have become the home of digitally enhanced, updated versions of traditional PIs, reproducing their status. Their texts are distributed by established media organisations, giving them both prestige and visibility. The web ecology facilitates updates, hyperlinks, archiving, and even some interactivity: most such posts allow for the possibility of comments. It is rare, however, that a blogging PI in this situation will answer comments; usually that is reserved for confrontation with another blogging PI, on the rather rare occasions when a debate emerges.

In the wider blogosphere citizens generally, as well as PIs, make use of blog and social media platforms and discussion sites. Even the by now the somewhat old-fashioned e-mail send-lists are still used to great effect: an individual can simply send out his or her own texts, and/or link to other texts, to a specific list of people, a 'small public', each of whom can respond to all others with comments and discussion. Efficient for a small network, this mode becomes unwieldy beyond a list of a few dozen participants, and it is here where blogging tools show their superiority for individuals who want to reach large numbers with their written thoughts (see Rettberg, 2008; Davis, 2009; Pole, 2010, for detailed treatments on blogging).

We should keep in mind that most blogs in the blogosphere are not political, but are rather based on, for example, personal, social, business, entertainment, consumption, or identity themes. One recent study (Caslon Analytics, 2011) found that less than 16 percent of US blogs had any connection with news or politics; the same source suggests that the reading of political blogs is not extensive among the general public. Yet, we can still point to a robust political blogosphere, and for PIs connected to major online media outlets, this form of blogging has become a dominant mode of expression in the new media landscape, supplemented by use of other platforms such as Twitter.

The digital generation

Generally speaking, traditional PIs have had to – and still must – go through various filters of quality control in order to gain access to a public. This has been integral to their status; they have not been 'just anybody'. The major online media institutions reproduce these older mass media mechanisms of editorial selection. While it is a democratic principle that everyone has the right to engage politically in the public sphere, editorial processes put restrictions on whose voice will be mediated – including in many online media organisations. However, elsewhere on the web, this has changed radically; just about anybody can in fact upload materials. Indeed, this open accessibility of speech gives credence to the claims about its democratic character. Thus, an important feature of the new media environment is precisely the ease of entry.

Thus, beyond the largely net equivalents of traditional mass mediated PIs, we find many people, mostly without elite status, running blogs on their own sites. If we sift through these bloggers, we will certainly find that a number of them could qualify as PIs in terms of their ambitions and the quality of their ideas. However, here we begin to encounter a significant grey zone: allowing for a degree of semantic indeterminacy regarding the criteria for a PI, I would suggest that there is a new generation of PIs emerging who differ from traditional PIs both in their adept use of the new media, and in their status as 'intellectuals'.

While most bloggers – and activists, advocates, special interest organisations, political debaters, and so on – make use of texts (albeit short ones, in particular on Twitter), we see a growing variety in online media production practices. Particularly younger people, with 'web roots', engage in a variety of media production practices. They use the web in more technically creative, multimedia ways, with audiovisual productions of various kinds, at times remixing materials from other mainstream or alternative sources. The contexts vary enormously, but even political/public sphere communication is being expressed in multimedia ways, often in the alternative political domain. These are still minority modes of representation, but they are growing. Most may not qualify as PIs today, but some will tomorrow. The multimedia angle evokes a comparison with politically oriented documentary filmmakers: it would not be stretching the definition too much to say that Michael Moore, Errol Morris, D.A. Pennebaker and Emile de Antonio are PIs, though generally the definition has not included media activities beyond text and spoken word. Yet, ideas can indeed be expressed in other ways beyond the classic linear text and its particular form of cognitive activity. There are other ways in which one can be intellectual, and the web forces us to reflect on what this term means today; I will return to this shortly.

This is a historically exciting development, though there are not only celebratory voices about the web's contributions to the spread of ideas and so forth, but also others with deep concern about its impact on our collective capacity to think, read and remember (see, for example, Carr, 2010). Intellectual activity inevitably evolves, we might assume, based on Enlightenment notions about progress, but can it erode – can reason survive in a multimedia digital world? This remains one of the big questions we will not be able to answer with any finality without historical hindsight (and some will no doubt argue that by then it will be too late). We have to live today with considerable ambiguity and accept in these matters that there will be a lower degree of consensus than in the past. At bottom, not just PIs but all citizens are becoming increasingly dependent on the new media technologies – and on web skills – for both knowledge and the development of critical thinking.

It remains true that some citizens are more intellectual, articulate, and imaginative than others in their political communication; these are the ones who tend to gain recognition within their circles and networks. They attract audiences, becoming opinion leaders of some kind – though just having an intellectual voice certainly does not guarantee that one will attract an audience. For those who do not gather an audience at once, the net can be seen as an important training ground, where they can gather experience and hone their craft (for example, by blogging). Whether or not society benefits from 'lowering the standards' and allowing more people to engage in whatever project is at hand, or whether it is better to let the experts stay in charge, is an old debate currently being replayed in the age of the internet. Thus, some today are horrified by the web-based onslaught of amateurs (e.g. Keen, 2006), while others claim that it is precisely the 'wisdom of crowds' and the participatory 'wikilogics' that we should support (e.g. Sunstein, 2008; Surowiecki, 2004; Tapscott and Williams, 2006).

'Web intellectuals'

Within the political blogosphere, elite bloggers, many of whom have strong connections with political and economic centres of power, and/or with major media organisations, account for only a small though highly influential sector. Academic blogging is a large sphere unto itself; sometimes it is directed towards politics (for instance, the Open Democracy Forum at supporters@opendemocracy.net). The majority have more mundane status, with some being closely connected with specific groups or parties as advocates or activists, while others operate independently. We also find umbrella sites that aggregate blogs according to themes, providing each with enhanced visibility. Among all of these are no doubt some whom we would be prone to classify as PIs. However, given the heterogeneity of intellectual activity we see in online public spheres, and taking into account the newer modes of multimedia and/or compressed textual expression, that category can begin to drift a bit in its meaning.

Yet, even if we don't want to stretch the notion of PIs too far, we still need to acknowledge the massive amounts of intellectual activity and energy we find in online public spheres. We might think in terms of a new version of PIs, a (usually) younger generation of 'web intellectuals' (as distinct from traditional PIs who may go online). They are public, but usually within more delimited online public spheres, which often build on the networks in which they operate. They are intellectual in varying ways, often with smaller storehouses of formal learning than traditional PIs, though I would imagine that many are less self-conscious about their intellectual status. Usually younger, they nonetheless often have political insight, an instinct for justice, and a communicative facility that builds on contemporary media culture. While less likely to reach extensive audiences than traditional PIs, they tend to have more interaction with those who experience their (multi-)media productions.

Web intellectuals are people with developed political identities, and with diverse origins (though the dominant socio-economic-ethnic-gender profiles tend towards the usual suspects). Though lacking elite status, they are contributing to the expansion (and evolution) of the intellectual character of the public sphere. The roles that they assume parallel those of traditional PIs: they act chiefly as opinion leaders, and do this via journalism, debate, cultural production, and political activism, with its dimensions of organising, mobilising, and inspiring. They become particularly visible during protest activities and revolt, where they combine political engagement with web skills and communicative creativity.

The notion of web intellectuals signals the continued importance of intellectual activity for democracy in regard to opinion formation, but involves a shift away from the more distinct and renowned figures we associate with PIs and the intellectual heritage on which they draw. Instead, the concept of 'web intellectual' suggests a more diffuse social category than traditional PIs; there are, by definition, more of them. Their intellectual modes can and do vary greatly. They are largely an online phenomenon (though in principle they could make use of the older mass media). They are probably mostly generalists, but certainly we can find many who build upon their specialised knowledge (e.g. environmental activists with ecological expertise); certainly some among them are also specialists in digital technologies. They mostly speak to, not with, the centres of power. Not least, I would assume that there is a growing number of cosmopolitan web intellectuals, as alternative politics increasingly engages in issues that cross national borders, and as transnational public spheres, albeit frail and vulnerable, continue to develop. No doubt members of diasporic populations are also found among the ranks of cosmopolitan web intellectuals. We certainly do not want to lose the traditional PIs, and from today's horizons this does not appear to be a danger. Yet online they are increasingly sharing the stage with an emerging cadre of web intellectuals, a development that thus far seems very beneficial for democracy.

Climates: Cultural and political

Modern problematics, anti-modern currents

These evolving practices – among PIs as well as the more diffuse category of civic intellectuals – take place against a backdrop of the structures of a shifting media landscape and digital public spheres. Another set of contingencies is to be found in the more general cultural and political climate of today, which is closely linked with the contemporary difficulties facing democracy that I discussed in Chapter 1.

We can begin by noting that in the prevailing cultural climate, there is a strong and growing strand of scientistic and technicist thought. In a sense this is not new; the faith in science and technology has been with us since the 18th century, as part of the Enlightenment tradition. However, its expansion becomes problematic when it gains hegemony in domains that ultimately have to do not with the physical realities of the world, but with values, that is, issues that have to do with how we should live. These have to be socially negotiated and have traditionally resided in the realm of norms, in politics. Increasingly such issues have become less areas of reasoned interpretation, and rather more the terrain of technical expertise. Habermas (1984/1987) refers to such developments as the 'colonisation' of 'the life world'. Scientific experts in the media address many areas of life – for example, economics, or even love relationships and child rearing – and offer guidance that makes use of discourses that often bypass reflection on values and politics. In the context of an evolution of this kind, the traditional normative discursive terrain of humanities-based PIs appears to be shrinking in many quarters.

Some elements of the Enlightenment legacy had been facing critical challenges at least since Nietzsche launched his interventions in the late 19th century, while many other critics expressed a loss of faith in this legacy in the aftermath of the horrors of the world wars and rationally administered genocide. Yet in the immediate post-WWII era of reconstruction, the belief in truth and progress within the Western democracies remained generally strong, especially in the US. In this context the status of 'ideas' retained its prominence and was linked to the notion of discussion and debate as vehicles for continually improving them. There was a cultural understanding that while we might not always be able to claim that we have the truth, we at least have the means to get ever closer to it and are thus equipped to participate in its discovery and in the march of progress.

Of course I paint this picture using a very wide brush, and I would also insist that we must avoid foolishly painting ourselves into a corner where we see only the 'end of civilization' and yearn for some mythic 'golden age' of the past. Yet even this very rough rendering should be sufficient to trigger recognition of some significant contemporary trends that stand in contrast to the Enlightenment faith that was previously prevalent. I would underscore that what I have in mind here is precisely some troubling trends, and these do not define the whole picture. Yet they are sufficiently widespread and sufficiently troubling that they should not be ignored. Debate and discussion in the public sphere, as countless observers have noted in recent decades, seems less and less guided by rationality, and the public is less inclined to pay attention to argumentation that requires effort. The belief in truth and progress, which has traditionally driven PIs, is certainly more problematic and complex today. While science and technology are still in a commanding epistemic position, there are counter-currents that harbour doubt and scepticism about the 'grand narratives' that science automatically brings with it progress. The Frankenstein metaphor is frequently evoked; the Faustian bargain often appears not to have been such a good deal, as we witness nuclear power disasters, anguish over genetic manipulation, a dangerously damaged environment, and so forth. In Ulrich Beck's (2009) terms, ours has become an increasingly fear-filled 'risk society', where we are continually making small and big gambles concerning our health, safety, and well-being, both individually and collectively.

Alongside of such problematisation of the Enlightenment we can also observe today forms of outright rejection of its key pillars; these at bottom challenge the premises of intellectual endeavour itself. In what might be interpreted as defensive cultural responses towards the dislocations of modernity, alternative grounds for knowing, such as New Age personal subjectivity, deep and unquestioning ideological conviction, or most commonly, religious faith, are blossoming. Religion on some fronts is contesting hard-won gains of the powers of reason; these conflicts are not just about ideas but can impact on, for example, health and well-being in a variety of ways; libraries, schools, and individual freedoms can feel growing constraints. In Europe and especially the US, for example, members of the Christian right can show a disdain for scientific facts and the logics and even basic rules of argumentation. The roots of this form of anti-modernism run deep in the social histories of specific religious currents, where strong elements of anti-rationalism have flourished, as Susan Jacoby (2009) illustrates in her analysis of the American situation. These diverse strands have led to a degree of uncertainty about basic Enlightenment principles in public culture that half a century ago seemingly had a more self-evident standing. More broadly, anti-secular fundamentalist religious strands of thought are globally advancing, altering the premises for public speech generally and PIs in particular.

Reason has certainly not vanished, and those who value it can find public spaces that validate and build upon its premises. If we find that it is less secure, at risk in some settings, we can simply avoid such contexts; this is singularly easy to do on the web, with its almost infinite multiplicity of spheres and the potential to generate ever new ones. Yet, the long-term consequences of such self-sectorisation cannot be healthy for democracy; there needs to be enough common ground to be able to speak about the importance and possibility of actually having a common ground. Suffice to say here that these trends, these cultural and political climates, risk diminishing the public dimension of PIs as well as the Enlightenment-based premises that intellectuals need to assume exist among their audiences.

The state of democracy

I discussed in Chapter 1 some of the deep problems facing democracy, and indicated how they were altering the dynamics of participation. By the early 1990s there was a general consensus among the Western democracies that their political systems were not working as they should. The list of issues was and is long; research has noted steady declines in voter participation, party loyalties, and civil society activities. There has been a growing distrust towards the political class, cynicism towards the system, and widespread feelings of disempowerment. Many citizens feel that the political parties offer no real options. While alternative politics offer significant response to these developments, it must be acknowledged that such activists thus far tend to account for only a small segment of the citizenry.

Traditionally, PIs have operated on the premise that they can reach informed audiences who will pay attention to them, that they can impact on public opinion, and that citizens' demands can be mediated into the political decision-making process. Moreover, PIs have banked on a degree of optimism and engagement on the part of citizens. As these premises begin to waver, as feelings of disempowerment spread, especially in the face of global economic crises, the basic *raison d'être* of PIs becomes less self-evident. In the face of such feelings of futility, critics of injustice and inequality who want to offer visions of a better world are met with a kind of response characterised by cynical reason (Sloterdijk, 1987): people often know very well what is wrong, how power holders abuse their authority, how economic policies favour the rich, and so on, but in the absence of a realistic alternative and a strong sense of civic agency, they will simply proceed as if they did not know. This of course sets up further roadblocks for the role of PIs – and political participation more widely.

Realignments

The notion of PIs will probably remain contested for the foreseeable future, but hopefully these reflections will help enhance the terms of the discussions. The older controversies about how to define and evaluate them remain. Today, however, the dramatic alterations of the media landscape, the attributes of the online public spheres, and the fact that many more citizens today are engaged in mediated intellectual activity using forms of expression that are facilitated by the digital technologies, means that many of the basic contingencies for PIs have changed significantly. While the traditional mode of PIs is still visible in the printed media, the emergence of the web as a terrain for the public sphere means that many PIs become visible online by mere virtue of the fact that most traditional media have online versions.

At the same time, the web offers opportunities for more innovative, multimedia forms of practice that begin to diverge from the model of the linear text – though this tends to be more common among the younger age cohorts, who no doubt dominate the ranks of the broader category of web intellectuals. Whether the advent of this more pervasive form of enhanced participation in online public spheres will result in an augmentation of the 'public' side of the PI phenomenon or an erosion of the 'intellectual' side – or simply a further late modern transformation of the character of online political discourse – remains to be seen. There are grounds for both positive and negative anticipation.

Fundamental to these developments is the current state of democracy. This is the context that at bottom gives the idea of PIs its meaning and legitimacy. Yet, as democracy continues to rush headlong into dark times, fuelled by cultural climates of irrationality and political uncertainty, the communicative space necessary for PIs to function effectively seems to contract. This in turn further contributes to the weakening of democracy. From the perspective of the role of traditional PIs as well as the newer, more diffuse web intellectuals, there are no doubt many possible ways forward. It would seem, however, that operating on two key fronts is paramount. These trajectories frame the challenge of functioning both intellectually and publically in new ways.

On the one hand, PIs must address the problems of democracy itself more specifically and not just involve themselves in particular issues or give their support to specific causes. As intellectuals, PIs are in a position to confront principles, values, social trends, and discursive strategies that undermine democracy and civic culture – as well as offering alternative visions for politics and society. This would of course be a multivalent, heterogeneous and pluralistic effort, though the particular erosion promoted by the coupling of market logic to democratic universalism would seem to warrant special attention. The point would not be to offer a one-size-fits-all ideological vision, but rather to put democracy per se on the political agenda, to make it a critical topic of public discussion. We do of course see some contributions of this kind today, but the point is that a much more concerted effort is needed. 'Democracy' has been to a great extent reduced to a form of incantation; it requires more critical reflection among broad ranks of citizens.

On the other hand, PIs need to successfully negotiate and use the digital media environment. They have to adapt and develop modes of communication that will reach audiences – and co-participants – on the web. For traditional PIs who want to move beyond the basic print format, this becomes a techno-creative challenge. For the newer PIs, the web intellectuals, this may involve retaining or retrieving sufficient degrees of Enlightenment rationality, such that political discussion remains possible, inviting, and meaningful – amidst the cacophonic yet ever-stimulating web environment.

5
Web Journalism and Civic Cosmopolitanism: Professional vs. Participatory Ideals

The world changes, and with it our understanding of it – even if the goodness of fit between the world in some 'objective' sense and our grasp of it will always remain problematic. One important factor in shaping the way we see the world beyond our own face-to-face experience is of course journalism, with its various institutions, practices, and representations. Journalism finds itself in a period of dramatic transition; indeed, the term 'crisis' has been a part of the discussions for some years now, applied to a complex field that is witnessing pushes and pulls from several directions, deriving from changes in, among other things, financial circumstances, technologies, media landscapes, audience use patterns, and notions of professionalism. (There is of course a vast literature on these themes; for recent contributions in the American context, see McChesney and Nichols, 2011; the current annual report *State of the News Media*, 2013; see also Russell, 2011; Waisbord, 2012). A specific development to be noted in this regard is that increasingly, journalism is not being done only by journalists. This is not historically new per se, but the magnitude and diversity of the actors and practices involved today are significant.

With the web, the range and even the intensity of participation in society can become enhanced; the terrains of consumption, popular culture, civil society, and the political become accessible for engagement. That journalism is rapidly becoming a robust field for civic agency is laudable from a general democratic perspective. Still, as we shall see, questions have to be raised about the significance of such participation in the ever-evolving state of journalism, given the centrality of this institution for the life of democracy. Moreover, if the primary terrain of such citizen involvement in journalism is that of civil society, it at times veers into the political, raising still further issues. If the criteria for professional journalism are being decentred, how should we view the alternatives on offer from the still inchoate vision of participatory journalism? Participatory journalism today takes a variety of forms, while mainstream journalism itself opens itself up to assistance and collaboration from citizens. These developments are far from controversial, and serve to further destabilise traditional definitions of the field and its profession. The reactions from within established journalistic institutions have certainly been mixed (see Lasorsa et al., 2012).

Participation both in and via media is extending going global, increasing the transnational character of many people's frames of perception; the 'world' is becoming more 'global'. Our mental maps are not only filling in more details in areas that were previously fuzzy or even simply non-existent, but we can also observe an increased understanding and even engagement in areas and issues that lie beyond national borders. If we examine the trend of increasing citizen participation in journalism in combination with the growth in global civic and political involvement, we direct ourselves towards one of the key frontiers in democracy's current development, especially if *political* participation is expressed in journalistic form.

This chapter will head towards that frontier and will take the route of cosmopolitanism. This term has emerged with a noticeable vigour in the past two decades, even if it remains overshadowed by the more familiar notion of globalisation. Despite its lack of full semantic security, cosmopolitanism explicitly addresses our expanding global awareness; at the same time it also incorporates normative and analytic dimension in regard to one's encounters with and action towards others. It thus has relevance for citizens' agency in global settings, leading us to the notion of what we can call civic cosmopolitanism.

In this chapter I explore the intersection of participatory journalism with the traditional horizons of the profession, framed by the theme of civic cosmopolitanism. While I indicate the social contingencies of cosmopolitanism, my main concern is to highlight and juxtapose these two sets of ideals, two normative frameworks for guiding practice in regard to journalism. To set the scene, in the first section I sketch some of the relevant contours of cosmopolitanism, underscoring the normative themes that it raises. The second section takes up one of the few conceptual efforts to establish a link between media, cosmopolitanism, and agency. In the final section I pursue an interface with horizons of civic cosmopolitanism and those of a dilemma-ridden professional journalism; I try to pull the strands together by elucidating the implications and the issues that ensue.

Cosmopolitan connections

In the 5th century BC, the Greek historian Herotodos wrote of his experiences in the multicultural world of his time. Interestingly enough, the award-winning Polish journalist Ryszard Kapuscinski, who passed away a few years ago, found great inspiration from Herotodos on how to encounter strangers in foreign lands. On his very first foreign assignment he was sent off to India – without a working knowledge of English. His editor gave him a Polish copy of Herotodos' book, a text he carried with him his entire professional life. Kapuscinski's last major publication has relevance here. In his *Travels with Herotodos* (2008) he recounts how this Greek, writing two and a half millennia ago, inspired him through the decades to encounter the other in an open, respectful and self-reflective manner, to try get a handle on the language being used, to understand the world through the other's frames of perception, and thereby to better understand the contours and limits of his own horizons. A splendid connection across time between two paradigmatic – and pragmatic – cosmopolitans.

Kapuscinski captures some key themes of contemporary cosmopolitanism: the normative element involved in dealing with geographically and/or culturally distant others, the capacity for self-reflection and empathy, and the evolution of one's own frames of reference. Cosmopolitanism offers an analytic angle for approaching issues about social perceptions of and relations with others in the world today. With the continuing integration of the world via the various 'scapes' and 'flows' of globalisation – albeit often in very uneven, unequal, and contested ways – the other, or rather the many others, come all the closer to us. Globalisation can thus be seen as the condition that raises cosmopolitanism to its renewed level of relevance. In this sense cosmopolitanism, as a moral perspective for looking at social behaviour towards others, takes on increasing relevance as global others increasingly become a part of our everyday worlds.

Global civil society actors

In looking at the range of global civil society actors and political movements, Davis (2010: 149) notes that compared to political parties, they tend to address a broader range of issues, offer more opportunity for genuine participation, and are less hierarchical and more inclusive. He has in mind movements that are generally 'progressive', which translates into mostly left-reformist, as opposed to right-wing or revolutionary politics. (Yet, he notes that this does not mean that such groups always function in a democratic manner). That many citizens are thus getting involved in what we might call global civil society, beyond party structures, and using the affordances of these highly sophisticated yet very accessible media technologies, marks a new and uncharted phase in the history of democracy. It opens up many possible lines of inquiry, and scholars are approaching these phenomena from a variety of angles.

In terms of organisation we encounter here the broad terrain of nongovernmental organisations (NGOs), non-profit organisations, activist networks, interest and advocacy groups of all kinds, including at times very amorphous social movements. Even alternative journalistic organisations figure here, the most well-known being Indymedia. The focus of their engagement likewise covers a broad span; some are engaged in social, religious, or cultural networking, for example, diasporic or religious groups. Others are involved in advocacy, for themselves or as representatives of larger causes or interest groups. A good number of these actors work in tandem with large established international organisations such as the UN or the EU, which actively consult with civil society organisations. Many such actors have become a significant factor at the level of policymaking.

There is also a large range of explicitly political actors, while the border between civil society and political life of course always remains very porous. Some give voice to long-standing, protracted conflicts, others air newly emerged ones, while yet others are working politically to alter the behaviour of governments, regulatory bodies or corporations, based on normative visions of global change. For some political actors religion is a motivational force. Many global civil society and political actors display healthy democratic profiles. Others may have goals or use practices that are questionable, even violent, in pursuit of anti-democratic goals. They by definition fall outside of the boundaries of civil society or democratic politics; however, there will no doubt always remain contested grey zones.

In short, there is an ever expanding domain of global civil society, and the literature on global civil society is of course extensive, but some recent contributions which convey summary pictures include Dartnell (2005); Eberly (2008); Keane (2003); Chandler (2006); Drache (2008); Scholte (2011); Thörn (2009); Walker and Thompson (2008). In particular, in the political realm, special attention should be given to the alterglobalisation movement, sometimes also called the global justice movement. It is massive in scope, yet there are strong efforts to coordinate many diverse groups, most noteworthy being the World Social Forum (WSF). With its stance of confronting neoliberal globalisation on many fronts, this meta-movement is of particular significance for the development of global society. The alterglobalisation movement generally, and the WSF in particular, has been made academically visible in recent years; see, for example, Acosta (2009); Gills (2011); Hosseini (2010); Maeckelburgh (2009); Pleyers (2011); Sen and Waterman (2007); de Sousa Santos and Rodriguez-Garavito (2005); Smith et al. (2007).

While the wide range of actors on the transnational stage has often been framed as manifestations of globalisation, we can shift conceptual lenses and see it as an expression of cosmopolitanism, indeed, even as specifically civic cosmopolitanism. In so doing, we let other dimensions of such participation move into the spotlight. Let us begin by exploring the concept of cosmopolitanism.

Probing a multivalent concept

One important line of inquiry addresses the vision of a more just and democratic world order (e.g. Archibugi, 2008; Gould, 2004; Sullivan and Kymlicka, 2007; Vernon, 2010). Among such authors, Held (2010) is a prominent voice, and he asserts the exhaustion of traditional politics, especially in the face of massive global problems such as climate change, the financial crisis, and human rights abuses. He argues that cosmopolitanism is the only realistic way forward. Others focus on a particular aspect of this larger theme, namely the notion of citizenship, and the issues of rights and inclusion in the contemporary global situation, not least in regard to the EU (e.g. Benhabib, 2004, 2006; Habermas, 2006; Morris, 2010).

Further, much of the contemporary discussion about cosmopolitanism ranges over moral theory and political philosophy (Breckenridge et al., 2002; Brock and Brighouse, 2005; Nussbaum, 2006); it often invokes the philosophy of Levinas, with its emphasis on responsibility to others, and places this moral horizon in a global context. These contributions are thus to a great extent characterised by normative discourses. Still other interventions address the sociocultural preconditions for cosmopolitanism and/or its subjective dimensions (e.g. Beck, 2006; Appiah, 2007; Hannerz, 1996). While some of the above authors engage with cosmopolitanism in a critical way, few explicitly frame it in terms of a confrontation with neoliberalism and its consequences, though there are some notable exceptions (e.g. Cheah, 2007; Dallmayr, 2003; Delanty, 2009; Harvey, 2009). Indeed, Harvey takes several authors, such as Nussbaum, Beck, and Held to task for what he sees to be their implicit collusion with neoliberalism. Similarly, Kendall et al. (2009) note a certain degree of political naïveté among many authors and a utopian tendency to construct a new world of tolerant and responsible citizens, while offering little analytic insight on how to deal with the major global divides – or ignoring them altogether.

In the pluralism of approaches to cosmopolitanism there appears a fundamental issue that has to do with the basic tension between universalism and the particular (or local, or national). Is there one set of cosmopolitan values and perceptions, a 'one-size-fits-all'? We can discern an unresolved tension between cosmopolitanism on the one hand as an expression of multiple empirical realities around the world, and on the other as a unitary global ideal, with universalist virtues. Universalist claims are at times vulnerable to critiques of embodying ethnocentrism or cultural specificity. Is the notion of a unitary normative vision inherently an expression of a camouflaged manoeuvre for cultural power?

Turner (2002) argues that cosmopolitan virtue basically encompasses pacifist values that preclude violence and promote human agency and dignity. He suggests that there is a great diversity of human happiness, but there is unity in suffering, and thus cosmopolitan virtue that comprises a fundamental opposition to human suffering becomes a position that goes beyond and yet unites different cultures and historical periods (Turner, 2002). If human rights exist to protect us all from suffering, then there are universal human obligations to oppose misery, to respect cultures of other peoples and to oppose governments that fail to protect human rights. Turner makes the cosmopolitan argument even more convincing by contending that the vulnerability of the human body provides a starting point for an account of human commonality and compassion as the basis for a cosmopolitan ethic. For him, The UN Declaration of Human Rights is obviously a very cosmopolitan document, which he builds into his argument.

Thus, one way of understanding contemporary cosmopolitanism is to see it as a response to ethnic cleansing and racial violence in the context of global dynamics that are creating ever greater gulfs between rich and poor. Such a virtue is expressed as obligations that flow from a recognition of the vulnerability of persons and of the precariousness of institutions within a globalised world. Turner thereby takes a clear stand against moral relativism. However, one could respond that Turner's position is 'easy': to reduce physical suffering is perhaps not so controversial. In situations that, for example, have to do with expressions of minority community membership in majoritarian cultural settings (for example, clothing that signifies religious affiliation), can we easily identify an operational universal ethic?

Delanty (2009) sees cosmopolitanism as a dimension in contemporary social processes that can serve as a normative critique of globalisation, and thus of capitalism. He underscores that cosmopolitanism can promote our capacity for self-reflection, and foster new ways of seeing the world when diverse peoples experience common problems. Distancing himself from more anthropological approaches, Delanty (2009) argues that the conflicts around 'difference' in the world today are less about culture and more about social and economic questions that have significant political implications. Yet the cultural can also articulate with power, as, for example, the critical tradition of post-colonialism demonstrates.

Post-colonialism, in ways similar to Cultural Studies (with which it at times blends together), is sensitive to how culture and the production of meaning are always bound up with relations of power. Post-colonialism, with its anchoring largely in the humanities, has not engaged much with the discourses of globalisation, which hover mainly in the social sciences (an exception is found in the collection by Krishnaswamy and Hawley, 2008), yet can help to alert us to the historical antecedents of a vast array of aspects where cultural power has relevance. It can cogently illuminate patterns of cultural influences, images of the other, identity processes, integration/assimilation, language use, institution-building, and so on in ways that are highly relevant – and often quite problematic – for the perspective of cosmopolitanism. Conceptually and empirically, cosmopolitanism cannot be reduced to a mere function of power, yet neither can power be ignored. If power is not obviously manifest, then it is always hovering there – in both micro- and macro-circumstances – as a potential on the threshold of becoming realised. Power evokes counter-power, so it is not simply a case of unidirectional and deterministic mechanisms, even if hegemonic positions are characterised by continuity.

Situated practices

Cosmopolitanism is also about practices, and has thus to do with individual agency. While this line of thought generally avoids unrealistic admonishments about finding or creating a mythic 'new cosmopolitan subject', it is nonetheless clear that many writers envision a particular set of culturally supported attributes that promote cosmopolitan agency. Smith (2007) makes use of Arendt's notions of 'world' and 'worldliness': these involve a capacity for self-reflection, enhanced care, and certain skills for relating to others. Self-reflection and irony (Turner, 2002) with respect to our own cultural context, origins, and values go hand in hand with a scepticism towards the 'grand narratives' of modern ideologies. In other words, tolerance of others must start from a position of scepticism about the ultimate authority of one's own culture. This does not imply that one does not or should not have a country or a homeland to identify with, but rather that one has a certain reflexive distance to it, that one can see it as but one of many possible homelands on the planet.

Such attributes are not completely unrelated to social position and power. Achieving such self-reflection and a sense of distance from one's own background and identity is usually not an inbred human trait. It is usually predicated on routine encounters with those significantly different from oneself. Such contacts and experiences are precisely what many less privileged and insular communities may lack. Indeed, many minority communities may justifiably feel threatened by majoritarian social patterns. The attributes of cosmopolitan agency, then, tend to connect at least in part to questions of social privilege, even if the relationship is complex; for example, migrant workers and diasporic groups develop versions of cosmopolitan attributes that differ from those who, for example, attend international academic conferences.

Another set of contributions underscores precisely the sociocultural preconditions for cosmopolitanism and its subjective dimensions (e.g. Beck, 2006; Appiah, 2007; Hannerz, 1996; Kendall et al., 2009). They also warn against a blanket, universalistic morality to be applied in every context. Dallmayr (2003) refers explicitly to the 'situated differences and motivational resources' in discussing our moral responsibilities to the world. Suitable agency in a cosmopolitan perspective is always contingent on circumstances and cannot be predefined; agency is always contextual. While the world order has fortunately agreed on the notion of human rights as a form of universalism, authors like Dallmayr remind us that the actual application of such tenets in concrete situations always involves choice-making. And beyond these overarching principles, our more detailed normative compass must be established anew in each concrete situation.

Empirical research reminds us that our expectations for fully fledged cosmopolitan consciousness should remain modest. Based on research with focus groups, Skrbis and Woodward (2007) found that 'ordinary cosmopolitanism' in Western contexts is expressed as an ensemble of discourses that are mobilised as everyday accounts. These accounts deal with such issues as cultural heterogeneity and global problems. However, rather than taking the 'high road' which leads to openness and hospitality to strangers, and puts generalised human needs ahead of national interests, many participants instead discursively frame cosmopolitanism as the attractive affordances of globalisation, such as travel and culinary diversity. Moreover, discourses about 'cultural loss' and the 'dilution of national culture' are widely in circulation. While their research underscores the obvious point that cosmopolitanism is as yet not a universal phenomenon, it also – and more interestingly – suggests that it is also possible to empirically study the concept as something socially constructed by concrete actors, contingent on specific contexts. Also, their work affirms the importance of cosmopolitanism as an everyday terrain of contested identities and communities.

Yet, the sociocultural angle also suggests that today one does not by definition have to be mobile to be cosmopolitan. While Kant was a famous promoter of cosmopolitanism and seldom ventured far beyond Köningsberg, today the local manifests more and more elements of the global in a variety of ways. Not least, we have access to the 'world' – via the media, with all their connections. Sociological common sense suggests that having contact with those different from oneself could help facilitate a cosmopolitan stance. Certainly the world – present and past – is full of examples of successful neighbourhoods, cities, states, and empires where tolerance and openness to difference has prevailed, where cosmopolitanism starts on one's own street. However, there is no guarantee, and we know that all too often encounters with the other can lead to closure, exclusion, and even violence, if the circumstances are not favourable. Cosmopolitanism is an admirable vision, but can never be taken for granted.

For our purposes here, cosmopolitanism offers a horizon on normative agency in the global arena. In accentuating the situatedness of agency, we can avoid predefined universalist norms. At the same time, there is a normative horizon, largely entwined with the values of democracy. Comprising an ensemble of relevant attributes, cosmopolitanism as a mindset still requires sociocultural circumstances to nurture it. Also, there is a strand within cosmopolitanism that links agency with democracy, and as citizens engage all the more in transnational issues in the global arena, the concept of civic cosmopolitanism takes on relevance. This form of participatory citizenship is very often manifested online, and increasingly engages in versions of journalism.

As an interesting and self-reflexive excursus, I can mention here that there are also calls from within the academic world for enhanced cosmopolitanism (see Godrej, 2011). To be genuinely 'open to the world' involves the ability to reflect upon and distance oneself from one's own frameworks, to see them as relative, and to be open to others. Obviously this is not always easy; most of us in some ways have to struggle with it. Beyond being 'cosmopolitan colleagues', the demands become more complex, as we move into the substantive aspects of our work. Godrej (2011) engages with this theme from the standpoint of political theory, where, as mentioned above, the notion of cosmopolitanism has re-emerged as an important normative dimension. There is a growing recognition that political theory should not continue in a mode that is at bottom Westerncentric; it needs to engage much more with 'non-Western' sources and circumstances.

He offers some reflections to help move our thinking forward. For one thing he advocates an avoidance of extreme binary categories: the 'Western' is by no means a monolithically constructed entity – it has many versions and inflections and builds on many traditions. Thus, cosmopolitan horizons generally, and political theorising in particular, must progress beyond simple dichotomies. Such perspectives must incorporate 'multiple selves and multiple others, variously located in multiple relations with one another' (Godrej, 2011: 123). The challenge is not to be locked into any one tradition but to have access to several, to access post-Eurocentric paradigms and begin to interact with them. Yet, if we reflect on the extent to which non-Western real-world political experience has actually served as a foundation for, or even entered into, political theorising in the West, the results look sparse. There have at times been efforts on the margins, but on the whole we still have far to go.

The mediapolis: A new site of agency

The mediapolis and civic cosmopolitanism

Oddly enough, the media have not figured extensively in the literature on cosmopolitanism. A step forward in making conceptual connections is found in Copus Ong (2009); see also Hier (2008). One major empirical effort to establish causal links between media use and cosmopolitan mindsets is found in Norris and Ingelhart (2009). Generally, they find that exposure to global media will promote cosmopolitanism. However, the authors underscore the research complexity of establishing causal relationships, and make the point that there are also many non-media variables at work. From another angle and with a focus on television news, Robertson (2010) looks at journalists/editors, news narratives, and viewers around the world to elucidate the complexities around identity and cosmopolitan horizons in the popular imagination. The more specific theme of recognising and identifying with distant others via news coverage of suffering is found in an extended theoretical essay by Boltanski (1999), while Chouliaraki (2006) addresses this theme in a more empirical manner. This literature demonstrates the media's importance for cosmopolitanism, while at the same time showing that the relationship has many dimensions.

An overarching, essayistic approach to the media's relevance for cosmopolitanism is found in Roger Silverstone's (2006) last major work, which strongly reflects the normative character of cosmopolitanism. Its point of departure is that the media play a decisive role in the constitution of late modernity and its forms of globalisation, and they thus lead us inexorably to reflect on cosmopolitanism, journalism, and democracy. For my purposes here, I want to highlight his basic ideas with an eye towards cosmopolitanism as a necessary element for civic agency in the modern globalised world, and the character of the media as a precondition for such agency.

In brief, Silverstone observes that the media are becoming what he calls 'environmental'; they can no longer be seen as simply discrete flows of messages or information, but rather take on the character of dense symbolic ecologies that penetrate just about every corner of our existence. What he terms the mediapolis is comprised of the vast communicative space of mediated global appearances. It is via the media that the world appears to us, and where appearance constitutes the world. It is through the media that we learn who we are – and who we are different from – and where relations between self and other are conducted in a global public arena. The media establish connections, relationships; they position us in the world (see Bakardieva, 2011, for another exposition and application of Silverstone's concept of mediapolis).

'Mediapolis' is both a normative and an empirical term. Empirically, it is something other than a rational Habermasian public sphere; it is cacophonic, with multiple voices, inflections images, and rhetoric – it resides beyond logic and rationality, and it cannot offer any expectation of fully effective communication (see Gardiner 2004, for a juxtaposition of Habermas with Bakhtin's rather different view of communication). The communications dynamic that Silverstone sees here he calls *contrapunctual*: each communicative thread gains significance at best only in relationship to others – together, the ensemble of tension-ridden, contradictory communicative interventions comprise the tumultuous whole.

Normatively, however, despite differences in communicative and other forms of power, the mediapolis demands mutual responsibility between producers and audiences/users, as well as a capacity for reflexivity on the part of all involved, including recognition of cultural differences. This moral response is expressed in our responsibility for thinking, speaking, listening, and acting. It of course raises issues of the kinds of reality created by the mediapolis, the kinds of publicness, who appears – and how – as well as who does not appear. There is clearly an element of media power here: definitional control lies most immediately with the media organisations, but Silverstone emphasises that there is still responsibility on all sides. Journalists, editors, and producers have a responsibility for the representations they offer, while audiences/users have an obligation to reflect on what they encounter and to respond in an ethical manner – both to the world portrayed and to the media.

The notion of mediapolis is thus a challenge to the inequities of representation, mechanisms of exclusion, the imbalances of media power (via both state and capital), and 'the ideological and prejudicial frames of unreflexive reporting and storytelling' (Silverstone, 2006: 37). The media, in their representations of the world, inevitably engage in what he calls boundary work: boundaries are constantly being drawn, reinforced, and altered between various constellations of 'us and them'. In underscoring the significance of morality and ethics, Silverstone means that moral dimensions should become a focus of analytic concern, just as social, political, and cultural perspectives are part of our analytic approach to the processes of communication.

From morality to agency

In all this Silverstone admits that we have some obvious questions to deal with, including that the public as such does not conceptually have a strong status, and, we might add, empirically is not politically very efficacious. Thought, speech, and action are disconnected and compromised by lack of contexts that afford practice, the erosion of memory, the weakness of analytic rigour, and increasingly, the absence of trust. Also, we witness patterns of withdrawal from the public realm, into the private; in fact, the decline in engagement has been a major dilemma confronting democracy. Silverstone's reflections on the political go well beyond traditional liberalism as understood in political philosophy, which underscores individuals' rights and their pursuit of private happiness. His is a political sensibility that puts him at home with republicanism, with its emphasis on individual development through democratic engagement and responsibilities towards collectivities.

Thus, the mediapolis becomes a sites not only for moral response, but, potentially, for practices, for civic participation. His notion that our responsibility is expressed in thinking, speaking, listening, and acting puts us directly in touch with the themes of civic agency and skills. The cosmopolitan moral agent must move beyond the state of merely thinking about his/her responsibility; s/he must enact and embody agency via some kind of action (which, in the context of the political, will often take the form of communication). Such a proactive social ethics, that demands engagement with and responsibility for global others, points us towards cosmopolitan citizenship, a concept which is strongly tied to versions of democracy. This link between cosmopolitanism and democratic civic agency – civic cosmopolitanism – involves translating the cosmopolitan moral stance into concrete political contexts that benefit not just our own interests but those of our globalised others in a democratic manner.

Silverstone's book, with its promotion of cosmopolitanism and its normative anchoring, invites us, in a compelling manner, to better conceptualise the links between agency and global responsibility in and via the media. He points out that the mediapolis contains institutions and organisations, which in turn are comprised of categories of people working in their identifiable roles in specific situations: journalists, editors of various sorts, owners, producers, programme directors, managers, accountants, lawyers, audiences, citizens, and so on. In short, we have sets of individuals who act as elements of larger institutionalised agencies. I emphasise the individual level not to signal a suspension of a sociological perspective, but to underscore the dimension of human agency, where moral reflection is in principle always possible. The differing horizons of these various social positions provide different contexts in terms of moral action.

In conceptualising the transition from moral response to civic agency via the mediapolis, we must of course be aware of the fundamental difficulties. The mediatisation of such global engagement can at times lead to a sense of personal disempowerment, especially when the range of possible practices seems narrow and one is largely positioned as a spectator, even if a very committed one (see Chouliaraki, 2012, for an insightful analyses of these circumstances). It is also worth reiterating here Dallmayr's (2003) caution in regard to moral universalism. He argues cogently that an excessive emphasis on moral universalism can lead us to ignore the contextual differences, the external constraints, that shape the specificity of human action. Moreover, he stresses the importance of actively promoting agency; cosmopolitanism thus becomes a part of a global, critical democratic project. He insists that, 'it is insufficiently moral – in fact, it is hardly moral at all – to celebrate universal values everywhere without also seeking to enable and empower people in their different settings and locations' (Dallmayr, 2003: 438). He thus advocates a turn to practice and participation, that is, to politics, broadly understood to include all forms of civic engagement – including journalism, I would add.

If we should be wary of moral universalisms, practice still needs norms and criteria to guide it. This gives rise to questions of which norms, and whose criteria? On what authority? These issues become quite concrete as we shift our focus to the terrain where civic cosmopolitanism encounters the practices and representations of journalism. A large range of non-professional actors – individuals and organisations – are doing forms of journalism that are a part of the global mediapolis. Some see themselves as doing journalism, albeit of an alternative kind (e.g. Indymedia), others define themselves as established civil society actors (e.g. the vast number of international NGOs), some are explicitly activist or at least advocacy oriented (e.g. institutionalised groups or social movements promoting human rights, environmental improvement, gender issues, whether or not under the broad umbrella of alterglobalisation), while others may be very much part-timers or even engage in one-off interventions via social media. In all this kind of journalistic activity, the civic impetus, with cosmopolitan dimensions, confronts, implicitly or explicitly, journalistic traditions.

Journalism and plural realities

To pull together the main threads of the discussion thus far: the web enables new forms of civic and political participation, and even if there are many contingencies that set limits on the character and extent of such participation, this marks a new historical phase in the history of democracy. Web-based democratic participation is also going global, and the horizon of cosmopolitanism invokes a normative dimension, underscoring a sense of responsibility towards distant others. As citizens, notably via digital media, are increasingly operating in transnational and/or transcultural contexts, we conceptualise the notion of civic cosmopolitanism, understood as the attributes associated with democratic participation in global contexts. Such agency is always contingent – there is no detailed normative handbook as to how to proceed, even if general moral precepts about universal rights are always relevant. At the same time, it is clear that the attributes of cosmopolitanism, such as empathy and self-reflection, have varying sociocultural origins and cannot be merely assumed. Nurturing these attributes can be seen as an ongoing project, one with no guarantees and no real endpoint, only a sense of importance and indeed urgency. Elements of this global participation venture into, mingle with, and challenge the field of journalism, while the institutions and practices of journalism already find themselves in a turbulent situation from pressures from a number of other directions as well. The question of which norms should guide journalism thus hovers prominently in our field of vision.

The journalistic turn

The use of the web for civic and political participation emerged at the dawn of the internet era and continues to grow (see, for example, Atton, 2005; Lievrouw, 2011). That civic online engagement should turn to journalistic forms comes as no surprise. Historically, of course, there have been innumerable versions of an alternative press or radical media, often connected to particular social or political movements (see, for example, Atton, 2002; Baily et al, 2007; Downing, 2000; Ostertag, 2007; Waltz, 2005). On the web, we see the continuation of these traditions, as well as the emergence of new ones, facilitated by the unprecedented technical affordances. Various forms of citizen-assisted journalism are encouraged by mainstream journalistic institutions, especially when their own journalists do not have direct access to unfolding events; the reporting from recent events of the insurrections in the Arab world are but one case in point. Participatory journalism has grown markedly in the past few years, as the news industry undergoes serious transformation, not least in regard to its use of social media. With non-journalists using platforms such as Facebook, Twitter, and blogs to generate and share journalistic material, journalism is gradually becoming more interactive, collaborative, diverse, partisan, and immediate. This has unquestionably deepened and broadened the public spheres of democratic societies – and helped challenge the power structure in authoritarian ones.

The situation of online journalism today is difficult to grasp in its totality. This sprawling domain is comprised of mainstream online media, alternative journalism sites, the blogosphere, social media, individual and group productions, including efforts by social movements and other activists and groups of every imaginable persuasion – political, religious, and life style advocates, hobbyists, and many more. All kinds of 'amateur' as well as 'para-' or 'quasi-journalism' are juxtaposing and blending with each other. Facts and opinions, debates, gossip, nonsense, misinformation, the insightful, the deceptive, the poetic, are all mixed together, scrambling the traditional boundaries between journalism and non-journalism.

There is a justifiably celebratory tone in much of the discussion about how the web facilitates the participatory character of journalism. However, we should try to keep a sober sociological eye on these developments. For one thing, it is perhaps easy to lose sight of just how prominent mainstream reporting still remains, particularly in foreign coverage. Also, much citizen-generated journalism operates symbiotically with mainstream material, even if commenting on or contesting it. Moreover, concerning citizen-assisted journalism, there is a strong tendency for the professionals to maintain a tight gatekeeping function and editorial grip on the submitted material, even if there are some signs of new formats and hybrid practices emerging in this context (Lewis, 2012; Thurman and Hermida, 2010). Looking at journalism in the blogosphere, Campbell et al. (2010) found that non-professional journalistic bloggers only very rarely generate original news; this happens mostly when the blogger has some kind of specialised knowledge or an unusual access to unfolding events. The authors also underscore that the vast amount of information available on the web can in itself serve to destabilise traditional journalism, in that it permits audiences to filter content according to their own values. On the other hand, bloggers do have the capacity to impact on the news agenda by reactivating or reframing news stories.

Despite the contingencies that limit the practices and impact of participatory journalism, such civic initiatives are altering the character of journalism and should be seen as a democratic asset. Yet these developments of course also give rise to many questions (see, for example, the collections by Papacharissi, 2009; Rosenberry and Burston St. John III, 2010; Tunney and Monaghan, 2010), not least among the defenders of traditional journalism. The issue of journalism's definitional boundaries becomes all the more acute as mainstream journalism simultaneously grapples with its professional identity in the wake of infotainment's hybrid formats and the marked increase in forms of opinion journalism. When the boundaries of journalism become unclear, the norms of its practices and the criteria for its evaluation in turn become slippery; this is especially the case when journalism turns explicitly activist (see Forde, 2011). For participatory journalism, often fuelled more by the ideals of citizen-driven democracy than by traditional professional values, the encounter with the cosmopolitan horizon provides both inspiration and uncertainty.

In simplified terms we could say that today we have two modes of journalism within the mediapolis, which coexist as a mixed system. On the one hand we have what is sometimes referred to as high-modernist journalism, with its origins in the institutions of the mass media. Its claim is to offer accurate and fair reporting about society and the world. It emphasises the distinction between facts and emotionality; it allows for rational judgement *and* moral response. However, the subject position of *spectator* is largely cemented; in the contemporary world it finds itself on the defensive, economically and culturally. On the other hand we have what might be termed late-modernist journalism, which emerges with interactive media. It claims to underscore experiential witnessing, authenticity, directness; it allows for networking, invites potential practice, encourages participatory narratives. 'Objectivity' gives way to a stream of many voices. (We could add that at the moment, citizen-assisted journalism, where citizens send in their material to established media organisations, represents somewhat of a hybrid between the two.) The strengths and weaknesses of each come into focus, and we can almost hear echoes of the intense debates that haves raged over the past decade or two.

Truth – and moral responsibility

Non-professional civic agents engaging in journalism in its many forms often refer explicitly to the ideals of democratic participation, perceiving themselves as embodying these ideals in their journalistic practice. At the same time, it is not possible to simply ignore the norms of journalism, even if today they are less fixed and more problematic than before. These norms remain ultimately tied to our understanding of democracy. And if that concept has also become more multivalent and contested, we need to continue to grapple with both journalism and democracy, in relation to each other. We can refract the interface of the ideals of journalism and participation through two dimensions: the epistemic issue of truth, and the moral dimension of witnessing.

A cornerstone of traditional journalism has always been its commitment to truth. Yet one need not be a professional philosopher to understand that the notion of 'truth' is fraught with difficulties. On a basic level, the description and characterisation of factual reality, of events and developments, is in principle not problematic, assuming the information is available. The number of civilians killed or wounded by a bomb, the location of the rebel headquarters, the extent of the proposed cuts in social services, are the kinds of facts that can be verified. Yet, even with so-called solid facts there can always be different ways of slanting them, giving them different significance by using different news frames, narrative structures, value premises, vocabularies, and so forth. As we move into the more complex domains of human activity and its meaning, reporting becomes open to still more contestation. Yet mainstream journalism tends to cluster its interpretive horizons fairly tightly. As socially situated storytellers, news organisations usually deploy well-embedded, taken-for-granted discourses that pre-structure much of the meaning to be conveyed, as, for example, Robert Fisk (2006) demonstrates in his coverage of the Middle East and in his critical reflection on Western reporting of it.

Language use is thus always already implicated in social horizons, pre-understandings, and power relations; ideologically charged discourses can shape the meaning of reported events, intentionally or otherwise. As Kant pointed out, the conditions of our knowing are always complex, and our knowledge of the world (and of ourselves) is always mediated and filtered in various ways. Despite its established professional routines, journalism is always confronted by the epistemic challenge of grasping and transmitting knowledge in an ever-changing world; the problem of knowing is never secure. To deal with this, particularly in a time when relativism is gaining some legitimate ground, practitioners of journalism need helpful tools for orientation.

One conceptual starting point lies in acknowledging that the truth may in fact be multidimensional. And if not all versions of the truth have equal validity even in our own eyes, others may see it still differently, depending on how they are situated in the world. Thus, for journalism's professional tradition, while the commitment to the truth remains crucial, this stance will not absolve it from having to deal with the plural nature of social reality. If the quest for the truth about the world remains paramount, journalism must increasingly pursue this by taking into account the multiplicity of valid frames of perception in the world today. Further, if the distinction between fact and value seems less self-evident today, the solution lies not in abandoning the idea of the distinction, but rather in finding more useful ways to conceptualise it. This is particularly important as the opinion side of journalism expands, even within mainstream journalism. Reporters need to be alert to how various frames of reference may distinguish between facts and values in concrete cases. For example, in the history of a given conflict, the different parties will most likely have internalised different histories of the hostilities, which shape their perceptions of the present.

The civic participatory thrust in journalistic activity tends to highlight interpretation and advocacy; this is democratically healthy, yet must be counterbalanced by a traditional trajectory that, while sensitive to multiple realities and modes of perception, emphasises the quest for truth. Tensions within the traditional journalistic ideals and norms are inevitable, but hopefully they will serve rather than hamper the goal of truthfulness in the context of an ever pluralising world.

Yet journalism cannot rest content with tackling the epistemic challenge of transmitting truthful renderings of reality. From the horizons of the mediapolis, we understand that it also has moral responsibilities to others. This can be formulated in a variety of ways, but in particular it is the function of witnessing that should be underscored. As Chouliaraki (2010) discusses, the testimonial service that journalism can provide makes use of factual information but addresses us in ways that invite affective response and reflection on possible practices. Ideally, witnessing puts us face to face with the situation of distant others, and not just as individualised spectators, but as part of constructed collectivities, of publics, who embody the potential for civic agency. Understood in this manner, journalistic witnessing – of both the participatory kind and the professional tradition – can be seen as a form of civic communication whose normative grounding is, fundamentally, the moral horizons of democracy. Journalism does not just inform, but at some level resonates with us emotionally and prefigures democratic agency.

In the contemporary cacophonic mediapolis of online global communication between individuals, groups, institutions, publics, and political cultures, as well as within national societies divided by political horizons, ethnicity, and culture, there are many voices telling many stories, and in principle there are many possible stories to tell about the same phenomenon. For journalistic activity, a cosmopolitan disposition is indispensible for dealing with such heterogeneity. This does not mean uncritically accepting everything at face value – but nor does it permit one to simply dismiss that which hovers beyond one's own immediate mental map. The tension between passionate engagement and a commitment to the truth is not always easy, but it remains central: Kapuscinski, for all his moral engagement in the people and situations about which he wrote, still struggled to maintain identity as a teller of the truth.

News narratives are not just vehicles for content, they have an epistemic dimension as well; narratives comprise ways of knowing and relating to the world, offering different horizons and experiences. A regime victim-turned-rebel fighting an authoritarian state will most likely, in a journalistic context, tell a different story from that of a foreign professional journalist who has just arrived in the country, especially if s/he makes use of local narrative traditions. One account is not necessarily more or less true than the other, but each can offer a specific version of reality. Also, the rebel in this case will most likely be a better source for journalistic witnessing; giving journalistic voice to his testimony puts us in the communicative domain of his realities, touches us at the affective level, and invites a moral response from us.

Journalism in a multi-epistemic world

Mainstream professionals as well as civic cosmopolitans need to come to terms with traditional journalistic criteria to see what can and should be salvaged, and what new elements need to be introduced. If the notion of objectivity is not so helpful these days, there are other traditional attributes or criteria that can at least help guide journalism closer to the truth, even if their application is not always easy: accuracy, which reminds us that the adherence to the facts as best understood remains indispensable; transparency, which requires self-revelation as well as self-examination, making visible the journalistic production process; and accountability, which involves checks and consequences for deliberate malpractice, such as lies and disinformation.

The most difficult classic virtue, however, may well be impartiality, which demands fair representation of differing voices and points of view. Those with journalistic practices imbued with political commitment will tend to downplay its significance, seeing their efforts as needed antidotes to dominant journalistic discourses. Yet even for those intent on adhering to the classic professional model, impartiality is becoming more and more difficult to maintain. In the mediapolis, it is not just concrete issues, beliefs, and worldviews that clash, but language and symbols as well. Finding a discursive position 'outside' those of the conflicting actors, a language use that is not already embedded and 'tainted' through its premises and historical associations, becomes increasingly difficult, for example, Western journalistic coverage of conflicts where religion plays a part is a typical minefield. (A useful collection of texts that explores these issues in conceptual and practical terms is found in Barkho, 2013). For all their difficulties, accuracy, transparency, accountability, and impartiality can continue to serve both professional journalism and participatory civic cosmopolitans; these criteria supply no easy solutions to many dilemmas, but can at least help to define the problems. While for many professionals these criteria are second nature, for many civic journalists learning to struggle with them to improve their practices would be an important step.

To this list of journalistic criteria we should also add the virtue of cosmopolitan reflection, that is, the mental exercise of understanding how one's view of reality is shaped by a range of specific factors and is thus always situated and limited. Such reflection articulates neatly with all the professional criteria, especially that of impartiality. It deepens one's awareness that there are indeed other, alternative ways of looking at the world – and that impartiality is thus a massive challenge. This is admittedly a tall order, given that within journalism there is much reality predefinition built into the narrative discourses used. One could say that a common attribute of mainstream professional journalism is that it often tends to represent the world via a seemingly unified voice. This is of course practical, and rhetorically, gives credence to its authority. However, it also fosters the norm of a singular version of the truth. It thus needs to deepen its sensitivity to what we can call the multi-epistemic nature of the modern world.

To analytically distance oneself from cemented taken-for-granteds about unitary truth is not simple, but not impossible. It is perhaps easier for some activist civic cosmopolitans, since they often have a background in critically confronting dominant media discourses. Yet even professional journalism is capable of it, and we see examples emerging. From the days of having local 'stringers' assist global news bureaus to the current situation where news organisations actively recruit material from anybody on the scene and make use of social media (albeit filtering and structuring this material according to their established practices), professional journalism is encountering more quasi- and non-professional voices who are telling viable journalistic stories. Journalism is becoming more multivocal, more collaborative, even if the professional desire to maintain editorial control remains strong.

It could be that what has been now set in motion is precisely a growing pluralism of voices; while it is not quite a seismic shift yet, a transformation is clearly under way. We see this, for example, in the various locally produced magazine segments that appear on the global news networks. Also, without idealising it, we could say that Al-Jazeera, for example, has developed a heterogeneous journalistic profile that takes a point of departure in its location in the Middle East, makes use of reporters and bloggers with a number of nationalities, and yet manages to resonate even with Western audiences. This suggests that today there are cosmopolitan options available – and that, significantly, there is a growing market for them. Fox News, of course, demonstrates that there are also markets for anti-cosmopolitanism. The world would probably not have been ready for either organisation two decades ago, which suggests something about the turbulent nature of the present historical situation.

The transformation is of course also manifested in the broad range of journalistic activity in the social media. How and where we draw the boundaries between journalism and non-journalism will remain a (hopefully fruitful) point of contention in the immediate future, but at present we recognise that blogs, Twitter, Facebook, and YouTube have become integrated into the public sphere. From these platforms we are today getting some important journalism that demonstrates a loyalty to the truth as well as compelling moral witnessing. This is evidenced, to take but one example, in the materials from the ongoing uprising in Syria, where most professional journalists are barred. While civic cosmopolitans mostly make use of the Web 2.0 affordances, some will no doubt in the future be entering mainstream journalism, further contributing to its evolution. In the meantime, as traditional journalism is becoming all the more reliant on citizens' use of social media, the boundaries of journalism are rendered yet more porous.

If journalistically inclined participatory civic cosmopolitans tilt their journalistic endeavours towards advocacy, the challenge becomes to preserve in some fashion the traditional journalistic virtues while at the same time pursuing their civic and political objectives. For professional journalists, the key challenge has to do with dealing constructively with the increasing number of social worlds that diverge from their own, where actors are emerging and making claim to be legitimate voices. We would be wise not to anticipate any swift resolution to the force-field between professional and civic ideals of online journalism; it is a dynamic that will continue to play out intensely in the years ahead, shaped and altered as circumstances evolve. But for the sake of democracy, we need a positive unfolding.

Part III
Critical Approaches

6
The Civic Subject and Media-Based Agency

Research on media and democracy mobilises a range of conceptual versions of the subject. This is often done out of habit, with a specific model becoming implicitly established in any given research tradition. This chapter argues that different theories of the subject can have different implications for our understanding of citizenship and democracy. In the previous chapters I have been making use of a model that leans towards post-structural and psychoanalytic grounding, but also with other components, and at this point it could be edifying to make explicit a broader range of options. My aim is not so much to sell my own views as to make visible and invite reflection on various possible notions of the subject as citizen, something that we (myself included) tend to take for granted. (For an illuminating presentation that also pursues this theme, but with a different agenda, see Corner, 2011: ch. 3).

Thus, the discussion here surveys a number of versions, deriving from a large and heterogeneous literature, and organises them under four themes: rationalism, reflexivity, transparency, and contingency. No one version is offered as the ultimate one, since all have something to offer and at the same time all have their limitations. However, I suggest that more attention should be paid to how we conceptualise the civic subject in our research, not least in regard to issues having to do with affect, the limits of reflexivity and self-transparency, the role of the unconscious, and the importance of contingency.

The unsettled self

The question of how we can best describe and characterise the human being found its first answers in the misty origins of religion. At some later point in human history, philosophy began grappling with what came to be called the subject, and in more recent intellectual history, psychology and other behavioural and social sciences also began addressing the question of the subject, or the self, as it tends to be called within these traditions. Some of these efforts made and make use of evidence from the natural and biological sciences to various degrees, others do not. Today there are many possible theoretical trajectories one can follow to provide a conceptual portrait of the subject. This can involve ontological, epistemological, and normative dimensions, as well as empirical-historical ones; the pathways are many.

The use of the notion of the subject in the context of political thought is a comparatively recent phenomenon. In English we still have a lingering earlier usage of the term from the feudal period, though it has become muted: the idea of a 'subject of the crown', that is, one who is subordinate to a monarchical power structure. However, as the Middle Ages waned, philosophical writings about the subject as a thinking and feeling creature gradually began to emerge, and later, as such horizons connected with the Enlightenment and the intellectual currents of the American and French revolutions, the sense of the subject as citizen, as political agent in a democratic context, gained ground. The specific attributes of this civic subject – as well as the ideal contours of democracy – were and remain contested, however, even if the debates do not always continue with sustained intensity.

It might be worth noting here at the outset that discussions about the subject run parallel to another very extensive topic, namely that of identity. Conceptual usage can vary among different traditions, but for most scholars today identity is seen as socially constructed, an ongoing process where the interface of people, their circumstances, and their experiences give shape to their sense of who they are, both to themselves and to others. The subject, on the other hand, is an analytic construct that tends to signify a more fundamental layer of the self, the basic 'who' behind identity work. Yet, as we shall see, even the core of the subject is seen as a social product within some traditions.

Efforts to specify parameters of the subject take on particular intensity in certain periods. For example, during the 1960s and 1970s, behaviouristic models of the self were vigorously challenged; there was a robust wave of 'French theory' that included Lacan's linguistic take on Freud, Foucault's post-structural notions of discourse, and Derrida's de-centring of meaning; concurrently feminism was putting a gendered wedge into patriarchy's masculine model of the universal self. A decade or so later, postmodern visions were airing a situated, reflexive, and composite sense of selfhood. Today, such contexts as globalisation, multiculturalism, post-colonialism, and new media developments also leave their traces. All this reminds us that our understanding of the self is not likely to be settled with any finality.

If we look beyond the explicit endeavours to define the subject, however, and turn our attention to the routine practices of much of the social and human sciences, including media studies, the picture is more complacent. The versions of the subject that are mobilised in different research contexts become entrenched, familiar, and ultimately self-evident. That there can be competing models, with different analytic implications, fades from view, and the turbulent waters of debate become still. Thus, most often we find a particular range of rather established conceptualisations at work, some more implicit, others more explicit.

In thus modestly stirring up the waters and reactivating concerns about the subject, I do not intend to 'resolve' anything, for in fact we will always have to deal with competing versions and interpretations. The civic subject is at bottom the human being acting in political contexts, and from the standpoint of theory, humans have proven themselves to be rather slippery creatures who (perhaps fortunately) continue to resist neat and total theoretical enclosures. Yet this is not to say that it does not matter which model(s) of the civic subject we operate with. It does make a difference, and I will try to show the implications in terms of democratic theory of some different versions. I also draw out some of the pertinent connections to the media as a way of further situating the subject in the dynamics of contemporary democracy.

The literature theorising on the subject is vast and spans many disciplines; even a cursory inventory would be far beyond the scope of this presentation (a brief, introductory effort of this kind is found in Elliott, 2008). Thus, my exposition will be simplified and suggestive rather than technical and exhaustive. Based on my reading of this literature, I will focus on what I see as four definitive themes in regard to the subject that point to key attributes that are decisive in any theoretical perspective. These themes at certain points may blur into each other; they are not always distinctly separable, but, expressed in varying conceptual language, they account for much of what is at the core of this literature.

The themes are: *rationalism*, which raises the issue of to what extent our subjectivity and our actions are steered by reason vs. emotion; *reflexivity*, a concept that points to the ways that we monitor and adjust our actions in social contexts, and the consequences this has; *transparency*, the degree to which we have access to our own subjectivity and can understand ourselves; and *contingency*, the issue of to what extent we as subjects are shaped by our contexts and circumstances. I devote more space to the first two themes, but that has to do with the need to establish a few orienting ideas, which are carried forward in the second two themes; there is no implicit signal that any one attribute is theoretically more significant than any other. It could well be, however, that rationalism and reflexivity have been dealt with more in the media literature and we need to pay more attention to transparency and contingency. In any case, as a shortcut approach, I think this set of attributes will suffice to usher us into the main topics of debate and offer a rough map of some of the terrain. I suspect that most readers will recognise at least some of the attributes that I address as well as the traditions from which they derive (and some no doubt will feel I have omitted one or more that are crucial). I conclude with some reflections on the seemingly protean civic subject.

Rationalism: An emotional issue

Liberal subjects

In every textbook on the history of philosophy the topic of rationalism occupies a prominent place. From the ancient Greeks, to Descartes and Spinoza, and on to Kant and the Enlightenment, rationalism has rightly been lauded as a major achievement of the human mind. Basically, rationalism holds that reason is the ultimate ground of knowledge and the foundation for all forms of justification. In terms of the subject, it could be said that the attribute of rationalism is both descriptive and prescriptive: Kant argues that humans have the capacity to attain freedom by pulling themselves out of their self-imposed ignorance. They both can and should do this, and this optimism of the Enlightenment view of the subject remains with us today. Rationalism has always had its critics – Pascal and Hume, for example, argued for putting faith foremost, and even Kant himself was concerned to redeem ethics and aesthetics from rationalism's negative impact. And Neitzsche's various dissections of knowledge, rationalism, and their relationship to power foreshadowed postmodernist and post-structural interrogation that came later. Weber, too, with his metaphors about the 'iron cage', warned about rationalism's dangers. Yet rationalism's position remains well-entrenched.

In traditional political theory (as well as in much mainstream economic theory), rationalism remains particularly strong, and is understood as the foundation of the subject as an agent. Theories about 'rational man' (and the gender bias had a surprising longevity) has been a leitmotif of liberalism from the start. Compared to the autocratic regimes of feudal societies, where the domination of the politically subservient subject was seen as ordained by God, rationalism was undeniably a great progressive development. Feminists have rightly countered the masculinist implication of rationalism, and aside from whatever might remain of the gender bias, we are still left with a view of the subject that is inexorably individualistic. The ultimate social and political unit of classic liberalism is the person, and the point of his/her existence is the pursuit of self-interest, predicated on rational grounds and with the stipulation to not harm others.

Western political philosophy has not been unanimously happy with this vision, and the strict rationalism (and its concomitant individualism) of the liberal civic subject has been challenged by alternative views of citizenship. Thus, feminists accentuate the gender dimension, communitarianism argues for the importance of shared values among civic subjects, and republicanism stresses the importance of participation and a sense of responsibility to the democratic system as a whole. These and other critiques of the liberal vision and its civic subject are not out to jettison rationalism, rather, they seek to modify its dominance in describing and prescribing a more realistic and democratically attuned version of the self (for overviews of theories of citizenship, see Isin and Turner, 2003).

What many critics object to is precisely the lopsided view of the subject that is constructed in liberal political theory, where rationality is given such prominence and the affective side of human existence is so ruthlessly suppressed. This fear of the emotions has an understandable origin: people can commit dreadful acts, not least in political contexts, under the sway of emotions. However, they can also do so while acting in a rational mode (the 20th century provides much gruesome evidence of this). Writers such as Marcus (2002) and Hall (2005) argue, almost in a common-sense way, that rationality and emotionality are linked, always co-present within the subject, and that people would be profoundly crippled as social agents if one or the other was missing, or if the dynamic between them was ruptured. Rationality should not be in the driver's seat with the emotions strapped in the back seat; both need to be co-pilots. As Marcus puts it: 'people are able to be rational because they are emotional; emotions enable rationality ... The practice of citizenship must acknowledge the role emotion plays in the development of rationality ... the effort to exclude passion will also undermine our capacity to reason' (Marcus, 2002: 7).

...And deliberative ones

The critique of excessive rationalism is also directed at a theoretical trajectory quite different from that of mainstream liberalism, namely the communicative action of Habermas (1984, 1987) and the tradition of deliberative democracy that is closely associated with it. Clearly, this development by Habermas and the subsequent take-off of deliberative democracy as a vision of how civic communication should proceed are major contributions to democratic thought. Yet, various voices have questioned not only the feasibility of his framework (that includes what he calls the ideal speech situation), but also its desirability. Between the lines of these debates we find different notions of the subject.

There is an extensive literature here, but the basic argument is that while Habermas' insistence on rationality in communication between citizens (and decision-makers) makes perfectly good sense on one level, there is concern that this can quickly become counter-productive. Obviously the public sphere degenerates when discussion becomes irrational, illogical, and nasty. Yet, conceptually locking in place this degree of rationalism within the civic subject can be constrictive of political talk and expression, and even function as a power factor against groups less well-versed in this register of communication. Also, political innovation involves new ways of framing and rendering social reality that can promote new ways of seeing and 'denaturalize' old ones. This involves the use of such communicative strategies as 'irony, personal narrative, aesthetic interventions, theatricality, and visibility' (Kohn, 2000: 425). Similarly, Gardiner (2004) contrasts Habermas with Bakhtin, who asserts that 'living discourse...is necessarily charged with polemical qualities, myriad evaluation and stylistic markers, and populated by diverse intentions' (Gardiner, 2004: 36).

Adherence to what we might characterise as a 'straight-jacket' of rational speech for the civic subject thus undermines the potential richness and vibrancy of political discussion in favour of an illusory ideal, and is likely to actually deflect civic engagement rather than enhance it. Certainly we value the civic subject's capacity for rationality the closer we come to formal decision-making processes, but subjects characterised by strict rationalism and/or affective incompetence will not enhance the vitality of the public sphere. This is markedly true in the age of Web 2.0, with all its possibilities for creative expression.

Technologically enabled and free-floating 'users'

Interestingly enough, the advent of the Internet has tended to promote an ambivalent understanding of the subject in this regard. On the one hand, there appeared various optimistic discourses about the liberating and inventive online practices that posited a rather flexible subject. It was argued that people could construct, reconstruct themselves, and even engage in identity play and fantasy via virtual social relationships, new forms of intimacy, and so forth (for an early version, see Turkle, 1995). One could escape from some of the unavoidable and confining markers of identity that characterise life in the off-line world. These strands of thought resonated with theories about the dramatic sociocultural changes signalled by concepts such as globalisation and postmodernism, rendering these notions of the malleable self particularly compelling in this context. A new sense of freedom was in the air (and online). Versions of such currents are still with us, as we shall see shortly. While this kind of theoretical exuberance did not have much direct impact on notions of citizenship and democracy (whose discourses tended towards more staid modes of theorising), the overall optimism it generated no doubt contributed to positive thinking about the net and democracy.

From another angle, however, discourses about 'users' were gaining ground at the expense of the concept of 'audiences', a major pillar in theories of mass media. The notion of the user does not offer any explicit theory of the subject, but it has come to play the role of a common-sense repository of a key characteristic of those who use digital media, namely that they are almost by definition empowered agents who make rational choices. There is nothing per se wrong with the term 'user'; the problems arise when this concept is plugged into social analyses of digital media and left under-theorised.

The user becomes a free-floating agent employing communication technology in a strategic, effective manner, but is too often bereft of any psychological traits or sociocultural specificity. We have instead a rather empty signifier that becomes a de facto repository for various assumed traits that are projected onto it from on the one hand informatics and other technical disciplines engaged in internet analysis and on the other marketing research. Seemingly the notion of user has drifted from these disciplines into media studies and the broader social sciences. Thus, this understanding of 'user' often correlates well with contemporary individualised, media-savvy consumers making rational market choices.

Affect and the popular

Overly rationalist views of the subject imply a restriction on his/her modes, registers of expression and representation. Still more significantly, such views imply that affect, as a terrain of the psyche, is neither a site nor a resource for the political. Another trajectory that challenges this walling off of emotional reality was formulated by feminists already engaged in their critique of the basic bourgeois configuration of public and private, where affect and emotions (along with women) belong to the private space of home and family (this strand of feminist political theory is exemplified, by, for example, Lister, 2003; Voet, 1998). The civic subject is gendered, a point that is not just an ontological abstraction but has political import: gender becomes a vector for democratic politics, and issues deriving from the private and personal domain could and should always be seen as legitimate topics of potential political contention. Further, this feminist intervention affords legitimacy to affect as a grounding of human experience and as a dimension of public expression.

The link to the media landscape becomes readily visible: the media obviously play an enormous, if increasingly complex and even contradictory role, in the definitions of gender, relationships, and intimacy (Gauntlett, 2008; Gill, 2006). Moreover, the gender theme has in recent decades given force to broader critical views that accentuate the centrality of affect and challenge the traditional view of strict separation between politics and the public on the one hand, and popular culture and the private on the other (see, for example, Street, 1997; Corner and Pels, 2003; Hermes, 2005; Van Zoonen, 2005). The critics insist that even if the domains should not be collapsed into each other, there is no fixed boundary between politics and popular culture. They are discursively structured in similar ways and they flow into each other, not least via the evolving genres and modes of representation in the media. Popular culture offers a sense of easy access to symbolic communities, a world of belonging beyond oneself that can at times be seen as preparatory for civic engagement, prefiguring involvement beyond one's private domain.

Thus, popular culture invites us to engage – with both our hearts and minds – in many questions having to do with how we should live and what kind of society we want. It allows us to process issues having to do with conflicting values, norms, and identities in a turbulent late modern sociocultural milieu. Moreover, many of the themes taken up by popular culture may seem more important and more personally relevant than the agendas on offer from mainstream politics. Finally, popular culture can serve to foster alternative conceptions of what actually constitutes politics and the political, generating reflections and engagement over other kinds of concerns and issues. In short, in this literature we find the contours of a civic subjectivity where affect and pleasure are always potential concerns of – and resources for – citizenship.

Reflexivity: The monitoring self

That people monitor their actions in order to suitably adapt them to the surrounding circumstances has always been a feature of the thinking subject. The modern concept of feedback, for example, captures this idea in regard to technical and biological systems and is also used in some branches of psychology. In the social and human sciences, the notion of reflexivity became somewhat of a buzzword in social theory in the 1990s. It extends and applies the idea of feedback, underscoring the process by which the individual examines and reflects on his/her life trajectory, scrutinising both the developments in the external world as well as inner psychological responses, and thereby adjusts and modifies specific practices and more overarching life strategies. On the surface all this may seem banal, but it has come to generate varying implications for how we understand the subject in the historical present. Fundamentally, the theme of reflexivity opens up the question of who is actually doing the monitoring, and who is being monitored.

Image management

One modern theorist who simulated a good deal of controversy in this regard is Erving Goffman. His micro-sociology is generally not associated with the specific domain of citizenship, but it does have salience. It was his first major publication (Goffman, 1959), entitled *The Presentation of Self in Everyday Life*, that established his reputation (and somewhat undeservedly overshadowed some of his later work), and in it Goffman shows how the self is at bottom performative. People strategically enact their identities, adapting different modes in different contexts, and they fine-tune the performances by monitoring the reactions of others. The self is thus seen as being aware of a distinction between itself and the roles, the public identities, it uses in different settings. This is obviously a far theoretic cry from the Habermasian interlocutor, who is geared towards openness and authenticity.

Goffman does not tell us much about the deeper self behind the publicly performed identities; it remains shadowy. The most we can really say is that it seeks to express and embody itself in social enactments and encounters. Does this necessarily have to mean that we are dealing here with a con-artist, a hustler, as is sometimes claimed? It seems to me that the Goffmanian agent need not be the ethical dark side of the one that Habermas and others envision, and were we to insert this subject into a context of democratic participation, it is not at all certain that this would be detrimental to such ideals. Goffman's subject can have innumerable agendas, aims, and ambitions, but s/he is decidedly committed to being a social participant. This subject is adept at the norms and moral frameworks of society, and there does not appear to be any reason to assume that s/he would break them any more than any other subject we might theoretically construct. Indeed, Goffman's subject, in his/her self-presentation, is actively involved in the construction and reproduction of society at the micro level, in ways that he implies are in fact similar to Bourdieu's perspective (Goffman, 1983).

A certain moral scepticism towards the Goffmanian subject no doubt derives precisely from its explicit status as knowingly performative. This seems to smack of manipulation, and if we invoke the norms of democracy, it can readily trigger alarm bells among some who are committed to deliberation and similar orientations. And yet: the notion of performance as central to democracy has ancient origins, and in modern times it is strongly associated with the work of Hanna Arendt (see Arendt, 1958). More recently, Mouffe (2005) has recast this performative notion of political participation in the theoretical horizons of radical democracy and discourse theory (which I will return to below). We have in Goffman a proto-decentred subject, one that operates with a multiplicity of identities, and one that at least need not be at odds with some version of the civic subject. Its self-monitoring, its social competence and adaptability can in fact be viewed as important assets for the sociality required for doing citizenship in specific interactive contexts of the public sphere.

Empowering reflexivity

If the natural habitat of Goffman's subject was the middle-class society of the mid-century US, a different perspective on reflexivity can be found in the writings of Anthony Giddens. As one of the most prominent and productive of contemporary sociologists, Giddens has devoted a number of his works to the areas of globalisation and late modernity; it is in this context that he has written about the contemporary self, most explicitly in Giddens (1991). Giddens' subject is seemingly always in the 'on' mode; reflexivity never sleeps, given the swirling settings and intense dynamics of the contemporary world.

This subject of course encounters difficulties, is confronted by many uncertainties, but at bottom is robust and brave, and can make sense of his/her circumstances in culturally alert and socially astute ways.

The biographical narratives that sustain identity and its lifestyles are always open for revision. The strategic interpretation of ever-changing (and to a great extent media-borne) cultural trends, norms, and values in late modernity is a key competence this subject possesses, as is the capacity to evaluate institutions, organisations, and technological developments.

This is a compelling, upbeat portrait of a self that is creative and adaptable in the face of often intense sociocultural turmoil, and largely in charge of his/her own life project. Giddens' work on politics (Giddens, 1998, 2000) is informed by these horizons, resulting in a rather optimistic vision of a renewed social democracy. Even leaving aside the fate of the Blair government with which he was associated, Giddens' views have not surprisingly elicited critiques from a number of corners. Chief among the lines of criticism are that this notion of the self bears a strong resemblance to the classic liberal individual, and that s/he seems excessively in control of his/her life. Power relations, for example, never really quite impinge on his/her lifestyle choices. Moreover, this subject is at one with her/himself – s/he is self-transparent, with no dark corners of repression, conflict, desire (the theme I take up in the next section). Where lives have increasingly become self-conscious projects to be navigated in stormy sociocultural seas, reflexivity is an obvious response. Yet the apparent efficacy with which Giddens imbues the subject seems rather independent of social position and cultural capital, while its political import remains muted.

Adrift in liquid modernity

Gidden's reassuring portrait of the late modern subject encounters a flip side in a literature that strikes a quite different tone. In the many works of Bauman and others (see, for example, Bauman, (2007); Young (2007); Elliott and Lemert (2006)), a gloomier picture emerges. The subject is seen as struggling against imposing forces that threaten to overwhelm its ability to function effectively. Reflexivity becomes not just a pathway to freedom, but at some moments a huge burden, at others an inadequate strategy. In continuously having to rethink their day-to-day living and overall life courses, people are challenged in ways they cannot always handle well. What Bauman calls the 'liquid' character of late modernity means that its fluid, ever-changing character generates a permanent state of uncertainty and profound ambivalence. A globalised and notoriously unstable capitalism alters economic realities, occupational structures, and employment possibilities. Shifting institutions and transient organisations, altered cultural patterns, values, and norms, eroding everyday milieus, all take their psychic toll in disorientation, anxiety, depression, and so forth.

The subject appears as a harried and vulnerable creature, scurrying desperately to fashion a stable life and identity via consumerism and other practices that are predestined to merely reinforce the problems. The media become accomplices to the overall pattern, with not even the internet offering any genuine alternative. The creative and adaptive character of the subject is not denied, but the forces s/he is up against are ominous. In terms of democracy, Bauman and others argue that genuine power is slipping away from the political institutions that represent the citizens and could demand accountability; the global corporate sphere can act in an increasingly independent manner in shaping the development of society. One might see this perspective as a kind of late modern update on the Frankfurt School, but it would seem that the subject that Bauman and others postulate here, with his/her greater resiliency and inventiveness, at least holds out somewhat more hope than the portrait of the ideological victim in Horkheimer and Adorno. In that sense, liquid modernity at least remains more open to progressive civic intervention than the social world described by early critical theory.

Performing subjects/subject to performance

Goffman, Giddens, Bauman, and others offer versions of a subject that is characterised by multiplicity and/or malleability, capable of shifting modes in different contexts. Other trajectories explore such topics in different ways, for example, Butler's (1990) notion of gender as a constructed and performative dimension of the self that transcends the sexed male and female body. A sort of radical post-feminism with overtones of Goffman and Foucault, her perspective sees the subject as enacting identity via society's prevalent discourses and codes. In this way, individuals strive to fill a psychic interior that in her view is ultimately empty. This is a decisive poststructuralist move: the reflexive self has no real core. Butler's is one major trajectory within queer theory (see, Wilchins, 2004, for a useful overview), a critical endeavour of its own, with a strong postmodern bent, that argues for the social constructedness of gender and sexual orientation and confronts notions of deviancy in these matters, seeing such labels as an exercise of illegitimate and oppressive power.

At first glance these developments may appear somewhat marginal to concerns about the civic subject, but they signal an important reformatting of the political terrain. The definitions of the subject with regard to the intimate realm of life – having to do with gender, sexual orientation, family, birthing, abortion, medical technologies concerning the body – have emerged from the private sanctums and increasingly become politicised issues. Thus, conceptions of the subject that incorporate civic engagement with these issues lead us into the emerging terrain that Plummer (2003) terms 'intimate citizenship'. We can see these inflections of the civic subject as theoretically ambitious vectors that can resonate with and align themselves with others that challenge rationalist positions and affirm the centrality of the private and the emotional reality in an expanded view of the political.

While the more fluid models of the subject have become more widespread, the question of whether or not at its core there is only some kind of vacuum remains controversial. Yet, it may well be that from the standpoint of the civic subject, this issue is 'academic'. That is, the philosophical premises about its essence need not de facto have direct practical consequences for citizenship and democracy (even if supporters of traditional Enlightenment and humanistic notions of the subject may become indignant about this apparent void). The performative tradition in citizenship puts the accent on public deeds and speech, less on personal views, or authentic feelings; it tilts away from the inner and focuses more on the public and observable. Indeed, the demand for authenticity in political speech could theoretically quickly short-circuit the life of democracy.

However, the introduction of the unconscious, which I discuss in the next section, involves postulating a different kind of split within the subject. In this radical step, we have not nothing at the inner core, but rather a very vigorous actor, whose dynamics with the conscious agent are complex to say the least – and thus of significance for the outcome of political performance.

Transparency and its limits

Enter the unconscious

The notion of reflexivity that Giddens and others work with suggests that the subject can monitor not only the social environment but also his/her own experiences and inner feelings, to a lesser or greater degree, and in that way make suitable adjustments in behaviour. While not necessarily promising full transparency of the self and its emotional world, this model of the subject is not saddled with any a priori limits in this regard. But what if the case were precisely the opposite – what if the subject *by definition* can never really achieve access to itself, and is always and inevitably cut off from full awareness of its own inner workings?

What if the subject cannot fully understand why s/he does and says all the things that s/he does?

This of course is the fundamental premise of psychoanalysis and its view of the unconscious. There are other versions of the unconscious, but the Freudian model, with its various revisions and offshoots, has incontestably become the dominant one. In the context of 19th-century Vienna and a Victorian society not at ease with its sexuality, while at the same time coloured by expansive industrial capitalism, the vigorous growth of science and technology, and a faith in man's (sic) rationality, the notion of the unconscious detonated a bomb. That people are to a significant extent shaped and driven by unacknowledged desires and fears, unresolved conflicts and guilt, emotional double binds, that the self is cloven between its conscious awareness and a murky, elusive unconscious, was all very unsettling, to say the least.

The alleged lack of transparency of the psyche in particular subverted the ideal of self-mastery and control. That the anxieties of the inner self are blocked from view by elaborate processes of repression and forgetting implies that people are to some extent always doomed to be strangers to themselves, even if psychoanalysis holds out the promise of gaining better insight into the workings of one's unconscious mind. The unconscious, according to Freud, is fundamentally geared towards pleasure, while being removed from the normal realities that govern our sense of the world. It has its own dynamics, which among other things, are apparently aloof to logical contradictions. Fear and desire, love and hate, respect and disdain, and so can all be co-present in regard to the same person, object, or set of beliefs. From this perspective one can understand that we humans confront serious obstacles to communicative ethics, intersubjectivity, and authenticity.

Over the years, Freud's core ideas have been vehemently debated, often rejected; within psychoanalysis a variety of revisionist schools emerged. Attempts have been made to integrate psychoanalysis with other currents, such as Marxism and feminism, treating it as an analytic tool that can be used for progressive purposes to counter various forms of social and political oppression. For other critical thinkers, such as Foucault and some feminist theorists (including de Beauvoir), the Freudian model is seen instead as part of the oppressive apparatus, a technology of control, or at best an approach that deals with individuals' problems while ignoring their larger societal origins. On the other hand, many writers have used psychoanalysis as a hermeneutic tool, an interpretive scheme for understanding how literature, culture, and media phenomena (e.g. advertising, political speech) address their audiences and resonate through the unconscious.

Opaque interiors: Contrasting vistas

Despite this rich tradition, mainstream democratic theory has tended to avoid theories about the unconscious. Some psychoanalytically oriented authors have been inspired by Lacan's reformulation of Freud, which, among other things, posits that the subject's selfhood is ultimately fictitious, being founded on a misrecognition of a unified, omnipotent self (deriving from the 'mirror stage' of infancy). This poststructuralist version of the Freudian self is thus seen as an imaginary projection, one that can lead the adult subject into problems such as narcissistic delusion, if it cannot come to terms with its earlier misconceptions.

The immensely energetic Žižek, using Lacan as a theoretic compass, emphasises this idea of a lack, or void, at the core of the subject. This subterranean trauma, which people are always (usually unbeknownst to themselves) trying to rectify via various forms of fantasy and imagined identities, becomes a central psychic dynamic that he uses to interpret all manner of contemporary life, including political developments (Žižek, 2008, 2011). He charts how in politics this profound sense of insufficiency mobilises pleasure and fear, and can lead people to respond positively to unsavoury and undemocratic appeals. This Freudian subject appears to be politically quite vulnerable, and democracy looms as a venture riddled with deficiencies that can never be truly rectified.

Yet, the upshot of the fractured and de-centred Freudian self can also lead in other directions. Castoriadis (1987) deploys the Freudian tradition but comes up with a rather different understanding of what limited self-transparency and the manifestations of fantasy can mean. In brief, he puts the creative powers of the unconscious in focus. While creativity per se is no guarantee for the normatively desirable, he makes a cogent argument for the constructive powers of the imagination. With regard to the self, to social relations, and to society generally, notably at the political level, Castoriadis asserts that in the incessant flux of non-logical, uncensored fantasy, the subject can generate identifications, make associations, and visualise connections that can break with established patterns of thought. Though this view of the unconscious retains its ambivalent or even contradictory character, his point is that such processes in the creative unconscious can still inspire progressive renewal at individual, social, cultural, and political levels. The glass of civic subjectivity is half empty in Žižek, and half full in Castoriadis; science cannot offer us any resolution (though our unconscious probably can).

The Freudian view of desire and pleasure has links to those notions that I discussed above. The Freudian frame, however, accords affect a much stronger and more volatile position, given that the unconscious usually slyly outwits conscious awareness and its rationalism. In regard to politics and communication, this means we need to analytically pay attention to not just information and formal argument, but also symbols, imagery, rhetoric, allegory, emotional pleas, ideology, and all the other communicative modes beyond the rational; it is through these that the civic subject takes on agency. We find such analyses in literary and cultural criticism, less so in media studies, and much less so in political science.

Contingency: The shifting subject

Post-structural premises

In contemporary social theory, the idea that action, phenomena, and events are 'contextual', that is, to some degree a product of the circumstances that give rise to and delimit them, has become commonplace. Today we even assume that our ideas and knowledge have their 'conditions' and that our knowing is always to some degree 'situated'; such a perspective can be derived from the critical Kantian view of knowledge (which I will return to in the next chapter). If these general premises are largely shared, it is precisely the degree to which contingency is operative that evokes disagreement. Seen from that angle, the post-structural tradition of Laclau and Mouffe's discourse theory (DT), which we encountered in Chapter 3, takes a strong stand in arguing for radical contingency across the board. DT's position is that there is no foundation or essence, no fixed meaning – for knowledge, language, subjects, or social phenomena. There are only possibilities, nothing is necessary. Not everybody would align themselves with such a stark version of contingency, and surely one can discuss if it might not be wise to assume *some* basic foundations, some givens, that we might use as a secure building block for our understanding of the subject (and much else in the world), but Laclau and Mouffe's uncompromising version has the asset of clarity. From there one can begin to tinker with it if one feels philosophically so inclined – or combine it with other perspectives, which would inevitably yield a compromise version.

If the Freudian horizon tends to steer our attention inward to the tumultuous terrain of the unconscious as the motor that drives the subject, post-structural thought tends to give greater weight to external factors, chiefly the dynamics of discourses and language – not only in the piloting of the subject but also in actually generating it. What is particularly interesting about DT as a critical enterprise is that it expresses a strong commitment to democracy. DT is foremost a philosophical enterprise, and Laclau and Mouffe's text is well known for being a rather daunting reading experience (for illuminating treatments, see Smith, 1999; Jørgensen and Phillips, 2002). Yet their project is explicitly democratic in its intent, and their text is worth the effort it demands. Their horizons also have obvious connections to the media, though these links have in fact only begun to be explored rather recently (see Dahlberg and Phelan, 2011; Carpentier and DeCleen, 2007).

Laclau and Mouffe's intervention in the mid-1980s is often described as both a post-structural and a post-Marxist effort to better align critical theory in keeping with historical realities. They emphasise the multiplicity and often shifting ground of subject positions in the modern world; social class becomes but one of many. Subjects – and their knowledge – are socially constructed, but these processes always take place framed by power relations. In this view, even the terms, categories, and typifications that we use in our construction of the social world are already implicated in power relations. The political, in a sense, precedes the social. In society, it is always some particular discourses that have hegemonic sway at any point in time; these strongly shape the ways subjects, knowledge, and politics are engendered (in his lexicon, Castoriadis writes about social imaginaries). The notion of discourse in DT can at first be confusing. While *discourse analysis* has become a ubiquitous methodological concept, in Laclau and Mouffe's lexicon discourse refers to social and material practices; it can thus have both linguistic and non-linguistic dimensions.

Connecting with democracy

Meaning is not just fluidly constructed and reconstructed by discourses, however; it is many times contested. DT's concept of antagonism centres on the conflict over meanings, definitions, and identities. It is here that politics arises. Prevailing (hegemonic) meanings and identities can be challenged, and at times are dislodged, or dissipated, via what the authors call 'dislocation'. In evoking agonism, the notion of democratic debate in the ancient Greek forums, Laclau and Mouffe show DT to have a communicative dynamic that aligns itself with democratic norms. In democratic politics, we should strive to have political adversaries, not enemies; in other words, there should be rules of the game that all can follow instead of resorting to violence. Political conflicts involve establishing boundaries between 'us' and 'them', giving rise to identities that are specific and contingent to the circumstances.

Some of these arguments appear in a more accessible form in Mouffe's own work on radical democracy (see, for example, Mouffe, 2005). Building firmly on DT's key ideas about meaning, identity, contingency and political contestation, Mouffe sets a course that challenges many elements of traditional liberal theory as well as Habermasian notions of deliberative democracy. In its commitment to a democratic vision and its procedures, radical democracy theory offers an alternative way of looking at, for example, citizenship, participation, and political discussion. This view admonishes us to understand and accept that conflict and the struggles for hegemony are inseparable from social life – the political can arise anywhere – and that there is no harmonious, non-conflictual future waiting for us. The civic subject must always remain alert.

In contrast to most post-structural thought, Laclau and Mouffe's discursively constructed and highly contingent subject is afforded a rather impressive degree of agency. Discourses can constrain, but they can also empower; this civic subject can act, make choices, and have political impact – collectively, via group identifications. There is a detailed conceptual apparatus within DT that can be empirically applied in regard to politics and the media (those ubiquitous carriers of discourses), particularly in examining alternative politics (Dahlberg and Phelan, 2011; Uldam, 2010). What DT does, and what Mouffe does in her extensions of it in her perspective of radical democracy, is to provide analytic tools for illuminating the forces and conditions that shape the subject and its political playing field, without any built-in predetermination. The view of democracy here is one that is urgent: DT's origins as a critical sociopolitical project are still visible. It points to powerful hegemonic positions that, in the name of enhanced democracy, need to be contested.

Composing the civic subject

So what do we do with all this? Clearly, no hard and fast conclusions are in order. I have been probing a large and diverse literature, drawing out specific features, similarities, and differences with regard to versions of the civic subject, and linking these to the media where this has been suitable. My aim has been to illuminate the connections with the contemporary terrain of late modern democracy. As we have seen, tracking the civic subject via the attributes of rationalism, reflexivity, transparency and contingency can offer lucid revelations of a theoretical subject that is often merely taken for granted. In many cases we can see a theoretically marginalised civic subject, one who, if brought out on the playing field, could function in different ways and have different impact in democratic processes.

How we conceptualise civic subjectivity has implications for the inflection we give to democracy. From the liberal rationalist ideal, to the deliberative model, to the interfaces with popular culture and affect, and on to various optimistic or dire views of late modern democracy, and on to the view of democracy as an ominous challenge to the unconscious or as an inherently unstable discursive construction, versions of the compatible civic subject hover close at hand. It will analytically help us to further explore these connections. Sometimes seen with optimism, at other times conveying regret, the self in these various traditions is often less of an explicit psychological portrait and more of a diagnostic metaphor for the state of democracy and of our societal condition. We might conceptually test various models, and evaluate the outcome, even inserting empirical data into these constructs. In any case we will have to accept that the 'real' subject no doubt will always to remain elusive to some degree; any version we might compose will always be but a partial rendering.

Yet, in valorising different elements in our portrait, we can illuminate different ways of enacting citizenship, and doing democracy, and see how that fits with our visions of the good society. Leaving the civic subject just a little open, slightly ajar, will also avoid unnecessary closure in the ways we think about democracy – and about ourselves as political actors.

7
Critical Media Research: Something Old, New, and Unfinished

Introduction: A critical resurgence

The etymologically related concepts of 'critical', 'criticism', and 'critique' figure in a number of different discursive contexts; there are three broad sets of usages of these terms. On the one hand, the adjective 'critical' is an attribute that is often associated with science, the arts, and the pursuit of knowledge more generally, a legacy of its largely Enlightenment origins (its roots of course go back to ancient Greece). It most often involves an analysis of the merits and deficiencies of a particular work, as in 'literary criticism'; such an analysis results in a 'critique'. On the other hand, these terms also cluster around political analysis of social and cultural phenomena, which signals the intellectual lineage that runs from Hegel to Marx, and on to a variety of traditions on the Left, including the Critical Theory of the Frankfurt School and many contemporary currents; here critique is seen as an emancipatory project that challenges domination.

The boundaries between these two realms are by no means watertight: conceptual tools from literary criticism can be and have been mobilised for critical textual analysis in political contexts, as has at times been the case in the critique of ideology. There is also a third usage, one that can be seen to hover between the two major traditions; this tradition derives from Kant and addresses the conditions, or contingencies, of our knowing. As I shall discuss, it is the interplay between what we can call the Hegelian and Kantian traditions of critique that are most relevant for critical media research.

Most fundamentally, critical social research – including that on the media – addresses and problematises power relations; such research is engaged and hence it is always in some sense 'political'. Before we get to critical media research, however, I want to briefly elucidate the notion of critique – the noun that anchors the adjective 'critical' – in a way that has underscores its basic relevance. Many authors have written lucidly on this topic over the years; there are a variety of strands and inflections, and in my view there is no 'ultimate' version. My own orientation leans a bit more towards the ecumenical than to the doctrinaire, while hopefully still retaining the decisive contours. And if much of what I say here is not startlingly new, hopefully it can at least help make these important ideas a bit more accessible and applicable.

Critical research today has its antecedents – traditions that we should be aware of and use to build upon. At the same time, it is also presented with intellectual innovation of various kinds. Thus, we must be steadily open to consider the new, the innovative, and not lock ourselves into rigid orthodoxies – while yet retaining that which is indispensable from the established traditions. And further: if critique is at bottom concerned with challenging unjustified power relations, its work is always unfinished, since societal circumstances are always evolving. We are continuously thrust into ever-changing situations, where power relations change, new asymmetries emerge, and new forms of domination take shape – requiring, in turn, new critical analyses.

Historically, various intellectual and political movements have been grounded on the notion of critique. In recent decades, however, the concept seems to have lost much of its punch, due no doubt to a number of factors, including the decline of the Left, the rise of neoliberalism, growing social uncertainties, the ironic sensibilities of late modernity, and not least the current global crisis, in which no clear political alternative has emerged to galvanise the many heterogeneous strands of opposition. Yet, if we live in difficult political times, this also means that critique has plenty to do and must ever be alert; indeed, the crises seem to have given rise to a much-needed resurgence and reinvigoration of critical thought, and I wish to connect with this energy in this chapter.

The first section of this chapter addresses the fundamental notion of critique, with a focus on its two basic and inseparable dimensions. Also, I offer a brief road map of key critical traditions and then illustrate the features of critique and the critical approach by highlighting a contemporary example, represented by Luc Boltanski. In the second section I briefly sketch how the logic of critique carries over into media and communication research, and manifests itself in four critical currents; I situate these currents against a sketch of the 'mainstream tradition' within the field. The third section probes deeper into one of the critical currents, namely the critique of ideology. It examines both the difficulties that eventually marginalised this current, as well as the persistence of key themes within it, which are manifested by versions of critical discourse analysis. In the final section I return to the notion of participation, first highlighting the significance of subjectivity in this regard, and then looking at how critical discourse analysis can add a useful methodological orientation. I close the section with a short overview of what critical media and communication research on participation might keep in its horizons.

In my discussions here I am covering considerable ground that builds on extensive literature. Much of the intellectual mapping that I do will no doubt be familiar to many readers, but I suspect that others will find it new – and hopefully useful. There are many traditions, strands, authors, and debates that are potentially pertinent to the discussion. I have been forced to be very selective in what I take up, and have had to leave much aside – with great regret. Thus, this chapter does not offer an encyclopedic overview, but rather uses a few signposts to chart one possible and hopefully fruitful course towards critical media and communication research and the intellectual legacies that have informed it. There are certainly other paths, with varying degrees of compatibility to my perspective. As for the incompatibilities, let us deal with them in a dialogical spirit of critical solidarity.

Critique: Roots and permutations

Orientations

The tradition of critique most fundamentally relevant for critical media and communication research is the one that winds its way from Hegel, through Marx, and all the subsequent forms of critical theories. It is centred on power relations, on confronting domination as an unnecessary and illegitimate restriction on human liberty and equality. Framed in terms of participation, this form of critique helps us to focus on features of specific situations that deny, deflect, or render ineffective forms of normatively justified democratic participation and the practices that embody them. This tradition, however, functions best in an interplay with the Kantian critique of the conditions of our knowledge.

In very compressed and simplified terms we can say that Kant argued (among many other things) for the importance of understanding how various factors condition that which we know and our ways of knowing; that is, he promoted epistemological reflection on the grounds of our own knowing. This is the core of his *Critique of Pure Reason* – that our knowledge of the world is never arrived at directly, but is always mediated in a number of ways. Today we understand that our sense organs, our mental processes, languages, specific cultural frames of perception, social location, and so on all impact on our knowledge and subjectivity. The Kantian tradition of critical reflection on the conditions that shape our knowledge does not figure prominently in the discussions about critical social theory or research, but I contend that it should. If critical research builds upon the interplay between normative reflection, methodological considerations, and intellectual labour, the Kantian critique has relevance for each of these three dimensions and the balance between them. Ignoring this aspect risks not only poor analysis but even a form of arrogance that critical scholars often attribute to 'positivists'. (Assertions about Marxism as 'the true science of society' come to mind.)

It could be said that critique should begin at home, that any self-conscious system of thought has an obligation to critically reflect, in a Kantian manner, on the grounds of its own knowing, its premises, and its value horizons. By the 1980s such discussions had become a part of the movement towards self-reflection within some areas of the social sciences, especially within cultural studies. One can see this development as a manifestation of the growing social constructionist sensibility within research, where the constructionist perspective becomes applied to the processes and findings of research itself. This disposition did not at first have too much impact on the various critical schools, except within some strands of feminism, though Foucault clearly argued that a key point in Kant's *What Is Enlightenment?* was precisely the difficulty of knowing one's own historical circumstances (Foucault, 1984).

This ambivalence on the political Left towards Kantian reflection is understandable, since an emphasis on the conditions of our knowledge ushers us quickly into relativism – the rejection of any notion of absolute truth or validity in favour of the role of contextual factors that shape our thinking. Historicism, a related notion that argues for the importance of historical context for understanding societal phenomena, also figures in this context. Such horizons can seemingly be debilitating for political projects by undermining certitude and thereby political energy as well. The debates over postmodernism within Left circles in the 1980s and 1990s often pivoted on this theme. Yet to underscore the contingencies of our knowing, indeed, the situatedness of our experience, need not lead to paralysis.

For one thing, we should distinguish between normative and cognitive relativism: even if our knowledge of the world is shaped by circumstances, we can at least claim more confidence in our values and moral compasses (even if these too are ultimately contingent). More significantly, human knowledge can only ever be the best possible that people can achieve under given circumstances; we are not omniscient beings, but the point is that we need not be gods to be political actors. Most forms of injustice, domination, and oppression in the world today are not so subtle and discreet that they generate epistemological conundrums. Certainly there are shades of grey, and in the broad terrain of identity politics, for example, it may be difficult at times to say which groups' claims about oppression are more compelling than those of others. However, the main problems confronting researchers are not so much about specifying injustice per se, but rather about finding possible paths for implementing change.

At a general level, we could say that in its best moments, critical social research manifests a fruitful reciprocity between normative reflection, methodological considerations, and intellectual labour. Normative reflection involves the analysis of the power relations in question and their moral status; basically, this comprises the explicit phase of 'critique'. Methodological considerations are intended to lead researchers to the most suitable approaches and procedures for the work at hand. There are always methodological options, and one needs to devise which one(s) best fit the research materials and questions at hand. The intellectual labour required obviously involves a number of elements, including the gathering and handling of data, discerning results, making analysis, finding suitable forms of exposition – all of which require a continual honing of craftsmanship. All three areas are necessary; a weakness in any one of these areas will undermine the quality of the work. The Kantian critique has relevance for each.

In addition, a Kantian view of knowledge connects readily with the more familiar social constructionism, which can help us in analysing how the dynamics of knowledge and of meaning-making – including subject positions, discursive horizons, values, and so on – among citizens serve to both facilitate and impede such change. Critical work often involves probing the discrepancies between surface appearances and underlying, deeper realities – a methodological approach emblemised in Marx's analysis of the commodity – and in such endeavours the contingencies and possibilities of knowledge and perception on the part of social actors remain a key dimension. This ushers us into the problems of participation and the role of media: people construct their social realities based on their (often mediated) experiences of the world. Yet, as we know, that which is socially constructed is not always so easy to de- or reconstruct as we might wish: discursive hegemonies are not to be underestimated. On the other hand, neither should we underestimate the power of counter-hegemonies.

Lineages and permutations

In terms of political strategy as well as research, the Left critical tradition has a number of ancestors as well as contemporary cousins, not all of whom are in agreement with each other in regard to politics, theoretical frameworks, and methodological premises. While it is far beyond my goal here to offer an intellectual history of these developments, I mention just a few of the many key themes and authors to suggest some the extensive diversity involved. From Marx's framework of historical materialism – where societal change is understood in terms of the social relations that shape the means by which the material foundation of life is produced – there have emerged a number of offshoots, but I would emphasise two basic intellectual lineages. One is the Marxist–Leninist trajectory and its Stalinist embodiment, which became the official ideology of the Soviet system and the communist parties elsewhere that accepted its leadership. This mode soon became a rather rigid body of thought, generally not very prone to Kantian self-reflection. Yet, even within this realm, there is a history of struggles between the orthodox defenders and those were branded 'revisionists' or 'deviant' (among the most prominent being the case of Trotsky).

The second and very heterogeneous tradition has become known as 'neo-', 'Western-' or 'critical Marxism'. While anchored in Marx, much of such work is concerned with further developing the paradigm in the face of its perceived analytic shortcomings – for example, the proletarian revolution that did not come about in the West, the catastrophe of World War I where workers of the world not only did not unite but killed each other in many millions, and the continuing tenacity of capitalist relations, increasingly sustained by ideological superstructures (such as mediated consumer culture). The history of neo-Marxism becomes quite intricate, with many currents mingling with as well as contesting each other. It includes various strands in political economy, represented by such authors as Samir Amin, (1976), Paul A. Baran and Paul Sweezy (1966), and Ernest Mandel (1975). More recently David Harvey 2006, 2011) has analysed the global financial crises. Perhaps more familiar to media researchers is the work of such major figures as Gramsci and the members of the Frankfurt School – notably Horkheimer, Adorno, and Marcuse – who emphasised cultural dimensions of power. Marcuse (1955) was also one of several theorists who mobilised Freud's psychoanalytic model. Generally, the sociological terrain where the space of subjectivity intersects with that of social structure remains fertile for social theory; both Bourdieu's notion of habitus and Gidden's concept of structuration plough this ground.

Jean-Paul Sartre (1991) links his existentialism to a version of Marxism. A bit later, Raymond Williams (1977) further develops the cultural dimensions of critical analysis. Louis Althusser (1969) can be seen as a pivotal figure, who on the one hand sought to define Marxism as a 'science of history' and condemned humanist and historicist interpretations of Marx, yet on the other began incorporating elements from the psychoanalytic theories of Jacques Lacan in shaping his own theory of ideology. Lacan's semiotic rendering of Freud is also central to a major contemporary figure – Slavoj Žižek. For example, he (Žižek, 2011) shows how politics responds to the contemporary crises in ways that manifest a series of psychoanalytic mechanisms: denial, anger, bargaining, depression, and acceptance. While this hovers at a rather lofty analytic level, it captures something of the dynamics working in the space of the unconscious. Today the descendants of the first generations of neo-Marxian scholars continue to work with a variety of revised interpretations and added elements, while forceful reiterations of the continued relevance of Marx's own work continue to appear (for instance, Eagleton, 2011).

A key force-field in the Marxian legacy has been the tension between what was called 'base' and 'superstructure'. In this couplet, base refers to the material foundations of society and the relations around them – that is, the domain of political economy. Superstructure takes us into the realm of culture, experience, and agency. If we reject a fully deterministic view, then we are left with a conceptual ambivalence that understandably can be difficult at times. One can argue, siding with some political economists, that it is indeed the economy that is determinant, but only 'in the last instance' – although it remains unclear when that instance actually presents itself. Those who emphasise the superstructure angle argue that we should target modes of culture, forms of representation, the dynamics of meaning-making, the internalisation of norms and values and so on to understand agency, not least in political contexts. Yet such approaches need to maintain a connection with political economic circumstances.

These processes within the superstructure are of course predicated on material circumstances, though in ways that may not always be obvious. The relationship between the two domains remains complex and can no doubt vary under differing circumstances. Even if we choose to operate outside a Marxian framework we are still confronted by the problem of accounting for the relationship between the material and the cultural/subjective dimensions of society. This is especially the case if we are concerned with social change, since this becomes important in understanding agency and participation. Ultimately we must deal with the logic of contingency, the absence of certainty, and the situatedness of action.

Points of contention

Disagreements continue on whether or not capitalism is ripe to be 'overthrown' or not in the current situation, and also on what a post-capitalist society could and should look like. The vast majority of Left groups are reformist rather than revolutionary; they do not perceive a popular-based uprising against capitalism itself as possible, but rather struggle to ameliorate specific problem areas; this is where they feel they can make a difference. Those committed to a more orthodox reading of Marx will argue that such approaches only put bandages on the problems but do not go to the root – namely, the capitalist system – and therefore do not constitute a genuine solution To which the reformists will argue that thinking about overthrowing capitalism in the present historical situation has no real anchoring in contemporary realities and their possibilities.

By the 1980s, the Marxian model, even in its more revised versions, was facing difficulties. The tensions between those who underscored the primacy of the political economy perspective and those who argued for the centrality of cultural and other dimensions continued to intensify. The emphasis on class as an analytic category was being confronted with critical analyses of other forms of domination and exploitation, which had to do with gender, ethnicity, sexual orientation, technocracy, and other dimensions of human existence that also involve power relations and manifest oppression. Oppositional groups and movements organised around such attributes were not only intervening politically but were also increasingly providing new guideposts for critical research. Even the view of power was being modified, as post-structuralist initiatives by Foucault (see Foucault, 2000) and others challenged the conceptual dominance of power as merely mechanisms of constraint embodied in traditional structures. They were proposing that power is also productive and enabling, and always invokes counter-power. Foucault, moreover, revived the Nietzschean idea of the inexorable ties between power and knowledge, further problematising the idea of Marxism as a privileged position from which to analyse society and history.

In the academic world, British cultural studies was emerging as a robust amalgam of various critical strands and developing an eclectic research programme. Integrating class analysis along with other elements such as Lacanian psychoanalysis, Barthes' semiotics, Foucault's post-structuralism, and then feminism, this movement spread globally, and for a while was a scene of considerable critical intellectual energy. (Some of this energy is still to be found there, but over the years this field grew rapidly and incorporated many currents that had less commitment to the critical project.) Other critical directions emerged in post-colonialism and studies of the subaltern, and more recently, queer theory.

It is noteworthy that early cultural studies explicitly emphasises the importance of grounding critical cultural analysis in a manner that can take into account culture's systemic features as well as its more voluntaristic aspects. In what became a classic article, Stuart Hall (1980) argues for a distinction between culturalist and structuralist strands of such research. The former treats experience as the foundation of culture, practice, and the process of meaning-making (or signification). The latter treats experience more as an effect of culture, and underscores the conditions that shape agents' practices; here Hall was incorporating structuralist arguments about language and the unconscious. Hall's point in making the distinction is to underscore that both perspectives are necessary (and once again we encounter the logic of contingency).

In regard to class, there has been and remains contention on the Left in regard to its analytic status. Fundamental, of course, is the reality of capitalism, in its various manifestations in the neoliberal global era. And if we are to deal critically with capitalism, we need to zero in on class, however much the surface manifestations may have been evolving over recent decades; the basic logics of political economy remain. At the same time, it is also obvious that in our societies today, class per se does not tend to be the prime flashpoint of political engagement. There are some exceptions: union politics still retain this as a horizon, even if conflict is often expressed in ritualised negotiations (while in the US, some state legislatures have been removing the right of public employees to strike). As discussed in Chapter 3, the OWS movement managed to put class on many people's mental agendas, even if the concept was somewhat submerged in the rhetoric of the 99 vs. the 1 percent and could not really establish a foothold in mainstream US political discourse.

If most people's political identity in liberal democracies does not pivot on class, other subject positions can nonetheless foster engagement. Thus, it would be misguided to hold off on political activity until an abstract future moment is ripe for class politics – when there is currently so much to be done on other political fronts. On the other hand, as the crises deepen, as economic issues become more central to greater sections of the population, and as the social gaps become ever wider, it is likely that more political response will begin to pivot precisely on class dynamics, rendering them more salient for political identity and practice.

In the meantime, using a variety of theoretical points of departure and emphasis, a broad range of critical scholars today – with varying relationships to the Marxian tradition – are addressing many central (and overlapping) topics, such as justice, political philosophy, democracy, imperialism, ethics, gender, and aesthetics. Among the more familiar names today are Zygmunt Bauman, Judith Butler, Nancy Fraser, Michael Hardt and Antonio Negri, Fredric Jameson, and Slavoj Žižek. There are happily many, many more, but even this small selection is indicative of the diversity of premises and approaches. We should not anticipate any fully unified critical school; rather what we see is a heterogeneous landscape where there will hopefully be more cooperation than in-fighting. Some of such conflict within critical circles has had to do with how the Marxian legacy is viewed and used. For example, Ernesto Laclau and Chantal Mouffe (2001) generated much controversy when their book first appeared in the mid-1980s; they offer what might be called a discourse-based social and political theory that is both post-structuralist and post-Marxist (from which I extracted a basic methodological approach in Chapter 3).

A contemporary example

To glean a bit more concretely what contemporary contributions to the critical project can look like, let us look at Luc Boltanski's (2011) much acclaimed volume *On Critique: A Sociology of Emancipation*, which has been translated into English from French. While it does not address media and communication (though Boltanski has written on the media in the past; see Boltanski, 1999), we find in it a contemporary version of post-Marxian critical analysis. As it grapples with and tries to come to terms with a number of issues, it illustrates the primary premises and concerns of the critical tradition. It is a concise, rather clear, and edifying example, and thus can serve as a useful model as a point of departure for discussing the contours of critical research. It will no doubt raise some questions among some critical scholars, yet this is inevitable – and ultimately healthy.

The perspective he develops here emerges from his previous work (notably Boltanski and Chiapello, 2005), including the collaboration with his mentor, Bourdieu. The volume addresses the perceived limitations of mainstream sociology, which have to do with how it positions itself – too often uncritically – towards the domination inherent in asymmetrical relations of power. These relations, being largely structural in character, may often elude perception from the horizons of everyday life. Boltanski acknowledges the classic methodological tensions between normative judgement and scientific research, navigating a coherent course between them. He sees it as necessary to move away from Bourdieu's critical sociology with its concept of habitus, whereby social actors strongly tend to internalise prevailing values and world views. While this can help account for the reproduction of structural social hierarchies, Boltanski argues that it fails to adequately account for social change. What he calls the pragmatic sociology of critique offers, instead, a view that underscores not only that social actors are capable of critique, but also that critical research must resonate with such critique and not merely derive from researchers' own (at times) grand horizons.

This too results in a tension: between the social actors who may not always possess critical insight and researchers who may have such perspectives in abundance. To deal with this problem, Boltanski sets his sights concretely on society's prevailing institutions, which he sees as the dominant definers of social reality in people's everyday lives. Institutions – not least in the context of the workplace – become the site of struggles and the key targets for critical analyses. They have vested interests that compel them to promote norms, values, societal perceptions, and 'truths' that favour their interests (other critical traditions would easily use the concept of 'hegemony' here). Such activities proceed through a wide range of routine mechanisms – conversation, reports, formalised procedures, official expertise, classification schemes, and so on (all of which many researchers would term 'discourses').

We can recognise here a critical version of the social constructionism tradition, where the reality constructed, according to Boltanski, is but a shrivelled and angled version of what the 'world' could actually be. And it is here critical analysis can intervene to help highlight power relations and 'render reality unacceptable'. Yet Boltanski also understands that daily patterns, stabilised worldviews, recognisable narratives and secure epistemological foundations – all of which institutions provide – are essential for society and community. So it is not a question of trying to wipe clean the sociocultural slate, but rather intervening where these patterns of social reproduction manifest dimensions of domination and exploitation. And in the age of neoliberal capitalism, there is no lack of targets.

Critique thus generates an eternal force-field with institutions; the two become in a sense locked together. From the standpoint of social actors, as their suffering and perceptions of injustice grow, they (presumably in dialogue with critical researchers) will manifest various forms of resistance and pursue a variety of strategy and tactics to confront the power of institutions and make them more accountable and just – a view reminiscent of Michel de Certeau (1984). The focus on institutions, which are run by specific groups of people, is a conscious turn away from targeting an abstract system, or class, which in his view rarely provides an empowering experience. This becomes, however, the major challenge, since today we live under what Boltanski terms complex domination – where institutions can shift and adapt as circumstances change. Yet, changing circumstances also mean that power and hegemonic positions are not and never can be eternal: cracks and fissures will appear, and the task of critique is to make them both visible and accessible to intervention.

Media research: Critical currents and questions

Continuities for media research

Boltanski's conceptual contribution to critical sociology has many obvious merits, and the attributes we discern carry over well into media and communication research. Indeed, in the past decades such characteristics have been manifested in a variety of ways in this field. First of all, his approach asserts the normative imperative of critique and confronts the negative consequences of capitalism. For critical media research, the critical problematisation of power relations in society at large and as manifested in the media landscape has obviously been central; the horizon of democracy, the vision of the public sphere, the premise of common interests and the centrality of participation have variously served as normative groundings for such research.

Also, Boltanski's overall logic runs parallel to a number of other related currents; there are many commonalities even if the vocabulary differs somewhat. It might have been edifying if he had pointed out the proximities of these other traditions, but on the other hand he did not engage in unproductive hair-splitting against others to make his own points. Significantly, the text unfolds in a self-reflexive (Kantian) manner, as an effort that builds on his previous work and his engagement with the work of others, not least his own mentor. It makes no claim to be the final word, and even its scientific character acknowledges its own situatedness; the critical reflection on its own position of knowing remains constantly alert. And it underscores that the critique of domination can never become a routine; it must conceptually and methodologically renew itself just as the phenomena it analyses adapt and change under evolving conditions.

Further, as with Boltanski, critical media research often zeros in on institutions – not only of the media, but also on the relationships between them and other institutions, such as the political establishment, the corporate and financial sector, the military, and so on. Political economy looms large in the institutional analysis of the media – elucidating how ownership, control, influence over policy formation, and so on impact on how media function. The present order – of which the media are central features – does indeed display Boltanski's notion of complex domination: media institutions have developed an impressive capacity to adapt their practices, to innovate, and to manoeuvre as social, political, technical, and cultural circumstances develop. In regard to the web, one could say that there have been a number of developments that have allowed for democratic expansions, as we noted in Chapter 2 (often in tandem with favourable circumstantial market logics), but as also indicated, these advances are in various ways under threat today. As crises deepen, the commercial logic can promote devastating consequences, as we see, for example, in the case of mainstream journalism.

While Boltanski adopts a class perspective, it is a revisionist one, as noted, and he advocates aiming the analytic lens at the culture of major institutions, explicitly the managerial elites who run them. Here one might expect some contention from some critical scholars. Yet Boltanski has previously demonstrated the utility of this focus on managerial culture as a way of understanding the logics of contemporary capitalism (see Boltanski and Ciapello, 2005). Some researchers may well choose to prioritise traditional critical political economy of the media, yet in my view both approaches can help us to understand the dynamics of the media landscape, and there is no reason why we have to choose one and reject the other.

Boltaski's self-reflexive style can serve critical media research well. He has obviously been struggling with the fundamental notion of critique – its normative foundations, its historical possibilities, its relationship to social science. This struggle for renewal and self-critique is laudable – just as it may also make things difficult. It is always easier to circumvent the Kantian issue about (self-)knowledge, and simply surge ahead with the critique of power relations. Yet convictions can be misplaced – and of course at the same time excessive self-reflection can become regressive and unproductive. There is perhaps an art to doing critical research – sensing when to take the initiative, when to pause and reflect, to be alert against the debilitating consequences of orthodoxy, and to incorporate innovative elements.

While there ever remains an urgent need for critique, it must also be acknowledged, as I mentioned earlier, that its power is not what it perhaps once was. The normal horizons of expectations in Western democracies are such that political scandal is common, but serious critique does not easily resonate. There is a sense that a normatively based analysis of injustice does not profoundly jar our expectations in today's world, jaws do not necessarily drop when we are confronted with the knowledge about systemic power abuse by an established institution in regard to their ongoing economic or political activities (see Brännström et al., 2011). In fact, the daily flow of critical revelations can entrench feelings of disempowerment. The German philosopher Peter Sloterdijk (1987) in his *Critique of Cynical Reason* argued that today we can see through a good deal of the prevalent deception and covert domination, yet this does not do much to alter our social actions. It could well be that the moral power of critique needs to be complemented with critical research that concretely can help empower people to act as political agents, as Boltanski argues for.

The heterogeneous mainstream

To speak of critical currents in media and communication research implies the existence of a non-critical counterpart, and even if the boundaries are not always sharp one can loosely refer to a 'mainstream' tradition that in turn consists of a variety of currents and sub-currents. (There are many course texts with overviews of this sprawling field; McQuail, 2010, the current edition of his classic treatment, is quite extensive.) While displaying considerable (and perhaps growing) heterogeneity in terms of theories, methods, and topics of research, what the mainstream currents share is a tendency to avoid the critical angle, understood in terms of questioning power relations, as well as to not address the grounds and implications of their own knowledge. While this is a strong tendency, there are of course always grey areas, and it should also be kept in mind that critical scholars can often make good use of quality research that may not have a critical focus or intent but still provides material and findings that are useful when framed by critical purposes.

The systematic study of the media arose in the early decades of the 20th century in the US, and the mainstream tradition today can be understood as the intellectual legacy of the pre-World War II American pioneers that spread globally. Despite its diversity, it is united in its basic adherence to largely social scientific methodologies and approaches to theory, though elements from the humanities are also a part of the field, and, more recently, elements from computer sciences as well. From about 1950 to about 1970, the mainstream tradition coalesced in the US and remained essentially unchallenged. Gradually, though, the heterogeneity of the field came to be seen as problematic; debate and uncertainty began to set in. Questions and contentions have been aired about the field's core, its boundaries, and the status of and relationships between various currents and traditions. One could say that the field of media and communication research remains a somewhat unstable signifier, even if today the demand and expectation for more field integration seem less intense. The large conferences suggest that a relatively harmonious coexistence among different currents prevails within the mainstream.

Yet we should also be aware of a new wave of heterogeneity in the field: many disciplines in the social, human, and technical sciences are now engaging in various ways with the internet and computerised communication, generating a good deal of intellectual and institutional ambiguity. We find that 'media research' is currently spread widely across the academic landscape; it is not just the prerogative of the field of media and communication. However, while the field may have suffered institutionally by its 'lack of discipline' across the decades, it is less certain that this has been detrimental to its intellectual growth, which significantly has permitted much theory to be imported from other fields.

As part of the contestations within the field that began around 1970, the critical trajectory has been the most vocal. The adjective 'positivist' has often been used by critical researchers, sometimes in a strict philosophy of science sense, at other times merely as an epithet, to highlight the absence of critical reflection and what they often see as the pretence of scientism – that is to say, the claim to be value-free. Critical researchers claimed that much of the dominant research was at least implicitly aligned with or actually supportive of prevailing societal arrangements – while posing as 'neutral' or 'objective'. The retorts to this of course charged the critical scholars with being 'biased' and 'political'.

The lines of critical media research are less nebulous than the field as a whole and are reasonably easy to trace. By the early 1970s such perspectives were robustly manifesting themselves and have continued to grow, albeit unevenly over the years, with new inflections being added. I will briefly take up three major trajectories here, just to sketch a map: *political economy, the public sphere tradition*, and what might be called the *culturological currents*. I probe a fourth one, the *critique of ideology*, in more detail in the next section. These lines of critical research, while fairly distinct from each other, should not be understood by any means as mutually exclusive; they can be combined and used in various ways. The work of many scholars illustrates this; for example, the work of the late Hanno Hardt (see, for example, Hardt, 1992, 1998) and Douglas Kellner (Kellner, 2005; Kellner and Hammer, 2009). Both scholars are thoroughly steeped in critical theory and related traditions, and in analysing the media they make use of a broad range of conceptual tools and approaches.

Critical trajectories

The *political economy* of the media has been from the start a central pillar, addressing ownership, commodification, (de)regulation, policy, and the links between economics and the social, political and cultural dimensions of modern life. The early work of such scholars as Dallas Smythe (1981) and Herbert Schiller (1975) opened up passages that scholars active today develop further (see, for example, Fuchs, 2011b; McChesney, 2008, 2013; Mosco, 2005, 2009; Wasko et al., 2011. A new introductory text is found in Hardy, 2013). The importance – and difficulties – of the policy dimension are highlighted in Freedman, 2008). A recurring thematic here is the tension between on the one hand, the capitalist logic of media development and operations, and on the other, concerns for the public interest and democracy; the field of journalism is of particular relevance here (see McChesney and Nichols, 2011).

For the most part, the political economy of the media does not anticipate the elimination of commercial imperatives or market forces, but rather seeks to promote an understanding of where and how regulatory initiatives can establish optimal balances between private interest and the public good, in hopes of redressing some of the worst power inequalities and promoting the democratic potential of media. Policy in the media field is shaped by the specific interests and actors involved, such as the state, commercial media institutions, the advertising industry, media production organisations, citizens' groups and other stakeholders. One can say that one key aim of critical political economy research is to engender a more democratic, equitable, and accountable power balance for citizens.

Another major – and quite familiar – pillar of critical media research frames the issues of media and democracy within the concept of the *public sphere*, a notion most associated with Habermas (1989), but one that figures in the writing of many authors (see Gripsrud et al., 2010, for a collection of key texts). In schematic terms, a public sphere is understood as a constellation of institutional spaces that permit the circulation of information and ideas, as well as the formation of public opinion and communicative links between citizens and the power holders of society. Habermas' (1989) historical analysis examines the structural evolution of public spheres as well as the character of their communicative activities, and can thus be said to straddle the base–superstructure divide.

Though the Habermasian model soon raised a number of issues, it has provided a strong critical foundation and normative horizon for thinking about the media, participation, and not least journalism, and has inspired countless research initiatives. The concept has some parallels with the liberal notion of the 'marketplace of ideas' and similar metaphors, and today it has entered into more mainstream usage where the problems of journalism are often discussed – though often at the risk of losing its critical foundations.

With the technological revolution of the digital age, political economic and public sphere analyses of media become all the more urgent (see, for example, Schiller, 2010; Curran et al., 2011; Mansell, 2012). The globalisation of media and media empires, the rapid convergence of digital technology and the web-based, mobile mediascape, and the crises in the traditional media, especially the press, have a profound impact on the present situation. I mentioned some of the issues around the web in Chapter 2; the legal contentions concerning such themes as conglomeration, privacy, surveillance, and copyright will no doubt be with us for a long time.

In the meantime, it is becoming increasingly clear that to merely insert the new technologies into the existing paradigms of mediated communication is conceptually inadequate. It is not just the case that in the era of Web 2.0 new questions arise as people can actively appropriate and creatively use media technologies for communication in unprecedented ways. Rather, as some argue, with the emergence of the computer the technology itself has become a 'participant' (Gunkel, 2012), and in some respects, can be said to take on agency. This ushers us into the realm of artificial intelligence, and, moreover, means that the field of media and communication is increasingly becoming interwoven with the broader landscape of digital technologies – and its legal and normative questions.

Probing the overlaps, specifying research areas, and defining field boundaries will no doubt become more complex as time goes on. From the wages and working conditions of the high-tech factories around the world to the ownership and control of private data, there is an immense digital arena in which critical media research should intervene; not least, class relations and conflict are embedded and manifested in this domain on a global level. The production, consumption, distribution, and innumerable uses of digital technologies embody power relations that at bottom are no different from those of the industrial age – perhaps only more difficult to discern and illuminate. Looking further afield, mediated communication has become part of the overall 'digital condition' of late modern society, where the new technologies not only provide new possibilities, but also raise very fundamental legal, moral, and political questions (see Wilkie, 2011 for a treatment of this perspective).

The critical *culturological current* is more difficult to deal with (and not just because of the cumbersome neologism); it encompasses a vast array of approaches with various origins. At its most fundamental, culturalogical efforts highlight the links between power and an array of concerns such as meaning, subjectivity, identity, and practices. Some contributions are part of the neo-Marxian efforts mentioned above, others are post- or non-Marxian. Many of these efforts could be put under the heading of cultural studies, but there are others that would not sit so comfortably there. Cultural studies itself has grown into a heterogeneous, multi-disciplinary field in its own right, where studies of the media are only a small part of its vast concerns. As cultural studies has expanded and become a global academic phenomenon mingling with many other academic traditions, the critical character of its earlier years, where issues of social and semiotic power were thematised, has not always remained consistently evident. For its part, critical culturological research in media and communication is clearly no neat category. Elements of it are certainly found within political economy and public sphere approaches, and one might rather see it as a general but diffuse tendency. It is certainly prevalent in the final critical trajectory, which I will take up in the next section, namely the *critique of ideology*.

Ideology and beyond

A boomerang concept

The critique of ideology is a major vector of the critical tradition. Yet the term itself has a decidedly dated feel to it ('It sounds SOOO "seventies!"' I once heard a student say). This is understandable, since there are a number of issues around the notion of 'ideology' that never seem to be resolved, and the term has been all but shelved in the past two decades. I have no particular investment in the term per se, but it strikes me that it refers to something that keeps coming back at us, despite our efforts to toss it away. This boomerang-like quality, I would suggest, has to do with the links between structures of meaning circulating in society and their role in helping to maintain power relations that are normatively problematic. These links are always of contemporary relevance, even if the phrase 'critique of ideology' today sounds too much like retro-chic or revivalism. In this section I first present a synopsis of the career of this concept; thereafter I chart some of the alternatives that have arisen in its place, and then discuss how we might fruitfully deal with the issues with which the concept confronts us.

We should keep in mind that with 'ideology', we have two basic traditions, which are largely not on speaking terms with each other: the descriptive and the critical. The descriptive is the familiar notion of ideology as the political platform or worldview of a person or organisation. It comprises a (fairly systematic or coherent) set of political ideas, with a positive valence, as in: 'The ideology of our party consists of ...'. Or, in a more historical light, we can see, for example, liberalism and socialism as two positive, programmatic ideologies (or complex, ideological traditions, to be more accurate).

The critical trajectory has always been the conceptually difficult one. Traditionally it has pointed to a distinction between reality, essence, or truth, and appearance, or falsehood, aimed at highlighting forms of distortion that in some way support the ruling class. It was often associated with the idea of 'false consciousness', that is, a miscomprehension of 'true' class interests. This of course begs the question of what is the 'truth', and the term began to wobble under increasingly sophisticated scrutiny. While the intellectual roots derive from Marx (and his studies of Hegel), the concept has been modified by successive writers in the neo-Marxian tradition, including the Frankfurt School, Gramsci, Althusser, Raymond Williams, and Jameson (see especially the probing critical cultural analyses in Jameson, 1981, 1991). The adaptation of Freudian psychoanalytic theory, later filtered through Lacan, has added to the mix: the psychic mechanisms of the unconscious, especially repression/denial, can take on relevance in understanding how ideology operates at the level of individual subjectivity.

Further elements were added from cultural theory, eventually signalling a growing entwinement of the critical and culturalist schools as manifested in early cultural studies. Developments in the theory of the subject, in language and semiotics were added by some authors to better account for the actual mechanisms of ideological reproduction. Growing epistemological reflection began to problematise simplistic notions of 'the truth' and our easy access to it. Jameson (2010: 357–363) discusses how the assumption that there can be a privileged space or position outside of ideology from which to analyse it in begins to erode in the face of a totalising global capitalism. Nobody, in his view, can situate themselves on 'the outside'; we are all already embedded.

All of these robust developments – and problems – found their way into media and communication studies, as the critique of ideology became part of the critical repertoire. Yet the difficulties with the concept of ideology basically mirrored the issues facing neo-Marxism more generally, as critiques based on premises other than class became prevalent. Thus, feminists could speak of the ideology of patriarchy within gender relations, and other groups, in a parallel logic, began to examine established meaning processes that contributed to their respective subordination or exploitation. The unitary utopian impetus of the emancipatory Marxian project was losing its edge. While many of the critics would not deny the importance of class relations in shaping the mediated symbolic environment and the impact this can have, it was the monopolistic stance that only the class perspective has merit that grated with the sceptics.

One of the more cogent efforts to recast the notion of ideology is found in Thompson (1990), who bases his work on the hermeneutics of Paul Ricoeur, where the perspective of the interpretive and historicist character of knowledge and analysis remains central (see, for example, the collection Ricoeur, 1981). Thompson removes social class as a privileged frame for ideology and argues that ideology should be understood as forms of communication or meaning-making that support *all* forms of social relations of domination. Moreover, the elucidation of social relations of domination remains ultimately, from Thompson's angle, a question of interpretation; that is, the 'truth' of such societal circumstances can never be defined a priori.

Thompson's notion of ideology remains perhaps too much of a question of attributes of media-based language, and he seems to be operating with a rather unproblematic unified interpreting subject who confronts the media, yet is offered little in the way of connections to agency and participation. While his contribution in the long run could not keep the critique of ideology on the research agenda, it nonetheless opens up the idea of ideology and its empirical investigation to a broader, post-Marxian critical approach, and underscores the reflexive dimension such analysis requires.

A final theme worth noting is that from non-Marxian directions voices were raised against the apparently passive view of people/media audiences implied in the concept of ideology: it was (somewhat unfairly) seen by some as a left-wing version of the basic stimulus–effect model, a charge frequently aimed at the Frankfurt School tradition. Though it is simplistic to say that the critique of ideology describes media audiences as passive dupes, it is perhaps a bit ironic that at about this time (in the early 1980s), as this critical trajectory was beginning to encounter serious difficulty, the view of the audience as active, sense-making agents was emerging, especially in the wave of reception studies. In the conceptualisations of how power is distributed between mass media and audiences, there was now a shift to see the audience as more empowered, less as victims, and capable of independent (and critical) interpretation.

From the perspective of media and communication studies, John Corner (2011) writes how since its heyday back in the 1970s, there have been various efforts to 'repair' the notion of ideology, to fix what has been troubling it and to relaunch it in new, improved versions. His point is that these efforts on the whole have not been fully successful; the term has been overloaded and overworked, bent in many different directions. It's probably time to let it sit, undisturbed, and not press it into service once again. He ends his discussion by underscoring the importance of 'further research and argument about the interconnections of meaning, value, social structure and power' (Corner, 2011: 151). I certainly concur with his programmatic proposal – even if we are still left with the problem of what to call such interconnections, which keep on demanding our analytic attention.

By another name?

However, as the concept drifted decidedly to the margins, another enterprise moved into at least some of the space it had filled. Critical discourse analysis (CDA) in its various versions began an ascendancy in the early 1990s, retaining some obvious links with the critique of ideology tradition (see, for example, Fairclough, 2010; for a recent collection with a methodological treatment, see Wodak and Meyer, 2009; van Dijk, 1998).

Van Dijk entitles his book *Ideology*, but reframes the concept in terms of discourse analysis and cognition – which simply reminds us that mapping intellectual trends is never a neat enterprise!). In simple terms, discourse can be understood as patterned ways of using language in specific social contexts to understand the world; when the patterns and contexts take on large societal proportions, some authors (for example, Foucault) deploy the term 'discursive formations'.

Significantly, theories of discourse underscore its constitutive character: discourses participate in the shaping of subjectivities, identities, social relations, objects, systems of knowledge, modes of cognitive and normative perception – while at the same time being shaped by such elements. One can say that discourse has become an analytic category within the broad tradition of social constructionism. Discourses can serve to help engender and sustain social order – as well as to challenge it – by solidifying patterns of meaning. Thus, discourses are more than just text; they are manifestations of (collective) social practice – while at the same time functioning as linguistic contexts, as symbolic environments for human action. Action, in turn, as the meaningful expression of agency, always has a discursive dimension to it.

In relation to the traditional notion of ideology and its problems, what this discursive turn accomplishes is that it dispenses with the dualism of true and false; it takes a constructionist view of language and treats all social contexts as having discursive dimensions. Further, it adds, varyingly, elements of more sophisticated theories of the subject. And in its critical version – CDA – it can be deployed for challenging relations of power. Fairclough sees CDA as investigating

> often opaque relationships of causality and determination between a) discursive practices, events and texts and b) broader social and cultural structures, relations and processes ... how such practices, events and texts arise out of and are ideologically shaped by relations and struggles over power ... how the opacity of these relationships between discourse and society is itself a factor securing power and hegemony.
>
> (Fairclough, 1993)

CDA examines the dynamics between three basic dimensions: text, discursive practice, and social practice/structures. Methodologically CDA is rather diverse and open; specific approaches tend to emerge in relation to the discursive object, its social contexts, and the problems perceived in this triad of text-practice-context. Yet methodology is also

greatly informed by theory; which involves precisely conceptual hori-
zons regarding the subject, identity, power, and societal arrangements.
For a useful interpretive overview of discourse analysis generally, see
Jørgensen and Phillips (2002).

From a somewhat different horizon, a number of key post-
structuralists working with their variants of discourse analysis made
it very clear that ideology critique should be seen as a thing of
the past; new methods and approaches render it obsolete. Their
Nietzschean inspiration lead them to take the view that critique ultimately leads nowhere, since the critical interpretation of masks merely
reveals ... more masks. And yet: what we might call the logics of ideology
critique remain in the work of for, example, Foucault and in Deleuze,
albeit in a discrete way – even as they explicitly distance themselves
from it (I build on Grant, 2011: 91–104). Foucault finds ideology a problematic concept; to distinguish between truth and appearance is a futile
task, he claims. Truth and its effects are products of historically specific
discourses that are neither true nor false, since we can only interpret
reality via one discourse or another; we cannot position ourselves or our
knowledge outside discourses.

However, in the *History of Sexuality*, Foucault (1990) argues that truth
can indeed be 'masked', obscured from us, not because we choose to
ignore it, or we misunderstand it. Rather, the mask derives from power
itself, which is 'tolerable only on condition that it mask a substantial
part of itself. Its success is proportional to its ability to hide its own
mechanisms' (Foucault, 1990: 56). The critical task thus becomes, he
argues, to unmask the mechanisms of power that have become hidden by dominant discourses; these 'subjugated knowledges' are to be
'revealed by criticism'. This does not, however, signal a return to an
earlier phase of ideology critique, as Grant (2011: 93) argues. Foucault
dispatches the distinction between appearance and essence. Pulling
away a mask does not reveal what *really* is, but rather what *also* is. But
it is precisely this which is significant; the issue becomes not one of
truth vs. falsehood, but rather between the visible, the accessible vs. the
opaque, the concealed. Similarly, Deleuze, like Foucault, also talks about
criticising mystifications; he writes about 'piercing masks' in order to
reveal motivations and strategies, of individuals and of power (Deleuze,
1986: 106).

So, these different (under)currents still insist on the logic of the critique of the links between power and meaning, while avoiding putting
class as such in a privileged position. The reasoning here seems to be
that while we can only challenge specific discourses with the aid of

other discourses, this does not have to lead us into a blind alley of complete epistemological relativism (as some critics argue). Discourses still provide us with useful empirical referents to the social world, even if knowledge becomes shaped by social and linguistic factors. Yet, as we can recall, this dimension of the contingent character of knowing was Kant's claim from the outset (though we need not classify him as a post-structuralist). Within the post-structural camp we have, moreover, the discourse theory (DT) of Laclau and Mouffe (2001), which takes as one of its points of departure the incessant force-fields of power between discourses, where hegemonic discourses can be confronted and challenged by those of a counter-hegemonic character.

Participation in focus

'Producing subjectivity'

At this point in the discussion it could be helpful to recall our key concern with participation and practices, since the issue of subjectivity is central to it. (Of course the critical orientation angle can and must be aimed at many other topics as well.) Highlighting the production of subjectivity in the critical analysis of communication becomes important precisely because participation requires certain modes of subjectivity. These modes have to do with the sense of self, an identity, as a political agent, one who is empowered and can perceive possible practices as meaningful and at least potentially efficacious, and who can insert him/herself into the discursive antagonisms of politics. Further, the specific political vectors of engagement – taking positions on particular issues – involve subject positions. Yet the subject is by no means a simple concept; in the previous chapter I contended that, analytically, the notion of the subject raises issues having to do with affect, the limits of reflexivity and self-transparency, the role of the unconscious, and the importance of contingency. These themes of the subject and the processes of political identities can and need to be worked into a methodological platform for the critical analysis of communication and signifying processes.

Thus, in leaving behind the notion of ideology and deploying its heirs, CDA and DT, we benefit from developing an approach with a constructionist, constitutive view of communication in social context. This allows us to look at how, for example, various social groups are 'invited' or, alternatively, 'disinvited' to participate. In other words we can probe how discursive patterns dynamically open up and stimulate political practice, or close it off via mechanisms of depoliticisation, exclusion, and disempowerment, mobilisations of fear, and so on. We can analyse how power relations tend to discursively 'nudge' subjectivity in certain directions. Moreover, we can explore how alternative, counterhegemonic discourses can challenge the hegemonic ones in concrete circumstances, becoming manifestations of agency nourished by civic cultures. What emerges is an approach that triangulates mediated texts and their interplay with discursive practices and the power relations of their social contexts – including, but not limited to, class dimensions.

A final note on subjectivity: the view that it is discursively engendered should not be seen as deterministic. Rather, we are looking at probabilities in the patterns of collective subjectivity deriving from discourses, but always allowing for variation, leakages, and contradictions. Discourses are never total, and they themselves are always contingent. Neither is this perspective reductionist in the sense of arguing that people are nothing more than expressions of prevailing discourses (to paraphrase an extreme position); luckily humans are far more complex than that. What we have here can be seen as another version of the classic motif in social theory of the force-field between structure and agency. I retain the idea of a subject-as-agent, albeit a socially constructed and contingent one. In analysing participation and agency more generally, I find it conceptually impossible to proceed without allowing for a degree of individuality and autonomy on the part of social actors.

The broader picture

The discursive aspects of mediated communication, and their links with power, meaning, and subjectivity comprise core dimensions of critical research on participation and media. Yet this is not the whole story; we need to map participation in media on to relevant broad changes in society, its political economic developments, its evolving institutions, shifting social patterns and mutable cultural climates, as well inserting media into the specific circumstances to be studied (for a more extensive treatment on a proposed research agenda in this area, see Dahlgren and Alvares, 2013). The analytic lens needs to put contingencies into the spotlight, showing how various factors shape and interplay with the phenomena under investigation.

While attention must be devoted to electoral politics and the vicissitudes of voter subjectivity and practices, I would advocate a strong emphasis on the expansive arena of alternative politics, informed by an understanding of contemporary political developments and their significance for democracy. Various corners of civil society, popular culture, and consumption should be targeted, in search of new modes of the political. The intersection of journalism and democratic participation generates new practices – and issues. Certainly the web, as an everyday domain for sociality and networking, becomes a premier topography for participation, by citizens generally as well as opinion-leading web intellectuals; in the process, the import of its various logics must be kept in view. Yet the analysis of participation must also attend to live assemblages – and their relation to media. Even examples of normatively questionable or anti-democratic expressions of political disposition should not be ignored.

Further, I would add here that in understanding web-based political agency, its conditions, practices, and subjectivity, a sense of the historical is important. This becomes especially significant when seeking to grasp where and how political memories and meanings cohere and are sustained, and how recollections of the past may both inspire and impede participation. It can even be relevant to attempt to understand how the dynamics of memory may be altered by the prevalence of web technologies. In particular, a familiarity with the chequered history of democracy and its struggles, both generally and in one's own setting, is an important backdrop in analysing participation.

In looking at the multifarious social world and its politics, its intricate interface with economic and ecological systems, we may need to consider using other, new paradigms or approaches; we should keep the conceptual doors open. Critical research indeed requires normative grounding, methodological focus, and intellectual craftsmanship; each element on its own can be difficult, and getting the balance between right in every case is no less a challenge. Yet, when critical research is at its best, it can yield not only practical knowledge and interpretive understanding, but also the inspirational insight that what exists can potentially pass, and what still does not exist may yet come to pass.

References

Acosta, R. (2009) *NGO and Social Movement Networking in the World Social Forum: An Anthropological Approach.* Saarbrücken: VDM Verlag.

Aday, S., H. Farrell, M. Lynch, J. Sides, J. Kelly and E. Zuckerman (2010) *Blogs and Bullets: New Media in Contentious Politics.* Washington, D.C.: U.S. Institute of Peace. Available at: http://www.usip.org/files/resources/pw65.pdf (Accessed 6 March 2013).

Adey, P. (2010) *Mobility.* Abingdon: Routledge.

Agamben, G. A. Badiou, B. Bensaïd, W. Brown, J-L Nancy, J. Rancière, K. Ross, S. Žižek, eds. (2011) *Democracy in What State?* New York: Columbia University Press.

Althusser, L. (1969) *For Marx.* London: Verso.

Amin. S. (1976) *Unequal Development: An Essay on the Social Formations of Peripheral Capitalism.* New York: Monthly Review Press.

Amnå, E. (2008) *Jourhavande medborgare. Samhällsengagemang i en folkrörelsestat.* Lund: Stdudentlitteratur.

Amnå, E. (2012) Active, Passive and Standby Citizens. The European Wergeland Centre. Available at: http://www.theewc.org/statement/active.passive.and.standby.citizens (Accessed 3 February 2013).

Anonymous (2011) 'On Public Intellectuals'. *Philosophy Compass*, 9 May. Available at: http://philosophy-compass.com/2011/05/09/on-public-intellectuals/ (Accessed 18 August 2012).

Appiah, K. A. (2007) *Cosmopolitanism: Ethics in a World of Strangers.* New York: Norton.

Archibugi, D. (2008) *The Global Commonwealth of Citizens: Towards a Cosmopolitan Democracy.* Princeton and Oxford: Princeton University Press.

Arendt, H. (1958) *The Human Condition.* Chicago: University of Chicago Press.

Arnstein, S. (1969) 'A Ladder of Citizen Participation'. *Journal of the American Institute of Planners* 35(4), 216–224. Also available online: http://lithgow-schmidt.dk/sherry-arnstein/ladder-of-citizen-participation.html (Accessed 3 February 2013).

Askanius, T. (2012) *Radical Online Video: YouTube, Video Activism, and Social Movement Practices.* Lund: Lund University, Studies in Media and Communication 17 (Ph.D. dissertation).

Askanius, T. and N. Gustafsson (2010) 'Mainstreaming the Alternative: The Changing Media Practices of Protest Movements'. *Interface: A Journal For and About Social Movements* 2(2), 23–41.

Askanius, T. and J. Uldam (2011) 'Online Social Media for Radical Politics: Climate Change Activism on YouTube'. *International Journal of Electronic Governance* 4(1–2), 69–84.

Atton, C. (2002) *Alternative Media.* London: Sage.

Atton, C. (2005) *An Alternative Internet: Radical Media, Politics and Creativity.* New York: Columbia University Press.

Badiou, A. (2012a) *Philosophy for Militants*. London: Verso.

Badiou, A. (2012b) *The Rebirth of History: Times of Riots and Uprisings*. London: Verso.

Baily, O., B. Cammaerts and N. Carpentier (2007) *Understanding Alternative Media*. Maidenhead, UK: Open University Press.

Bakardjieva, M. (2010), "The Internet and Subactivism: Cultivating Young Citizenship in Everyday Life," in T. Olsson and P. Dahlgren (eds.), *Young People, ICTs and Democracy: Theories, Policies, Identities, and Websites*. Gothenburg: Nordicom, pp. 129–146.

Bakardieva, M. (2011) 'Reconfiguring the Mediapolis: New Media and Civic Agency'. *New Media and Society* 14(1), 63–79.

Baran, P. A. and P. M. Sweezy (1966) *Monopoly Capital: An Essay on the American Economic and Social Order*. New York: Monthly Review Press.

Barber, B. R. (2011) 'Occupy Wall Street – "We are What Democracy Looks Like!"'. *Huffington Post*, 11 November. Available at: http://www.huffingtonpost.com/benjamin-r-barber/occupy-wall-street—we-a_b_1079723.html (Accessed 24 February 2013).

Barkho, L., ed. (2013) *From Theory to Practice: How to Assess and Apply Impartiality in News and Current Affairs*. Bristol: Intellect.

Barkho, L. (2010) *News from BBC, CNN, and Al-Jazeera*. Cresskill, NJ: Hampton Press.

Barnett, Clive, Paul Cloke, and Nick Clarke (2010), *Globalizing Responsibility: The Political Rationalities of Ethical Consumption*. Oxford: Wiley-Blackwell.

Bauman, Z. (2007) *Liquid Times: Living in an Age of Uncertainty*. Cambridge: Polity Press.

Bauman, Z. (2011) *Collateral Damage: Social Inequalities in a Global Age*. Cambridge: Polity Press.

Baym, N. K. (2010) *Personal Connections in the Digital Age*. Cambridge: Polity Press.

Beck, U. (2006) *The Cosmopolitan Vision*. Oxford: Blackwell.

Beck, U. (2009) *World at Risk*. Cambridge: Polity Press.

Beck, U. and E. Beck-Gernsheim (2002) *Individualization: Institutionalized Individualism and its Social and Political Consequences*. London: Sage.

Beer, D. (2009) 'Power Through the Algorithm? Participatory Web Cultures and the Technological Unconscious'. *New Media and Society* 11(6), 985–1002.

Benhabib, S. (2004) *The Rights of Others: Aliens, Residents and Citizens*. Cambridge: Cambridge University Press.

Benhabib, S. (2006) *Another Cosmopolitanism*. New York: Oxford University Press.

Benkler, Y. (2006) *The Wealth of Networks: How Social Production Transforms Markets and Freedom*. New Haven, CT: Yale University Press.

Bennett, W. L. (2012) 'The Personalization of Politics: Political Identity, Social Media, and Changing Patterns of Participation'. *The Annals* 664(1), 20–39.

Bennett, W.L. and A.Segerberg (2011) 'Digital Media and the Personalization of Collective Action: Social Technology and the Organization of Protests against the Global Economic Crisis'. *Information, Communication & Society* 14(6): 770–799.

Bennett. W. L. and A. Segerberg, (2012) 'The Logic of Connective Action: Digital Media and the Personalization of Contentious Politics'. *Information, Communication & Society* 15(5): 739–768.

Bennett, W. L. and A. Toft (2009) 'Identity, Technology, and Narratives: Transnational Activisim and Social Networks'. In P. Howard and A. Chadwick, eds. *The Handbook of Internet Politics*. New York: Routledge, pp. 246–260.

Bennett, L., C. Wells and D. Freelon (2010) 'Civic Media: The Generational Shift from Mainstream News to Digital Networks'. In L. Sherrod, J. Torney-Purta and C. Flanagan, eds. *The Handbook of Youth Engagement*. Hoboken, NJ: Wiley-Blackwell, pp. 393–424.

Bennett, L., C. Wells and D. Freelon (2011) 'Communicating Civic Engagement: Contrasting Models of Citizenship in the Youth Web Sphere'. *Journal of Communication* 61(5), 835–856.

Berger, B. (2011) *Attention Deficit Democracy : The Paradox of Civic Engagement*. Princepton, NJ: Princeton University Press.

Boltanski, L. (1999) *Distant Suffering: Morality, Media and Politics*. Cambridge: Cambridge University Press.

Boltanski, L. (2011) *On Critique: A Sociology of Emancipation*. Cambridge: Polity Press.

Boltanski, L. and E. Ciapello (2005) *The New Spirit of Capitalism*. London: Verso.

Borg, C. and P. Mayo, eds. (2007) *Public Intellectuals, Radical Democracy and Social Movements*. A Book of Interviews. New York: Peter Lang.

Boyd, D. and Crawford, K. (2012) 'Critical questions for Big Data: Provocations for a Cultural, Technological and Scholarly Phenomenon'. *Information, Communication and Society* 15(5): 662–679.

Brännström, L., A. Johansson, S. Rider and M. Rönnblom (2011) 'What is the State of Critique Today? A Conversation with Anders Johansson, Sharon Rider and Malin Rönnblom'. *Eurozine* (2011-10-12). Available at: www.eurozine.com/articles/2011-10-12-johansson-en.html (Accessed 10 January 2013).

Brighenti, A. M. (2010), *Visibility in Social Theory and Social Research*. Basingstoke: Palgrave Macmillan.

Breckenridge, C. A., P. Sheldon, H. K. Bhabha and D. Chakrabarty, eds. (2002) *Cosmopolitanism*. Durham and London: Duke University Press.

Brock, G. and H. Brighouse, eds. (2005) *The Political Philosophy of Cosmopolitanism*. London: Cambridge University Press.

Butler, J. (1990). *Gender Trouble*. London: Routledge.

Campbell, V., R. Gibson, B. Gunter and M. Touri (2010) 'News Blogs, Mainstream News and News Agendas'. In S. Tunney and G. Monaghan, eds. *Web Journalism: A New Form of Citizenship?* Brighton: Sussex Academic Press, pp. 31–47.

Captain, S. (2011) 'The Demographics of Occupy Wall Street' Fast Company, http://www.fastcompany.com/1789018/occupy-wall-street-demographics-statistics#disqus_thread (Accessed 24 February 2013).

Caren, N. and S. Gaby (2011) 'Occupy Online: Facebook and the Spread of Occupy Wall Street'. *Social Science Research Network*. Available at SSRN: http://ssrn.com/abstract=1943168 (Accessed 6 March 2013).

Carpentier, N. (2011) *Media and Participation: A Site of Ideological-Democratic Struggle*. Bristol: Intellect Publishers.

Carpentier, N., P. Dahlgren and F. Pasquali (2013) 'The Democratic (Media) Revolution: A Parallel Genealogy of Political and Media Participation'. In N. Carpentier, K. C.Schröder and H. Lawrie, eds. *Transforming Audiences, Transforming Societies*. Abingdon: Routledge.

Carpentier, N. and B. D. Cleen (2007). 'Bringing Discourse Theory into Media Studies'. *Journal of Language and Politics* 6(2), 265–293.

Carpentier, N. and E. Spinoy, eds. (2008). *Discourse Theory and Cultural Analysis*. Cresskill, NJ: Hampton Press.

Carr, N. (2010) *The Shallows: How the Internet Is Changing the Way We Think, Read and Remember*. London: Atlantic Books.

Caslon Analytics (2011) *Blog Statistics and Demographics*. Available at: www. caslon.com.au/weblogprofile1.htm#many (Accessed 18 August 2012).

Castells, M. (2010) *Communication Power*. Oxford: Oxford University Press.

Castells, M. (2012) *Networks of Outrage and Hope: Social Movements in the Internet Age*. Cambridge: Polity Press.

Castoriadis, C. (1987) *The Imaginary Institution of Society*. Cambridge, MA: MIT Press.

CBS News (2011) 'Poll: 43 Percent Agree with Views of "Occupy Wall Street"', 25 October. Available at: http://www.cbsnews.com/8301-503544_162-20125515-503544/poll-43-percent-agree-with-views-of-occupy-wall-street (Accessed 24 February 2013).

Chandler, D. (2006) *Constructing Global Civil Society: Morality and Power in International Relations*. Basingstoke: Palgrave Macmillan.

Chatfield, T. (2009) 'The World's Top Intellectuals on our Website'. *Prospect Magazine* September. Available at: http://www.prospectmagazine.co.uk/prospect-100-intellectuals/ (Accessed 18 August 2012).

Cheah, P. (2007) *Inhuman Conditions: On Cosmopolitanism and Human Rights*. Cambridge, MA and London: Harvard University Press.

Chouliaraki, L. (2006) *The Spectatorship of Suffering*. London: Sage Publications.

Chouliaraki, L. (2010) 'Ordinary Witnessing in Post-Television News: Towards a New Moral Imagination'. *Critical Discourse Studies* 7(4), pp. 305–319.

Cleland, S. and I. Brodky (2011) *Search and Destroy: Why You Can't Trust Google*. St. Louis, MO: Telescope Books.

Cohen, J. and A. Arato (1992) *Civil Society and Political Theory*. Cambridge, MA: MIT Press.

Coleman, S. (2007) 'From Big Brother to Big Brother: Two Faces of Interactive Engagement'. In P. Dahlgren, ed. *Young Citizens and New Media: Learning for Democratic Participation*. New York: Routledge, pp. 21–39.

Coleman, S. (2013) *How Voters Feel*. New York; Cambridge: Cambridge University Press.

Coleman, S. and J. Blumler (2009) *The Internet and Democratic Citizenship*. New York: Cambridge University Press.

Corner, J. (2011) *Theorising Media: Power, Form and Subjectivity*. Manchester: Manchester University Press.

Corner, J. and D. Pels, eds. (2003) *Media and the Restyling of Politics*. London: Sage.

Corpus O. J. (2009) 'The Cosmopolitan Continuum: Locating Cosmopolitanism in Media and Cultural Studies'. *Media, Culture & Society* May 31(3), 449–466.

Costanza-Chock, S. (2012) 'Mic Check! Media Cultures and the Occupy movement'. *Social Movement Studies* iFirst article 1–11, 2012. Available at http://dx. doi.org/10.1080/14742837.2012.710746 (Accessed 23 February 2013).

Couldry, N. (2010) *Why Voice Matters: Culture and Politics After Neoliberalism*. London: Sage.

Couldry, N. (2012) *Media, Society, World: Social Theory and Digital Media Practice.* Cambridge: Polity Press.

Cowen, T. and V. D. Rugy (2012) 'Reframing the Debate'. In J. Byrne, ed. *The Occupy Handbook.* New York: Backbay Books/Little, Brown and Co, pp. 411–421.

Crouch (2011) *The Strange Non-Death of Neoliberalism.* Cambridge, Polity Press.

Curran, J. N. Fenton, D. Freedman, eds. (2012) *Misunderstanding the Internet,* Abington, Routledge.Dahlberg, L. and S. Phelan, eds. (2011) *Discourse Theory and Critical Media Politics.* Basingstoke: Palgrave Macmillan.

Dahlgren, P. (2009) *Media and Political Engagement.* New York/Cambridge: Cambridge University Press.

Dahlgren, P. and C. Alvares (2013) 'Political participation in an age of mediatisation: toward a new research agenda'. *Javnost/The Public* 20(2) 47–66.

Dallmayr, F. (2003) 'Cosmopolitanism: Moral and Political'. *Political Theory* 31(3), 421–442.

Danowski, J. A. and D. W. Park (2009) 'Networks of the Dead or Alive in Cyberspace: Public Intellectuals in the Mass and Internet Media'. *New Media and Society* 11(3), 337–356.

Dartnell, M. Y. (2005) *Insurgency Online: Web Activism and Global Conflict.* Toronto: University of Toronto Press.

Davis, A. (2010) *Political Communication and Social Theory.* Abingdon: Routledge.

Davis, R. (2009) *Typing Politics: The Role of Blogs in American Politics.* New York: Oxford University Press.

de Sousa Santos, B. (2005) 'Beynd neoliberal governance: the World Social Forum as subaltern cosmopolitan politics and legaity'. In B. De Sousa Santos and C. A. Rodriguez-Varaviti, eds. *Law and Globalization from Below: Towards a Cosmopolitan Legality.* Cambridge: Cambridge University Press, pp. 29–63.

Dean. J. (2010) *Blog Theory.* Cambridge: Polity Press.

Dean, J. (2012) *The Communist Horizon.* London: Verso.

de Certeau, M. (1984) *The Practice of Everyday Life.* Berkeley, CA: The University of California Press.

Delanty, G. (2009) *The Cosmopolitan Imagination: The Renewal of Critical Social Theory.* Cambridge: Cambridge University Press.

Deleuze, G. (1986) *Nietzsche and Philosophy.* London: Continuum Books.

DeLuca, K. M., S. Lawson and Y. Sun (2012) 'Occupy Wall Street on the Public Screens of Social Media: The Many Framings of the Birth of a Protest Movement'. *Communication, Culture & Critique* 5(4), 483–509. Available at: http://onlinelibrary.wiley.com/doi/10.1111/j.1753-9137.2012.01141.x/ (Accessed 6 March 2013).

Dezner, D. W. (2008a) 'Public Intellectuals 2.0'. *Foreign Policy* 13 May. Available at: http://drezner.foreignpolicy.com/posts/2008/05/13/blogs_public_intellectuals_and_the_academy (Accessed 18 August 2012).

Dezner, D. W. (2008b) 'Am I Defining Public Intellectuals Down?' *Foreign Policy* 12 June. Available at: http://drezner.foreignpolicy.com/posts/2008/06/12/am_i_defining_public_intellectuals_down (Accessed 18 August 2012).

Downing, J. (2000) *Radical Media: Rebellious Communication and Social Movements.* London: Sage.

Drache, Daniel (2008) *Defiant Publics: The Unprecedented Reach of the Global Citizen.* Cambridge: Polity Press.

Dwyer, T. (2010) 'Net Worth: Popular Social Networks as Colossal Marketing Machines'. In G. Sussman, ed. *Propaganda Society: Promotional Culture and Politics in Global Context*. New York: Peter Lang, pp. 77–92.

Eagleton, T. (2011) *Why Marx Was Right*. New Haven and London: Yale University Press.

Eberly, Don E. (2008) *The Rise of Global Civil Society: Building Communities and Nations From the Bottom Up*. New York: Encounter Books.

Edwards, M. (2009) *Civil Society*, 2nd ed. Cambridege: Polity Press.

Ehrenreich, B. and J. Ehrenreich (2012) 'The Making of the American 99 Percent and the Collapse of the Middle Class'. In J. Byrne, ed. *The Occupy Handbook*. New York: Backbay Books/Little, Brown and Co, pp. 300–310.

Elliott, A. (2008) *Concepts of the Self*, 2nd ed. Cambridge: Polity Press.

Elliott, A. and C. Lemert. (2006) *The New Individualism: The Emotional Costs of Globalisation*. Abingdon: Routledge.

Elliott, A. and J. Urry (2010) *Mobile Lives*. Abingdon: Routledge.

Etzioni, A. and A. Bowditch, eds. (2006) *Public Intellectuals: An Endangered Species?* Lanham, MD/Oxford: Rowman and Littlefield.

Fairclough, N. (1993) *Discourse and Social Change*. Cambridge: Blackwell.

Fairclough, N. (2010) *Critical Discourse Analysis*, 2nd ed. Harlow: Longman.

Feenberg, A. (2010) *Between Reason and Experience: Essays in Technology and Modernity*. Cambridge, MA: MIT Press.

Feenberg, A. and N. Freisen, eds. (2012) *(Re)Inventing the Internet: Critical Case Studies*. Rotterdam: Sense Publishers.

Fisher, M. (2009) *Capitalist Realism: Is There No Alternative?* Ropley, Hants: Zero Books.

Fisk, R. (2006) *The Great War for Civilization: The Conquest of the Middle East*. New York: Harper Perennial.

Forde, S. (2011) *Challenging the News: The Journalism of Alternative and Community Media*. Basingstoke: Palgrave Macmillan.

Foucault, M. (1984) 'What is Enlightenment?' In P. Rabinow, ed. *The Foucault Reader*. New York: Pantheon Books, pp. 32–50.

Foucault, M. (1990) *The History of Sexuality vol. 1: An Inyroduction*. New York: Vintage Books.

Foucault, M. (2000) *Power (The Essential Works of Foucalt, 1954–1984)*, vol. 3. New York: The New Press.

Fraser, N. (1992) 'Rethinking the Public Sphere: A Contribution to the Crtitique of Actually Existing Democracy'. In C. Calhoun, ed. *Habermas and the Public Sphere*. Boston: MIT Press, pp. 109–142.

Freedman, D. (2008) *The Politics of Media Policy*. Cambridge: Polity Press.

Fuchs, C. (2011a) 'A Contribution to the Critique of the Political Economy of Google'. *Fast Capitalism* 8.1. Available at: http://www.fastcapitalism.com (Accessed 12 February 2013).

Fuchs, C. (2011b) *Foundation of Critical Media and Information Studies*. Abingdon: Routledge.

Fuchs, C. (2012) 'Some Reflections on Manuel Castells' Book Networks of Outrage and Hope: Social Movements in the Internet Age'. Triple 10(2)775–795. Available at: http://www.triple-c.at/index.php/tripleC/article/view/459 (Accessed 18 February 2013).

Gauntlett, D. (2008). *Media, Gender and Identity: An Introduction*, 2nd ed. Abingdon: Routledge.

Gardiner, M. E. 2004. 'Wild Publics and Grotesque Symposiums: Habermas and Bakhtin on Dialogue, Everyday Lide and the Public Sphere'. In N. Crossly and J. M. Roberts, eds. *After Habermas: New Perspectives on the Public Sphere*. Oxford: Blackwell Publishers, pp. 28–48.

Geiger, K. and M. Reston (2011) 'Mitt Romney Sympathizes with Wall Street Protesters'. *Chicago Tribune* 11 October. Available at: http://www.chicagotribune.com/news/politicsnow/la-pn-romney-wall-street-20111011,0,4608358.story (Accesses 12 December 2011).

Gerbaudo, P. (2012) *Tweets and the Streets: Social Media and Contemporary Activism*. London: Verso.

Gewen, B. (2008) 'Who is a Public Intellectual?' *New York Times* 11 June. Available at: http://artsbeat.blogs.nytimes.com/2008/06/11/who-is-a-public-intellectual/ (Accessed 18 August 2012).

Giddens, A. (1991) *Modernity and Self-Identity: Self and Society in the Late Modern Age*. Cambridge: Polity Press.

Giddens, A. (1998) *The Third Way: The Renewal of Social Democracy*. Cambridge: Polity Press.

Giddens, A. (2000) *The Third Way and Its Critics*. Cambridge: Polity Press.

Gill, R. (2006) *Gender and the Media*. Cambridge: Polity Press.

Gills, B. K., ed. (2011) *Globalization and the Global Politics of Justice*. Abingdon: Routledge.

Glynos, J. and D. Howarth (2007) *Logics of Critical Explanation in Social and Political Theory*. Abingdon: Routledge.

Godrej, F. (2011) *Cosmopolitan Political Thought: Method, Practice, Discipline*. New York: Oxford University Press.

Goffman, E. (1959) *The Presentation of Self in Everyday Life*. New York: Doubleday, Anchor Books.

Goffman, E. (1983) 'The Interaction Order'. *American Sociological Review* 48, 1–17.

Goldberg, G. (2010) 'Rethinking the Public/Virtual Sphere: The Problem with Participation'. *New Media and Society* 13(5), 739–754.

Goodman, A. and D. Moynihan (2012) 'Occupy the media: Journalism for (and by) the 99 Percent'. In J. Byrne, ed. *The Occupy Handbook*. New York: Backbay Books/Little, Brown and Co, pp. 256–264.

Gould, C. C. (2004) *Globalizing Democracy and Human Rights*. New York: Cambridge University Press.

Grant, J. (2011) *Dialectics and Contemporary Politics: Critique and Transformation from Hegel Through post-Marxism*. Abingdon: Routledge.

Gray, J. (2009) *False Dawn: The Delusions of Global Capitalism*. London: Granta.

Green, J. E. (2010) *The Eyes of the People: Democracy in an Age of Spectatorship*. New York: Oxford University Press.

Grimmelmann, J. (2008) 'Facebook and the Social Dynamics of Privacy'. *Ciberdemocracia.es*. Available at: http://www.ciberdemocracia.es/recursos/textosrelevantes/facebook.pdf (Accessed 10 March 2013).

Gripsrud, J., M. Hallvsard, A. Molander and G. Murdock, eds. (2010) *The Idea of the Public Sphere: A Reader*. Lanham, MD: Lexington Books.

Gunkel, D.J. (2012) 'Communication and Artificial Intelligence: Opportunities and Challenges for the 21st Century'. Communication+1.1(1) article 1.

Available at: http://scholarworks.umass.edu/cpo/vol1/iss1/1/ (Accessed 2 May 2013)

Gustafsson, N. (2012) 'The Subtle Nature of Facebook Politics: Swedish Social Network Site users and Political Participation'. *New Media and Society* 14(7), 1111–1127.

Habermas, J. (1984, 1987) *Theory of Communicative Action*. vol. 2. Cambridge: Polity Press.

Habermas, J. (1989) *Structural Transformation of the Public Sphere*. Cambridge: Polity.

Habermas, J. (2006) *The Divided West*. Cambridge: Polity.

Habermas, J. (2008) 'An Avantgardistic Instinct for Relevances: Intellectuals and their Public'. *Social Science Research Council: Public Sphere Forum* Available at: http://publicsphere.ssrc.org/habermas-intellectuals-and-their-public/ (Accessed 18 August 2012).

Hall, C. (2005) *The Trouble with Passion: Political Theory Beyond the Reign of Reason*. New York: Routledge.

Hall, S. (1980) 'Cultural Studies: Two Paradigms'. *Media, Culture & Society* 2, 57–72.

Hands, J. (2011) *@is for Activism: Dissent, Resistance and Rebellion in a Digital Culture*. London: Pluto Press.

Hannerz, U. (1996) *Transnational Connections: Culture, People, Places*. London: Routledge.

Hardt, H. (1992) *Critical Communication Studies: Essays on Communication, History and Theory in America*. London: Routledge.

Hardt, H. (1998) *Interactions: Critical Studies in Communication, Media, & Journalism*. Lanham, MD: Rowman & Littlefield.

Hardy, J. (2013) *Critical Political Economy of the Media*. Abingdon: Routledge.

Harvey, D. (2006) *A Brief History of Neoliberalism*. Oxford: Oxford University Press.

Harvey, D. (2009) *Cosmopolitanism and the Geographies of Freedom*. New York: Columbia University Press.

Harvey, D. (2011) *The Enigma of Capital and the Crises of Capitalism*. London: Profile Books.

Harvey, D. (2012) *Rebel Cities: From the Right to the City to Urban Revolution*. London: Verso.

Hay, C. (2007) *Why We Hate Politics*. Cambridge: Polity Press.

Hearn, J. (2012) *Theorizing Power*. Basingstoke: Palgrave Macmillan.

Held, D. (2006) *Models of Democracy*, 3rd ed. Cambridge: Polity Press.

Held, D. (2010) *Cosmopolitanism: Ideals and Realities*. Cambridge: Polity Press.

Hermes, J. (2005) *Re-Reading Popular Culture*. Oxford: Blackwell.

Hier, S. P. (2008) 'Transformative Democracy in the Age of Second Modernity: Cosmopolitanization, Communicative Agency and the Reflexive Subject'. *New Media & Society* 10(1), 27–44.

Hindman, M. (2009) *The Myth of Digital Democracy*. Princeton, MJ and Oxford: Oxford University Press.

Hitchens, C. (2008) 'How to be a Public intellectual'. *Prospect Magazine* May. Available at: http://www.prospectmagazine.co.uk/2008/05/what-is-a-public-intellectual/ (Accessed 18 August 2012).

Hosseini, H. S. A. (2010) *Alternative Globalizations: An Integrative Approach to Studying Dissident Knowledge in the Global Justice Movement*. Abingdon: Routledge.

Hurenkamp, M., E. Tonkens and J. W. Duyvendak (2012) *Crafting Citizenship: Negotiating Tensions in Modern Society*. Basingstoke: Palgrave Macmillan.

Isin, E. F. and B. S. Turner, eds. (2003) *Handbook of Citizenship Studies*. London: Sage.

Jacobs, R. N. and E. Townsley (2011) *The Space of Opinion: Media Intellectuals and the Public Sphere*. New York: Oxford University Press.

Jacoby, R. (1987) *The Last Intellectuals: American Culture in the Age of Academe*. New York: Basic Books.

Jacoby, R. (2008) 'Big Brains, Small impact'. *Chronicle of Higher Education* 54(18), p. B5 January. Available at: http://chronicle.com/article/Big-Brains-Small-Impact/11624 (Accessed 18 August 2012).

Jacoby, S. (2009) *The Age of American Unreason*. New York: Vintage Books.

Jameson, F. (1981) *The Political Unconscious: Narrative as a Socially Symbolic Act*. Ithaca, N.Y.: Cornell University Press.

Jameson, F. (1991) *Postmodernism: The Cultural Logic of Late Capitalism*. Durham, NC: Duke University Press.

Jameson, F. (2010) *Valences of the Dialectic*. London: Verso.

Joffe, J. (2003) 'The Decline of the Public Intellectual and the Rise of the Pundit'. In A. M. Melzer, M. Arthur, J. Weinberger and M. R. Zinman, eds. *The Public Intellectual: Between Philosophy an Politics*. Lanham, MD/Oxford: Rowman and Littlefield, pp. 109–122.

Jørgensen, M. and L. Phillips (2002) *Discourse Analysis as Theory and Method*. London: Sage, pp. 24–59.

Journal of Communication (2012) Special Issue: Social Media and Political Change, 62(2).

Juris, J. S. (2012) 'Reflections on #Occupy Everywhere: Social Media, Public Space, and the Emerging Logics of Aggregation'. *American Ethnologist* 39(2), 259–279.

Kadushin, C. (2012) *Understanding Social Network: Theories, Concepts, and Findings*. New York: Oxford University Press.

Kapuscinski, R. (2008) *Travels with Herotodos*. London: Penguin.

Keane, J. (2003) *Global Civil Society?* Cambridge: Cambridge University Press.

Keane, J. (2009) *The Life and Death of Democracy*. London: Simon & Schuster UK.

Keen, A. (2008) *The Cult of the Amateur*. New York: Doubleday.

Kellner, D. (2005) *Media Spectacle and the Crisis of Democracy*. Boulder, CO: Paradigm Publishers.

Kellner, D. and R. Hammer, eds. (2009) *Media/Cultural Studies: Critical Approaches*. New York: Peter Lang.

Kendall, G., I. Woodward and Z. Skribis (2009) *The Sociology of Cospopolitanism: Globalization, Identity, Culture and Government*. Basingstoke: Palgrave Macmillan.

Knebel, J. (2012) 'Bored with Occupy – and Inequality'. *Fairness and Accuracy in Reporting*. Available at: http://fair.org/extra-online-articles/bored-with-occupy8212and-inequality/ (Accessed 24 February 2013).

Kohn, M. (2000) 'Language, Power, and Persuasion: Towards a Critique of Deliberative Democracy'. *Constellations* 7(3), 408–429.

Kraidy, M. (2010) *Reality Television and Arab Politics: Contention in Public Life*. *Cambridge*. New York: Cambridge University Press.

Krishnaswamy, R. and J. C. Hawley, eds. (2008) *The Postcolonial and the Global*. Minneapolis: The University of Minnesota Press.

Kuziemko, I. and M. I. Norton (2012) 'Where is the Demand for Redistribution?' In J. Byrne, ed. *The Occupy Handbook*. New York: Backbay Books/Little, Brown and Co, pp. 280–285.

Laclau, E. and C. Mouffe (2001) *Hegemony and Socialist Strategy: Towards a Radical Democratic Politics*, 2nd ed. London: Verso.

Le Nouvel Observateur (2010) Special issue on: Le Pouvir Intellectuel. No. 2376, 20–26 May.

Lasorsa, D., S. C. Lewis and A. E. Holton (2012) 'Normalizing Twitter: Journalism Practice in an Emerging Communication Space'. *Journalism Studies* 13(1), 19–36.

Lewis, J. (2011) *Crisis in the Global Mediasphere: Desire, Displeasure and Cultural Transformation*. Basingstoke: Palgrave Macmillan.

Lewis, S. C. (2012) 'The Tension between Professional Control and Open Participation: Journalism and its Boundaries'. *Information, Communication and Society* 15(6): 836–866.

Lievrouw, L. A. (2011) *Alternative and Activist New Media*. Cambridge: Polity Press.

Limbaugh, R. (2011) 'Occupy Wall Street Cooks Join the 1%, Refuse to feed the Homeless'. Available at: http://www.rushlimbaugh.com/daily/2011/10/27/occupy_wall_street_cooks_join_the_1_refuse_to_feed_the_homeless (Accessed 24 February 2013).

Ling, R. and J. Donner (2009) *Mobile Communication*. Cambridge: Polity.

Lister, R. (2003) *Citizenship: Feminist Perspectives*, 2nd ed. London: Macmillan.

Loader, B. and D. Mercea, eds. (2012) *Social Media and Democracy*. Abingdon: Routledge.

Lovink, G. (2011) *Networks Without a Cause: A Critique of Social Media*. Cambridge: Polity Press.

Lukes, S. (2005) *Power: A Radical View*, 2nd ed. Basingstoke: Palgrave Macmillan.

MacKinnon, R. (2012) *Consent of the Networked: The Worldwide Struggle for Internet Freedom*. New York: Basic Books.

Maeckelburgh, M. (2009) *The Will of the Many: How the Alterglobalisation Movement is Changing the Face of Democracy*. London: Pluto Press.

Maia, R. C. M. (2012) *Deliberation, the Media and Political Talk*. New York, NY: Hampton Press.

Mandel, E. (1975) *Late Capitalism*. London: Verso Books.

Marcus, G. (2002) *The Sentimental Citizen: Emotion in Democratic Politics*. University Park: The Pennsylvania State University Press.

Marcuse, H. (1955) *Eros and Civilization: A Philosophical Inquiry into Freud*. Boston: Beacon Press.

Marden, P. (2011) 'The Digitalised Public Sphere: Re-Defining Democratic Cultures or Phantasmagoria?' *Javnost/The Public* 18(1), 5–20.

Mansell, R. (2012) *Imagining the Internet: Communication, Innovation, and Governance*. Oxford: Oxford University Press.

Mason, P. (2012) *Why It's Kicking off Everywhere: The New Global Revolutions*. London: Verso.

Mattoni, A.(2012) *Media Practices and Protest Politics: How Precarious Workers Mobilise*. Farmingham, UK: Ashgate Publishing.

McChesney, R. W. (2008) *The Political Economy of Media: Enduring Issues, Emerging Dilemmas*. New York: Monthly Review Press.

McChesney, R. W. (2013) *Digital Disconnect*. New York: New Press.

McChesney, R. W. and J. Nichols (2011) *The Death and Life of American Journalism*. New York: Nation Books.

McKenzie, P. J., J. Burkell, L. Wong, C. Whippey, S. E. Trosow and M. McNally (2013) 'User-Generated Content 1: Overview of Current State and Context'. *First Monday* 17(6). Available at: http://www.firstmonday.org/htbin/cgiwrap/ bin/ojs/index.php/fm/article/view/3912/3266 (Accessed 10 March 2013).

McNally, M., S. E. Trosow, L. Wong, C. Whippey, J. Burkell and P. J. McKenzie (2013) 'User-Generated Content 2: Policy Implications'. *First Monday* 17(6). Available at: http://www.firstmonday.org/htbin/cgiwrap/bin/ojs/index. php/fm/article/view/3913/3267 (Accessed 10 March 2013).

McQuail, D. (2010) *McQuail's Mass Communication Theory*, 6th ed. London: Sage.

Meikle, G. and S. Young (2012) *Media Convergence: Networked Digital Media in Everyday Life*. Basingstoke: Palgrave Macmillan.

Melzer, A M., J. Weinberger, M. R. Zinman, eds. (2003) *The Public Intellectual: Between Philosophy and Politics*. Lanham, MD/Oxford: Rowman and Littlefield.

Michael, J. (2000) *Anxious Intellectuals: Academic Professionals, Public Intellectuals, and Enlightenment Values*. Durham, NC and London: Duke University Press.

Micheletti, M. (2003) *Political Virtue and Shopping: Individuals, Consumerism, and Collective Action*. London: Palgrave Macmillan.

Miège, B. (2010), *L'Espace public contemporain*. Grenoble: PUG.

Moores, S. (2012) *Media, Place and Mobility*. Basingstoke: Palgrave Macmillan.

Morozov, E. (2011) *The Net Delusion: How Not to Liberate the World*. London: Allen Lane.

Morris, L. (2010) *Asylum, Welfare and the Cosmopolitan Ideal: A Sociology of Rights*. Abingdon: Routledge.

Morris, P. (2002) *Power: A Philosophical Analysis*, 2nd ed. Manchester: Manchester University Press.

Mosco, V. (2005) *The Digital Sublime: Myth, Power and Cyberspace*. Cambrdige, MA: MIT Press.

Mosco, V. (2009) *The Political Economy of Communication*, 2nd ed. London: Sage.

Mouffe, C. (2001) *The Democratic Paradox*. London: Verso.

Mouffe, C. (2005) *On the Political*. London: Routlege.

Naughton, J. (2011) 'Britain's Top 300 Intellectuals'. *The Guardian* 8 May. Available at: http://www.guardian.co.uk/culture/2011/may/08/top-300-british-intellectuals (Accessed 18 August 2012).

Negt, O. and A. Kluge (1993) *The Public Sphere and Experience*. Minneapolis: University of Minnesota Press.

Neumayer, C. (2013*) When Neo-Nazis March and Anti-Facists Demonstrate: Protean Counterpublics in the Digital Age*. Unpublished PhD, Copenhagen: IT University.

Newman, A. (2011) 'Big Soros Money Linked to "Occupy Wall Street" '. *The New American* 5 October. Available at: http://www.thenewamerican.com/ usnews/politics/9269-big-soros-money-linked-to-occupy-wall-street (Accessed 12 December 2011).

Norris, P. and R. Ingelhart (2009) *Cosmopolitan Communications: Cultural Diversity in a Globalized World*. Cambridge: Cambridge University Press.

Nussbaum, M. (2006) *Frontiers of Justice: Disability, Nationality and Species Membership*. Cambridge, MA: Belknap Press.

Oblak-Črnič, T. and J. Prodnik (2012) 'The Internet's Biases and the (dis)Empowered Web Audiences'. Paper presented at the 30th EURICOM Colloquium on Communication and Culture, Piran, 15–16 Nov.

Oboler, A., K. Welsh and L. Cruz (2012) 'The Danger of Big Data: Social Media as Computational Social Science'. First Monday 17(7). Available at: http://www.firstmonday.org/htbin/cgiwrap/bin/ojs/index.php/fm/article/view/3993/3269 (Accessed 10 March 2013).

Ostertag, B. (2007) *People's Movements, People's Press: The Journalism of Social Justice Movements*. Boston: Beacon Press.

Papacharissi, Z., ed. (2009) *Journalism and Citizenship: New Agendas in Communication*. Abingdon: Routledge.

Papacharissi, Z. (2010) *A Private Sphere: Democracy in a Digital Age*. Cambridge: Polity Press.

Papacharissi, Z. and E. Easton (2013) 'In the Habitus of the New. Structure, Agency and the Social Media Habitus'. In J. Harley, J. Burgess, A. Bruns, eds. *A Companion to New Media Dynamics*. Hoboken, NJ: Wiley-Blackwell. Also available at: http://tigger.uic.edu/~ zizi/Site/Research_files/HabitusofNewZPEE.pdf (Accessed 15 February 2013).

Pariser, Eli. 2012. *The Filter Bubble: What the Internet is Hiding From You*. London: Penguin.

Pasquali, F. (2011) 'Participating Audiences, Authorship and the Digitalization of the Publishing Industry'. *CM: Communication Management Quarterly* (21), 203–219.

Paybarah, A. (2011) 'Survey: Many Occupy Wall Street Protesters Are Unhappy Democrats Who Want More Influence'. *Capital* 18 October http://www.capitalnewyork.com/article/culture/2011/10/3790409/survey-many-occupy-wall-street-protesters-are-unhappy-democrats-who- (Accessed 24 February 2013).

Pleyers, G. (2011) *Alter-Globalization: Becoming Actors in a Global Age*. Cambridge: Polity Press.

Plummer, K. (2003) *Intimate Citizenship*. Seattle and London: University of Washington Press.

Pole, A. (2010) *Blogging the Political: Political Participation in the Networked Society*. New York: Routledge.

Posner, R. A. (2003) *Public Intellectuals: A Study of Decline*. Cambridge, MA: Harvard University Press.

Putnam, R. (2000) *Bowling Alone: The Collapse and Revival of American Community*. New York: Simon and Schuster.

Quinnipiac University (2011) 'Occupy Wall Street less Unpopular than Tea Party', 3 November http://www.quinnipiac.edu/x1295.xml?ReleaseID=1670 (Accessed 12 December 2011)

Rainie, L. and B. Wellman (2012) *Networked: The New Social Operating System*. Cambridge, MA: MIT Press.

Ricoeur, P. (1981) *Hermeneutics and the Human Sciences: Essays on Language, Action and Interpretation*, ed., trans. J. B. Thompson. Cambridge: Cambridge University Press.

Reigert, K., ed. (2007), *Politicotainment: Televison's Take on the Real*. New York: Peter Lang Publishers.

Rimbert, P. (2011) 'La pensée critique dans l'enclos universitaire: Enquete sur les intellectuells contestaires'. *Le Monde Diplomatique* (682) January, 1.

Robertson, A. (2010) *Mediated Cosmopolitanism: The World of Televison News*. Cambridge: Polity Press.

Rosanvallon, P. (2008) *Counter-Democracy: Politics in an Age of Distrust*. Cambridge: Cambridge University Press.

Rosenberry, J. and B. S. John III, eds. (2010) *Public Journalism 2.0: The Promise and Reality of a Citizen-Engaged Press*. Abingdon: Routledge.

Russell, A. (2011) *Networked: A Contemporary History of News in Transition*. Cambridge: Polity Press.

Sachs, J. D. (2012) 'Occupy Global Capitalism'. In J. Byrne, ed. *The Occupy Handbook*. New York: Backbay Books/Little, Brown and Co, pp. 462–474.

Sandel, M. (2012) *What Money Can't Buy: The Moral Limits of Markets*. London: Allen Lane.

Sartre, J.-P. (1991) *Critique of Dialectical Reason*, vol. 1 London: Verso.

Schiller, D. (2010) *How the Think About Information*. Champaign, IL: University of Illinois Press.

Schiller, H. (1975) *The Mind Managers*. Boston: Beacon Books.

Scholte, J. A., ed (2011) *Building Global Democracy: Civil Society and Accountable Global Governance*. Cambridge: Cambridge University Press.

Segerberg, A. and W. L. Bennett (2011) 'Social Media and the Organization of Collective Action: Using Twitter to Explore the Ecologies of Two Climate Change Protests'. *The Communication Review* 14, 197–215.

Sen, J. and P. Waterman, eds. (2007) *World Social Forum: Challenging Empires*. Montreal: Black Rose Books.

Shirky, C. (2008) *Here Comes Everybody: The Power of Organizing Without Organizations*. London: Allen Lane.

Silverstone, R. (2006) *Media and Morality: On the Rise of the Mediapolis*. Cambridge: Polity.

Skrbis, Z. and I. Woodward (2007) 'The Ambivalence of Ordinary Cosmopolitanism: Investigating the Limits of Cosmopolitan Openness'. *The Sociological Review* 55(4), 730–747.

Sloterdijk, P. (1987) *Critique of Cynical Reason*. Minneapolis and London: University of Minnesota Press.

Small, H. (2002) *The Public Intellectual*. Oxford: Blackwell.

Smith, A. M. (1999). *Laclau and Mouffe: The Radical Democratic Imaginary*. Abingdon: Routledge.

Smith, J., M. Karides, M. Becker and D. Brunelle (2007) *Global Democracy and the World Social Forums*. Boulder, CO: Paradigm Publishers.

Smith, W. (2007) 'Cosmopolitan Citizenship: Virtue, Irony and Worldliness'. *European Journal of Social Theory* 10(1), 37–52.

Smythe, D. W. (1981). *Dependency Road: Communications, Capitalism, Consciousness and Canada*. Norwood, NJ: Ablex Publishing.

Somers, M. R. (2008) *Genealogies of Citizenship: Markets, Statelessness, and the Right to Have Rights*. Cambridge: Cambridge University Press.

Song, F. W. (2009) *Virtual Communities: Bowling Alone, Online Together*. New York: Peter Lang.

State of the News Media (2013) Pew Research Centre Project for Excellence in Journalism, Ninth Annual Report. Available at: www.stateofthemedia.org

Straume, I. (2011) 'The political imaginary of global capitalism'. In S. Straume and J.F. Humphrey, eds., *Depoliticization: The Political Imaginary of Global Capitalism*, pp. 27–50. Malmö, Sweden: NSU Press.

Street, J. (1997) *Politics and Popular Culture*. Cambridge: Polity Press.

Striphas, T. (2009) *The Late Age of Print: Everyday Book Culture from Consumerism to Control*. New York: Columbia University Press.

Sullivan. W. M. and W. Kymlicka, eds. (2007) *The Globalisation of Ethics.* New York: Cambridge University Press.

Sunstein, C. (2008) *Infotopia: How Many Minds Produce Knowledge.* Oxford: Oxford University Press.

Surowiecki, J. (2004) *The Wisdom of Crowds.* New York: Anchor Books.

Swartz, D. L. (2003) 'From Critical Sociology to Public Intellectual: Pierre Bourdieu and Politics'. *Theory and Society* 32(5–6), pp. 791–823.

Tapscott, D. and A. D. Williams, (2006) *Wikinomics: How Mass Collaboration Changes Everything.* New York: Portfolio (Penguin).

The Communication Review (2011): Special Issue: Twitter Revolutions? Addressing Social Media and Dissent 14(3).

The Huffington Post (2011) 'George Soros says he Sympathizes with Occupy Wall Street Protesters' 3 October. Available at: http://www.huffingtonpost.com/2011/10/03/george-soros-occupy-wall-street_n_992468.html (Accesses 24 February 2013).

Thompson, J. B. (1990) *Ideology and Modern Culture: Critical Social Theory in the Era of Mass Communication.* Cambridge: Polity Press.

Thompson, J. B. (2010) *Merchants of Culture: the Publishing Business in the Twenty-First Century.* Cambridge: Polity Press.

Thörn, H. (2009) *Anti-Apartheid and the Emergence of a Global Civil Society.* London: Palgrave Macmillan.

Thorson, K., K. Driscol, B. Ekdale, S. Edgerly, L. G. Thompson, A. Schrock, L. Swartz, E. K. Vraga and C. Wells (2013) 'YouTube, Twitter, and the Occupy Movement: Connecting content and circulation practices'. *Information, Communication & Society* 16(2), 1–31. Available at: http://www.tandfonline.com/doi/abs/10.1080/1369118X.2012.756051 (Accessed 6 March 2013).

Thurman, N. and A. Hermida (2010) 'Gotcha: How Newsroom Norms are Shaping Participatory Journalism Online'. In S. Tunney and G. Monaghan, eds. *Web Journalism://A New Form of Citizenship?* Brighton: Sussex Academic Press, pp. 31–47.

Tunney, S. and G. Monaghan, eds. (2010) *Web Journalism: A New Form of Citizenship?* Brighton: Sussex Academic Press.

Turkle, S. (1995) *Life on the Screen.* New York: Weidenfeld and Nicholson.

Turner, B. S. (2002) 'Cosmopolitan Virtue, Globalization and Patriotism'. *Theory, Culture & Society* 19(1–2), 45–63.

Turow, J. (2011) *The Daily You: How the New Advertising Industry is Defining Your Identity and Your Worth.* New Haven and London: Yale University Press.

Uldam, J. (2010) *Fickle Commitment: Fostering Political Engagement in the 'Flighty World of Online Acivism'.* (Unpublished PhD dissertation). Copenhagen: Copenhagen Business SchooUrry, J. (2007) *Mobilities.* Cambridge: Polity Press.

Vaidhyanatha, S. (29011) *The Googlization of Everything: (And Why We Should Worry.* Berkeley, University of California Press.

van Dijk, J. (2012) *The Network Society*, 3rd ed. London: Sage.

van Dijk, J. (2013) *The Culture of Connectivity: A Critical History of Social Media.* Oxford: Oxford University Press.

van Dijk, T. (1998) *Ideology.* London: Sage.

van Zoonen, L. (2005) *Entertaining the Citizen: When Politics and Popular Culture Converge.* Lanham, MD: Rowman & Littlefield.

Vernon, R. (2010) *Cosmopolitan Regard: Political Membership and Global Justice*. New York: Cambridge University Press.

Vobič, I. (2012) *Global Trends of Online Journalism in Slovenian Print Media*. Ljubljana: PhD dissertation, Faculty of Social Science, University of Ljubljana.

Voet, R. (1998) *Feminism and Citizenship*. London: Sage.

Waisbord, S. (2012) *Reinventing Professional Journalism*. Cambridge: Polity Press.

Walker, J. W. St. G., and A. S. Thompson, eds. (2008) *Critical Mass: The Emergence of Global Civil Society*. Waterloo, CA: Wilfrid Laurier University Press.

Waltz, M. (2005) *Alternative and Activist Media*. Edinburgh: University of Edinburgh Press.

Wasko, J., G. Murdock and H. Sousa, eds. (2011) *Handbook of Political Economy of Communication*. Oxford: Wiley-Blackwell.

Weschler, L. (2012) 'Enough with Occupying Wall Street: It'sTtime to StartPpreoccupying Wall Street'. In In J. Byrne, ed. *The Occupy Handbook*. New York: Backbay Books/Little, Brown and Co, pp. 397–410.

Wilchins, R. (2004) *Gender Theory, Queer Theory: An Instant Primer*. Los Angeles: Alyson Publications.

Wilkie, R. (2011) *The Digital Condition: Class and Culture in the Information Network*. New York: Fordham University Press.

Williams, R. (1977) *Marxism and Literature*. London and New York, Oxford University Press.

Wimmer, J. (2012) 'The Times they are a-changin'': The Digital Transformation of 'Classic' Counter-Public Spheres'. *CM: Communication Management Quarterly* 23, 5–22.

Wodak, R and M. Meyer (2009) *Methods of Critical Discourse Analysis*, 2nd ed. London: Sage.

Young, J. (2007) *The Vertigo of Late Modernity*. London: Sage.

Žižek, S. (2008) *For They Know Not what They Do: Enjoyment as a Political Factor*. London: Verso.

Žižek, S. (2011) *Living in the End of Times*. London: Verso.

Žižek, S. (2012) *The Year of Dreaming Dangerously*. London: Verso.

Index

Note: page numbers in **bold** indicate major discussions